The Other Great Depression

Praise for *The Other Great Depression*

"An urgent, nervous, heartfelt book. . . . Lewis writes with an addict's jumpy restlessness, staggering from hurt to hurt, from tensely jokey confession to confession, from twitchy spiritual discovery to discovery."
—*Entertainment Weekly*

"Richard Lewis's writing completes what his stand-up and acting began. He is the voice of reason and sanity in a world of treason and insanity. He makes me squeal and sob in the same sentence. He is my rock 'n' roll prophet." —Jamie Lee Curtis

"Wrenching . . . Wonderfully written and truthful."
—*Houston Chronicle*

"Richard Lewis may just be the Franz Kafka of modern day comedy."
—Mel Brooks

"Richard Lewis transforms the run-on sentence into an art form. Linguistically twisting phrases created by cerebral synapses that seem to connect from some primordial psychosis, Lewis never stops. At least onstage. And now in print." —*The Boston Globe*

"Intimately self-confessional. . . . A heartfelt series of essays in which the comedian—well known for the neuroses that seem to define his life and his comedy—unveils the emotional turmoil from which his humor (and his disease) springs. . . . " —*Westchester Journal News*

"Richard was always the best and the brightest . . . and now you can add to that, the most honest." —Dennis Miller

"Touching . . . brutally honest . . . insightful and thought provoking . . . Most books by comedians tend to be light, brainless, quick and dirty vehicles to capitalize on their success . . . While Richard Lewis's book certainly has its share of laughs, it's also a hard-hitting look at one man's life—warts and all." —*The Buffalo News*

"Mesmeric—a dizzying ride on the R&L Express. Don't miss it."
—Lou Reed

THE OTHER GREAT DEPRESSION

How I'm **Overcoming**, on a Daily Basis,

at Least **a Million Addictions** and **Dysfunctions**

and Finding **a Spiritual** (*sometimes*) **Life**

RICHARD LEWIS

 PublicAffairs   *New York*

Published in the United States by PublicAffairs™,
a member of the Perseus Books Group.
First PublicAffairs edition published in 2000.
Authorized paperback reprint published by Plume, a member of Penguin Putnam Inc., in 2002.
First PublicAffairs paperback edition published in 2008.

Designed by Mark McGarry
Set in Meridien

Library of Congress Cataloging-in-Publication Data
Lewis, Richard, 1947–
    The other great depression: how I'm overcoming, on a daily basis, at least a million addictions and dysfunctions and finding a spiritual (sometimes) life / Richard Lewis.
        p. cm.
    HC: ISBN-10: 1-891620-93-2
    PB: ISBN-13: 978-1-58648-604-4
    1. Lewis, Richard, 1947–   2. Lewis, Richard, 1947– —Alcohol use.
    3. Comedians—United States—Biography.   4. Alcoholics—United States—Biography.   I. Title.
    PN2287.L443 A3 2001
    792.7'028'092—dc21
[B]
                                                                00–045836

10 9 8 7 6 5 4 3 2 1

This book is dedicated to all the people in my life who *really* got to know me, allowed me to be myself, stuck around with unconditional love and support while I struggled to find out who my *authentic* self was.

But mostly, it's to those angels who didn't fly away when I was soulless, hopeless, and ruled by booze during my maddening, self-centered, *intoxicated*, dark days. By the grace of God these folks are still in my corner, years after I have acquired some sobriety, faith and serenity, and still support my daily surrender to this ruthless disease of alcoholism, which—although in check a day at a time—will forevermore be hanging around waiting to destroy me if I'm not vigilant. These *winged pals* have made it possible for me to experience the greatest gig I ever had . . . *recovery*.

And finally, my book and prayers are dedicated to those of you living lives of addiction and despondency to whom I want simply to say, *"If I can change, you can change. Take it from me, someone who was once convinced that I was forever doomed . . . miracles are out there for the sickest of the sick. Life can actually become precious."* What a concept, huh?

But it's a sad man my friend who's livin'
in his own skin and can't stand the company.

—Bruce Springsteen, *Better Days*

Contents

Part 2: The Middle

Part 3: Another Beginning

Prologue

Roswell, New Mexico, 1947

FADE IN:

Many would have you believe that the United States government has been covering up incontrovertible proof that extraterrestrials landed in Roswell, New Mexico, in 1947 and the thing that bothers me the most about this possible cover-up is not my fascination with UFOs but the fact that that was the year I was born, and that I have no proof or documentation of precisely when I allegedly came out of my mother's womb; so on a few rare, serene occasions, I have thought that maybe a lot of my issues and psychological problems have nothing to do with my upbringing or even being chemically unbalanced but rather arise from the fact that *I'm not from this earth.*

FADE OUT:
THE END

Introduction

After nearly twenty-five fun-loving, excruciating years of devoting myself solely to expressing my innermost feelings publicly for laughs, attention, and a living (when money actually changed hands), it suddenly dawned on me that not only wasn't I being as honest with my audience as I thought I was, but, much more importantly, *I wasn't being honest with myself,* and was actually spiraling out of control as a raging alcoholic.

Since the laughs and I almost died for good, more than a decade ago, I have gone through a daily "recovery" and with it a remarkable transformation. It is with this change, and the clarity it brought, that I became hell-bent on finally—being as fearlessly and rigorously honest as I could be—going back to the womb in my head, and writing a book of my reflections from the past up to the present day. Memoirs, if you will, on the wondrous and oftentimes insane journey I never had the courage, sobriety, or faith to share before.

I figured out while writing my autobiography that I chose applause over tears and booze over fears. So I have this story to tell to anyone who wants to laugh or cry or maybe even (dare I be so bold) be enlightened, about how someone (me), who has been chronically depressed, anxious, and ultimately alcoholic, survived and moved on to a new life, still crazy but finally with a bit of hopefulness and contentment added to the mix.

PART 1: The Beginning

There's a **Candle** in My Belly, Thank God

It happened during a week when my family wasn't exactly having a winning streak on our home court. I mean, there was a lot of tension; so much tension that I remember hiding under my covers for most of it. They hardly noticed. The sounds of arguing came in through the crack under my bedroom door, even though I put a lot of blankets and shit under it to keep the noise out. I was Davy Crockett and I had my own little Alamo going on, man. I also had the screwball Mets on the radio from the West Coast so New Jersey boys hiding from their adolescence could feel better, secure in the knowledge that as bad as childhood seemed, the '62 Mets were worse. I loved them for that. I loved that brave, mostly ridiculous team of aging stars and young players who seemed to be doing bad Jerry Lewis impressions most of the time. So did the Dodger fans, the bastards lucky enough to have my Brooklyn Dodgers playing out of uniform as their home team. They were screaming even louder than my family. I could hear them over the little portable radio that I crammed up against my ear in the dead of night.

Oh, *that night*, when none of the yelling in the house made any sense at all and I felt like I was just going to bust. Just blow up. Right there in bed. Like a tiny float in the Jewish Macy's parade trying to show off to the other giant floats that it had something to say too! I could much more easily understand why the people in L.A. were screaming than everyone downstairs. They had Sandy Koufax. We had a history of angina.

I tried to drown out the horrifying noise downstairs by turning up the radio on the taunting screams of the fake Dodger fans. I lay on my bed as if I were lying in state as members of my family continued their filibuster on happiness, unaware that I was praying for something better for me. I don't really know who I was praying to but I know I was praying because I had my hands clasped together like I thought you were supposed to.

And I didn't know what exactly I was praying for but maybe it was love because whatever kind of love I was supposed to be getting by birthright wasn't happening. I mean, should a fourteen-year-old kid be praying in the middle of the night like this? It sure didn't feel right.

And then, it happened. I got this image. There was this silly little candle in my belly. I didn't know whether to scream or laugh so I shut up. I just lay there, quietly. The candle seemed to burn brighter the more I thought about it. And the more I thought about the candle, the less I heard the yelling, from both coasts.

It's easy now to guess what it meant. I think it had to do with faith. With faith in myself—but I got the strength from an unknown place. Maybe God. Maybe some kind of god that was my own special God. The kind of God I groove with today.

But back then I wasn't so sure. The sense of nothingness I'd had inside me for so long made me want to scream for understanding. But who would hear me? Not the people downstairs. Who would understand? I surely didn't understand.

I knew only one thing for certain. I didn't want to be like them. I had very little idea why they seemed so unhappy but suddenly it became very clear, frighteningly clear . . . I had to fly solo. It was that simple. I was getting lost, real lost, and as I reached out for help the only thing that answered the call was this candle. There was a candle in my belly, thank God. And I came to realize, in miraculous fashion, while Koufax was mowing down my heroes, that if the candle ever went out, I would probably either feel dead or BE DEAD.

When I was lying on a gurney in an ER thirty years later, in much the same position but this time hallucinating from excess cocaine use, the compassionate intern looked down with soulful eyes, and right after brushing my drenched hair back off my forehead, sweetly said, "You're so funny, Mr. Lewis. What are you doing this for? Why are you doing this?" I knew. I knew all right. I'd gone to the hospital because I honestly feared that if I didn't, I would die at home, and also, just as importantly, for the first time, I really didn't care who knew that I had a serious problem. I rarely did those kind of hardcore drugs (I loved alcohol) but whatever it was that got me to be that reckless and feel that hopeless had to be confronted. Somehow, I chose life over death.

Now I know what it means to hit bottom. Rock Bottom. And there was a candle in my belly, thank God.

Oh, yeah. Koufax pitched a no-hitter.

Prince of **Pain, Jr.**

Sure I quit drinking and felt like I gave birth to myself, but I still have more problems than you can shake a shrink at. I didn't come by that moniker I'm known by, "Prince of Pain," just because I spent most of my life doing charity work and helping good-natured Amish people build barns.

So, just who is the man behind this catchphrase? Well, I can comfortably admit to being a mammal but any more than that is speculation. Yet, I feel honor bound to take a wild stab at an answer, which is why I am writing this book about myself. There lies the problem. Me. Every shrink's wet dream. *"Take my dysfunctions, please."*

If pushed, I guess I'd have to admit to being one twisted, lucky motherfucker. I'm just your basic bad-postured, guilt-ridden ball of confusion with a trace of paranoia, self-loathing, and a little faith thrown in for some good taste.

I'm certain that a big part of my authentic being was kidnapped early in life, then got stuck in a kind of suspended animation when I

6 RICHARD LEWIS

became alcoholic. I have been trying to unravel the haze ever since. To be frank, that is *the main reason* I decided to write this memoir. Stopping carousing was the beginning of kind of a new funk for me. One with more dignity and yet still very foggy. One with unsure clarity.

I wish I could rid myself of any responsibility for my past behavior by saying I was abducted by an infamous cult, COCKTAIL, that took a fairly decent guy and slowly but surely ran his egocentric life down on Booze Standard Time. But I can't.

One morning back in the late seventies I woke up (curiously enough) with tens of thousands of bags of bar snacks all over my apartment floor, and I had no idea how they got there. I could have easily (after a big night out on the town) and for no sound reason taken them home with me; but I couldn't remember, and still can't. I have forgotten a lot of things. A lot of things are painful to recall but also essential to recall if I don't want to relive them again. In any event, it's kind of hard to piece things together from my past—like who I am—with all that alcohol in the way. They say "Don't look back," but even if I chose to, I doubt my own recall would earn me a Pulitzer Prize for accuracy.

But in sobriety, one thing *is* really clear to me. It's very hard to lie about anything anymore. Not little white lies . . . those are still easy. I'm talking about your big, fat, in-your-face, manipulative untruths. The kind where my intentions are to alter people's perceptions of who I am, even if I'm not drinking anymore. If I'm going to do that shit, I might as well get loaded. Why hang around just to be a sober asshole? It might beat death but it isn't much of a life. So in this book, I'm telling all the truths I can remember, even the ugliest ones.

I must've been in a lot of pain to begin with to want to drink so much. It took courage for me to get off the sauce. It takes a different kind of courage to make amends to people who were on the receiving end of all kinds of emotional abuse and irresponsibility that stemmed from my self-centered, fear-based, alcoholic lifestyle. Yeah sure, I cleaned up, and think that I have made most of my important amends to people; but if I'm not careful, at any moment, I can act unprincipled in the blink of an eye. And *without* even drinking. It was a hell of a lot easier to be an obnoxious alcoholic than to try, on a daily basis, to be a more decent, recovering human being. When you're unconscious there's not much to think about.

Man, do I have *war stories!* We all do. "Saving Private Lewis" took a lot of work. What a lot of wasted time I spent, slowly killing myself and needlessly hurting others. I blame nobody except me and my own lack of faith—at the time. And now a sober man, a nicer man, I can take no credit for anything, except the faith that I've acquired.

My current therapist (as opposed to those I've probably outlived or who chose to leave their profession after spending a little time in session with me) always knew I was an alcoholic, and much to her credit, always wanted me to be the one to say it out loud and admit it, first.

I couldn't, even when I knew, for many, many years.

Eventually, my armor started to weaken, along with my health and sanity. Always yearning to come totally clean to at least one person I trusted not to use it against me, I spilled the beans and told her that I *thought* I had a drinking problem.

Like she didn't *know* that I had a drinking problem. I remember so vividly how my denial felt that day in her office, when she looked squarely at me with an all-knowing but lovely smile that on this day was accompanied by an uncharacteristic bit of uneasiness in her eyes.

"Richard, I have an idea. Why don't you carry a diary with you this week and just jot down when you drink, how much, and what time of the day it is?"

She then continued the session with her usual, pleasant countenance, but I must have looked like Edvard Munch's stunt double. I knew right then and there, after this *locomotive of reason* hit me right smack in the denial, that I was letting my life get away. I was scared out of my mind. How could I feel so in control and yet feel so *out* of control? What a nightmare! I just couldn't fathom how to change a single thing that would make me feel better—without a drink. Sitting there paralyzed with fear, I couldn't wait to run out and go to a familiar bar and make believe everything was okay.

After the session, heading to the watering hole and being somehow conscious that I was running away from stability, I managed to grieve over the fact that I could never see my shrink again in this condition. Her brilliance and unconditional support made it impossible to lie to her anymore. Even if I didn't understand yet what I didn't want to lie about. Besides, what would be the point? In a brief moment of clarity, I silently acknowledged that if I was indeed an alcoholic, then it would be a dangerous charade to fabricate a "healthy man's drinking diary," which I had of course considered.

But I didn't. Nor could I stomach coming in the next week and reading something like, "Monday Morning . . . 7:45 A.M. . . . 5 glasses of Moët & Chandon with a little orange juice . . . Alone in house . . . What was I feeling? . . . Have no idea . . . Just mindlessly watching the Weather Channel."

How humiliating! How much shame! Who needed it? I just didn't have the balls yet to tell her the truth. Everyone knew but me, and I was the last one to find out.

So in a dyslexic display of honesty, I quit therapy. And for every second I spent away from my then ex-therapist (who had the acumen to never call me while I was on my inebriated, soul-searching journey), I at least knew that someone else knew that I was living a lie, and that helped me feel strangely less hopeless. (Never in my wildest dreams did I think that *anyone* else had the slightest notion of what kind of fog I was in. Ha! You have to be in quite a fog to be in *quite* a fog.) But most importantly, I knew that I had to be the one to want to change. I knew it, somewhere down deep buried in my subconscious, but by the time it traveled to my behavior, I had no controls; nor did I care one bit whether I was killing myself or hurting others. Even more insane, the *last* thing I thought about was who I might kill while driving high and living so recklessly in the vicinity of other people's lives.

This Prince of Pain me somehow justified my living out my own comedic hyperbole. Fueled by the disease of alcoholism I drank harder than ever, as if to give more life to my deadened perspective of existence. I became increasingly more reclusive. I thought that simply by hiding and drinking alone (or with an unconcerned lover) I wouldn't threaten my career or get people on my ass.

When you go months and months without returning calls and make endless excuses why you can't meet people who care about you in person, it's often only a matter of time before the eulogies begin to flow, and after a touching spot on the *News at Eleven*, you're history.

If I had to make a joke I'd say that even my own *shadow* started to get circles under its eyes. That's not even that funny. It wasn't really meant to be. It's just hard for me to be dead serious. I ran away from my feelings for so long that to this day I am still playing catch-up on events that happened decades ago.

I was a mess; and without faith, your addiction parties like there's no tomorrow. Today I live for today. Before I lived to drink. Regardless of how sober I was a lot of the time or what pleasure I brought to some, or how successful I might have become, getting high was at the center of things. There was a healthy man trying to get out of my aching, tormented body but he couldn't find the exit. The disease was in high gear and had a life of its own. My individuality, upon which I prided myself so, was being drowned out for no good reason. Even when I stared at my bloated face, overweight body, and scared eyes in the bathroom mirror and promised myself for what seemed to be the millionth time to stop drinking, I now know that I was only making that pledge to someone else. It wasn't me talking. And it wasn't even me listening. I was going through the motions of living. That I finally had a breakthrough and got the chance to begin thinking that there might be another way to live is truly a wonder.

I now believe in miracles and in a God. The biggest part of getting my soul back was the jump-start provided by my best friends. They finally had the nerve to slam the door on my sickness and tell me in no uncertain terms that if I couldn't stop killing myself, *they at least* wouldn't watch me do it anymore. *I love you guys. I love you guys. I love you guys.*

So, I'm still the Prince of Pain, but I've got my life and (lucky me) even my old shrink back. *I love her too.* God, I hope she doesn't over-analyze that.

I'm still a lunatic, but I'm a *recovering lunatic*. My life is crazier, yet happier and more productive than ever before. Shit happens all the time but what a pleasure that I don't create most of it anymore. What a pleasure it is to just try to do the right thing and see what happens. What a joy to feel free of the prison of alcohol abuse! How happy I am to finally let nature take its course. No more enemas for me. I like a good bowel movement with the best of them but only if it's meant to be. It's out of my hands, so to speak.

It's so much easier now to let the universe take care of itself with-out thinking like I used to, that I had something to do with it. I'm just one fuckin' happy universal tourist.

Yes, as frightened, addicted, obsessive, and hopeless as I was, hav-ing a today is pretty *awesome*. And for any of you out there suffering, and feeling certain like I did that you can't get through the day with-out getting high, why don't you first see what a day can look like clean—before you close the door on living for good.

I'm still pretty fucked up, and oftentimes I'm still a mess emo-tionally, yet now I'm a *proud mess*. I wouldn't want to be any other way. I always dug standing out in a crowd, and with all the pain and suffering and insanity out there, I figure that if my calling was to sur-vive all those "dates from hell" (or anything else "from hell") and boast about it, grandiose or not, then *"I'll gladly die on the couch for your problems."*

Martyrdom can be a trip. Sometimes entertaining. Even fun if I'm sober enough to appreciate the laughs. I'd much rather be the Prince of Pain than the King of Jesters. Those clowns never know when to get off stage. They'd rather die out there with their stupid, fucking hats on.

Thank God I knew when to take mine off. No joke.

Mistaken **Identity**

It all started two minutes after being yanked out of my mother's womb in unorthodox style through the not-yet-in-vogue C-section; taken by surprise, and ill prepared for all the commotion; without any opportunity to make up my own mind on the subject of whether I felt like coming out or not.

From the first words I *thought* I heard—"It's a boy. S*hit.*"—I had the indelible impression that I had already let the world down. I immediately felt like I was the spanking new owner of a strange "Shroud of Lewis" that was tragically and magically ingrained into my early nakedness, which caused me to feel not only sweaty and ill at ease but unsure of myself as well.

It seemed that almost immediately following my unseemly entry to civilization, I was forced to *meet and greet* everyone. At least fifteen relatives surrounded me as I lay inside my humiliating, see-through, *preemie* housing, displaying an excitement and happiness that appeared totally put on and maybe even scripted. I'm convinced now that shrieks of disappointment or looks from my parents indicating sentiments like "just our luck" or "fuck, like we really need another one," would have been more refreshing and up front and probably would have helped me psychologically in the long run.

Later, I was displayed on a horrible-looking, "touristy" blanket—one my grandparents got at a World's Fair—which was sloppily placed beneath my cute little ass. It wasn't the ugliness of the embroidery or whatever they call this mundane type of "art form" that bugged me but rather that the embroidery on it depicted FDR sitting in front of his familiar fireplace, chatting with his usual passion. This, I swear, even at the tender age of forty-eight hours, pissed me off, and gave me horrific vibes of what I would grapple with later when I was old enough to understand the infinite gravity of the

Holocaust and just how appallingly slowly the U.S. responded to the Nazis during FDR's presidency.

And to make my early outlook even more tortured, I took the heat for nearly killing dear old Mom. I mean, give me a break! It was purely unintentional! What was I supposed to do, stay put until it was safe to come out more traditionally?

Hey! I'm no baby! I'll concede, yes it is true, my mother did go through hell having me, and okay, it nearly did her in. There I've said it again. I've said it a thousand times! So let me once again apologize. That's the least a martyr can do.

And yet, I could never express *enough* regret. Throughout my childhood, I was repeatedly reminded in front of company that my mother was lucky to be alive. Sure they disguised this pronouncement as a cute family joke, but I knew that they really meant it: My umbilical cord symbolized a tether to my mother's hell.

But hey, what about me? It's no picnic not coming through the main door. Apparently the vagina was closed for the summer and I had to make the scene via a sneaky and humiliating secret bloody passage . . . What a mess! It looked like a Sam Peckinpah film made for *Sesame Street.* So forget the cigars! Molotov cocktails would have been more appropriate. And at the risk of sounding too *Hollywood, I* was the one who got all the bad press!

I know my birth on June 29, 1947, was more about *me* than anyone else, but oddly enough, it seemed to have *nothing* to do with me.

One day, many years later, desperately seeking attention and some revenge for my hurt feelings as a newborn, I made a toy model of my whole oozing birth using a doll that I stole from my sister's room. I poured ketchup all over it and then, for the topper, smeared it with gooey gelatin from a jar of Mom's® brand gefilte fish. Mom's® was far and away my favorite gefilte fish brand. I was always taken by the picture of the sweet, understanding woman on the label. If that image could've come to life, and been *my* mom, I would have done cartwheels for her. Anything to make her happy!

My real mom would've made a big stink about it, had she known, and would have gotten everyone else in the family on her side. Even if her feelings *were* hurt she probably wouldn't have expressed them (Yikes! Did she have low self-esteem first?!) and I probably wouldn't have understood *anyway* and then I'd be made to feel guilty for feeling alienated in the first place. To her, my pain was all about her. In fact, now that I think about it, from my earliest recollection on, my agony and unhappiness always seemed to be about how it affected everyone else *but* me. It soon became easier to feel responsible for others than to take responsibility for myself. I was lost with no hope of being found. If I *were* found wandering aimlessly in the street, I wouldn't even have known who to tell the policeman I was. Curiously, I would've known my address but not my identity. It was too confused. I was living inside a Sunday *New York Times* crossword puzzle.

To be fair, I don't think that anyone else in my family (or so I gathered from eavesdropping) had *any* idea who they really were either, and so no one could really express themselves *to* each other.

My family got real comfortable speaking in some do-it-yourself, circuitous tongue. I used to get motion sickness just standing quietly and listening.

"Kennedy just got shot, go rake the leaves."

"Put on a warmer coat, do you want to kill your father?"

"If we can send a satellite up into space you can at least make your bed!"

"Don't accidentally wet the bed on *purpose!*"

Sadly, the family resorted to consulting Dear Abby–type columns instead of going to family therapy (this would have been way too embarrassing had word gotten out in the neighborhood).

I'm not sure to this day whether I felt that anyone meant any harm. They just didn't mean anything. I was left to fend for myself without any idea who that was. To this day I'm most proud of the fact that I'm *self-made.*

Set 'em Up, Joe

If I could have figured out how to wear stilts and do an impression of an adult, I'm certain that I would have started drinking alcoholically probably somewhere around grade school. If there weren't age limits in bars and some money-hungry manager thought that having kiddie seats installed for Happy Hour *was* a good idea—maybe turning the TV on to the afternoon cartoon shows and putting some Walt Disney hits on the jukebox—I would've been there in a flash.

Certainly, I would rather have spent my childhood hanging out in a bar than going to Little League practice or being forced to pretend that hanging out in the woods with my fellow suburban Cub Scouts was a way to get badges instead of an assortment of rashes. After making pitiful-looking lanyards—none of us knew what a lanyard was when we were handed our initial assignment but we were finally enlightened by a pot-smoking, assistant scout leader—I opted to blow off the key chain idea (as depressed as I already was) and instead make a real large one, in the shape of a noose.

Yes, when I reflect on my childhood it's clear that I would have started drinking then if I'd only had the know-how. I would happily have taken up residence in a nice air-conditioned wine cellar with a small kitchen and decent john, rather than go through adolescence the more traditional way, being tormented by almost everyone around me and following leaders who had their own compasses stuck up their assholes.

My inevitable boozing seemed to be foredoomed. I sensed that almost everyone seemed whacked anyway, sober or not, and I had to contend with their bullshit from a very early age. There were so many mixed messages, it was nearly impossible to decipher a lucid one. The *straight and narrow* was something I had to find all by my lonesome. Nothing made sense. Even more devastating, I rarely made sense to myself.

I know the family was bugged because my early arrival threw everyone's social calendar all out of kilter, plus it was right in the middle of a heated pennant race and my father couldn't have been too thrilled. I mean, he worked his ass off and baseball gave him lots of pleasure and, well, to get this "designated whiner" prematurely couldn't have left him too electrified.

I wish I could have crawled to the nearest sandbox with a liquor license to drown away my guilty sorrows with some of the good shit that I couldn't get from my mother's breasts. I almost lucked out. This new formula potion was the rage and there was an outside chance I could pour a little whiskey in it when no one was looking. The only problem was, I couldn't come close to getting to that closet on top of the sink without making a scene. I told you I needed stilts. And of course I still had some trouble getting my hands to grasp objects or to master the coordination required for pouring. Instead, I had to lie there just crying and dreaming about how one day I would medicate the shit out of myself and not give a flying fuck what I felt or what anyone else thought of me.

That day couldn't come soon enough. And when it did, I grabbed a drink with as much gusto as I grabbed my cock from the moment I discovered it could get me *off*.

He's Soooo **Creative**

Yeah, that's what my mom always said. I guess she could've been right about the guy, I mean, what the fuck did I know? I was only about six or seven. He smiled, he entertained, he mocked his brother, all the while dressed in suits that Elton John would rip off twenty years later. She watched him with a reverence I felt so lacking in my life, from anyone. She'd try valiantly (yet carelessly at the same time) to make a tasty egg-salad sandwich for me, always with the brand of mayonnaise I hated, while digging Liberace on the tube with one eye, and half watching herself ruin the wretched meal with the other.

Quite frankly, all I expected (and usually received) was that I could get this smelly light repast without her relentless and unconditional praise of the show (it made me jealous) or, God forbid, any small talk that would serve only to make me feel smaller. So after scoring the imitation prison food I would quickly skulk down to the basement, where we had the big TV set that resembled a monitor from outer space in a bad Japanese sci-fi flick, remarkable at the time because it supposedly didn't need rabbit ears, the antennas for better reception, hurrying so as to not miss the beginning of a movie that was to have a profound impact on my life.

Yankee Doodle Dandy was going to be on again in a few minutes, on this cool show, *Million Dollar Movie,* which oddly enough, on some weeks, played one movie three times a day. And since this was my week off from school, I'd planned to watch Cagney twenty-seven times. No one seemed to care because no one seemed to be home. Even when they were home, everyone was in their own *world,* as far back as I can remember. Even the Mohel who *did me* at my briss (I seem to recall with horror) was not only trying to cut my dick off, but chanting beautifully *at the same time,* almost as if he was cutting a demo to get on some hot, new Yiddish recording label. If that was an early feeling of being castrated, what fun for my shrinks all these years.

I think the thing that somehow hooked me, while in a trance, after watching that film for days on end, thinking of not much else, was just how impenetrable George M. Cohan seemed to be as he worked with such blind integrity for what he wanted. I just loved how hard he tried to score and be authentic. *I just loved him for that.* Little did I know (while stuffing Mallomars down my throat at an alarming rate) that not only would I one day grow up and discover that I was an alcoholic, workaholic, and had an eating disorder for good measure, but that everything in my life was going to become secondary to having someone think that I was *soooo creative.*

And I almost paid for it with my life but, wahoo, here I am. And yeah, I think I am creative. Just like that beautiful ceramics teacher who would rove from school to school in our district twice a year.

She'd give us kids a break from the mundane and titillate us with her red lips and sexy, perfumed scarf as she leaned over our little desks (the same ones we would hide under when we thought Khrushchev had too much to drink and was trying to blow us up again). She would see our van Gogh–like ashtrays, made by mistake of course. At least mine were. Her cleavage became more of a vision than my own work. Her beauty was somehow a kind of oasis to conquer and feel fulfilled by; not at all (well, a little) in a sexual context, but as something that I could control and enjoy, something to make me feel I could have something worth calling my own. I didn't want breasts, I wanted a passion. She seemed creative because she turned me on in my mind. She gave me something to want. Something seemingly unattainable.

Years later, I found myself with the nightmare of having to become *sooooo creative* on my own. I soon realized that trying to make a living as an artist brings with it a world of critics who force you into a position of defending your own free will. As a young student, my accidentally impressionistic ashtrays sucked, but van Gogh's paintings were never sold while he was alive. Franz Kafka didn't want any of his work published even after he died. Maybe more disheartening from a human standpoint, Richard Lewis didn't even think anyone would care if he created a fuckin' thing. Least of all himself.

I slowly but surely encountered a very thin line between having the courage to express my personal feelings for a buck, and self-destructing under the pressure of practically everyone else around me. They looked at me like any attempt to be *sooooo creative* was a self-delusion. The endless lack of support and incredulity from 99.99 percent of those I knew, even those who claimed to love me, left me questioning whether or not I had any guts, or worse, a point of view. That sounds as trite as it was insidious and emotionally crippling.

Looking back on it now, as a full-blown, middle-aged, functioning anxiety collector, I can admit without cringing that my parents had their fair share of tremendous qualities, yet, being human much of the day, had more than just a handful of flaws as well. Much to my dismay and confusion, some of those flaws of my parents (I won't name names), and those shared by other close family members, seemed to inject my wavering courage to become a comedian with some sort of "You gotta lot of nerve gas." It was as if something made them tell my pediatrician to inoculate me with a vaccine to keep me from believing in myself. It was hard to shake, this feeling of always being on the wrong side of a decision, particularly in my early twenties, after graduating college and being tossed back into the unreal world. My God-given right to become me, the *sooooo creative* me, whoever the fuck that was going to be, was obviously going to have to be encouraged by strangers.

Growing up, as far as my mind could see, my outlook was that either I was always wrong and never did the right thing, or if I did, it was either never enough or I should find some reason to hide it. I was in a constant state of dissatisfaction. Like man, even if I just checked into the Nirvana Hotel I'd be looking for reasons to check out, immediately. This kind of irrational fear clouded so much of my vision that I was virtually blinded to my own insights, even with my 20/20 eyesight and healthy brain, before I got to kindergarten.

Yup. That's why I had a need to become *sooooo creative*. I had to give birth to myself.

Talk about born-again Jews. *L'chaim.*

He Only **Hit Me Once and I Didn't** Even **Cry**

. . . Dad cried though. He cried a lot. At least that's what my mom frantically reported back to me, her baby boy, about an hour after the incident.

Physically speaking, I was fine. He really didn't even hit me that hard, and I *did* deserve some sort of punishment, given what an asshole I was being that night.

The reason I didn't cry was because I was so petrified that he had used his belt for the first time, and as soon as he started to pull it out of his beautiful, silk slacks, the only way I could escape the fright was to imagine that it wasn't happening. I was sort of numb to any real impact it might have had on me. It never should have happened but his sons were acting like idiots and embarrassing the shit out of him in front of his cronies.

Downstairs, about ten close friends of my parents, who routinely came over for kosher food, gossip, and gin rummy, were unaware of the drama unfolding a few floors above, and kept company with my poor, stressed-out mother. She valiantly tried to keep them happy, at the same time sensing the nightmare of a potential early death upstairs. Given my dad's weak ticker, I suspect Mom was much more concerned with losing a husband than an offspring. Given how I already felt about myself in general, I could hardly blame her.

The brief and rare violence sort of went in slow motion. Dad appeared more like Lee J. Cobb in *On the Waterfront* to me than anything real, and taken by the intensity of it all, I felt more like a theater patron than a bad boy.

Sure, there was a little bit of shock that set in for a few moments, but I didn't feel as frightened as I might have because my brother, the other rabble-rouser, also experienced Dad's frustration and wrath, and having his company sort of diluted the overall panic. There was a safety-in-numbers thing going down between us even though it was just the two of us.

We were somewhere around the ages of David and Ricky Nelson. For some reason that night we seemed to be acting crazily irresponsible and not caring if we humiliated our folks. We simply refused to give a civil "yes" to the scores of pleas from our parents to go to bed. After six or seven snotty "no's" we were ushered away in a furious energy field of my old man's pure will.

I don't remember whether it was my older brother or me who was more to blame for that dark night, but, regardless, the eerie part is that it was one of the few times I can recall, to that point in my life, when I knew with any clarity that I had taken an action (albeit clearly for attention) and gotten a result. As scary as that was, it also actually made sense. In my house, it was very unusual to take an action—good or bad—and actually get a consequence that bore some relation to it. For example, thousands of times I'd been warned that I *might* give him a heart attack if I didn't do what I was told, but this seemed totally irrational and had nothing remotely to do with my behavior and, furthermore, it never happened.

Maybe that's why the belt seemed almost amusing to me. I actually *was* a jerk-off that night and yet it was almost a relief to have some kind of cause and effect, in a home where perhaps only parapsychologists, or maybe archeologists, would have had an outside chance of unraveling any understanding as to why things were said, or why people responded the way they did. An unspoken veil of confusion always lurked in my childhood home, and might have prompted me to joke at the time, the world's youngest comic, "Hey, I'll tell you, talk about anxiety, every room in my house is a wreck room." The central feeling of my adolescence was never quite being sure if my feelings or reasoning counted. This left marks deeper, and more emotionally scarring, than anything a belt could ever do. I felt like a little prizefighter, always on the ropes, trying to defend myself for merely acting decently if whatever I've done or said didn't perfectly reflect my parents' sense of things or put them in a good light. For some odd and ultimately hurtful reason in their psychological makeup, it was hard for them to allow me to be myself without it almost always becoming adversarial if who myself was didn't agree with them on every point. If I ate this I should've eaten that. If I went to work with my father, it was either "about time" or "I'm not really cut out for the job." If I felt sick and wanted to stay home from school I was immediately doubted. It was like being in a matrix of control and early on I fought my way out with jokes and isolation. I remember my mother bought me these atrocious-looking green pants and I just couldn't even think about wearing them but she raised such a stink I wore them anyway, feeling like shit all day until a very cool and hip teacher friend of mine made me see the ludicrousness of it all and it was yet another occasion when laughter became more and more of an antidote to crushed feelings of identity. One day I was supposed to help my father box and wrap a ton of shit in the basement in preparation for storage and he didn't allow me to tie one box; instead, he wanted me to watch "how it was done." I became increasingly insecure about expressing my own feelings or even being capable of doing much of anything and thank God I was a good athlete, had a sense of humor, and the young girls dug me or I might have dug a hole for myself and never come out. The more adulation I got from outside the family the better I felt, and yet the more I felt I needed my family to see what was good about me. But they didn't. Thus, most success meant nothing because they didn't know how to make me feel like I deserved it.

Trust me, babe, *it's lonely at the bottom*. How was I supposed to act when I had no idea how or why? My only choice, it became increasingly clear, was to look for that same hole Alice found in Wonderland so I could split from my own Confusionland, get the hell out of that environment and find some impartial people—delicious strangers, even if they had to look like fucking *talking playing cards*. Emotional beggars can't afford to be choosers.

Although I was needy for the right attention, I still managed to be simultaneously paranoid about my trick knees. Because if and when I ever found that white rabbit and jumped down that hole after him toward my hopeful salvation, it seemed like quite a long way and who has time to get knee-pads at a potential turning point in your life like this? Surprise! Surprise! I never found the hole except the one I was already in.

Still, I'm sorry, Dad. I really am sorry. I'm sorry that I made you cry that night, and the few other times, but I swear on your grave that I had no idea who I was or what you or anyone else expected of me. I also didn't know that the deck was stacked and the house always won. Your house. *The House that Guilt Built.*

Just like in Las Vegas. The house always wins there, too. You know I headlined a few times in Vegas? I made a lot of bread, too. Ain't that something, man? You were gone a long time by then, but you would probably have been proud of me, even though it was a tough room. Just like in the old days, at home, when I used to perform in front of the clan for attention.

Funny, I never stopped performing, even when I wasn't getting paid for it. And I swear, Pop, it kills me that you were never alive to see me on stage. I bet you wouldn't have ever cried or dropped dead because of that. I bet you would have applauded. I wish you could have lived to be there.

I guess I never told you this until now but I never really felt like a man in front of you. Come to think of it, I don't think I ever felt like much of a man until I got on stage. Imagine that, Dad? I bet if I'd only had the balls to tell you that when you were alive, you would have been cool about it and would have made it all better. And I bet you would have liked me more, too. I'm right, aren't I? Come on, I know you're listening. Really. You see, I'm spiritual now. I swear. Isn't that a good thing? . . . Fine, play hard to get. But it better be a good thing because, man, it's been a *long road to serenity* and just a hop, skip, and a jump to the bar down the street and insanity. You know what? I have a feeling you know about this shit already without me telling you.

But I don't think you know that I was always left feeling like the little kid you hit with that cool, big belt of yours, on that night I acted like a schmuck in front of your friends.

Anyway, I was too confused to apologize to you back then, but I prayed, after Mom told me you were crying, that you knew I sort of didn't know what the fuck I was doing. I never knew really, like I said; not until I went on stage. Not until I became a comedian. People always tell me what guts it must take to be a stand-up. Now *that's* a joke. Between you and me, it's the easiest fucking thing I've ever done or ever will do. It's like I had no choice; it just came naturally. I rarely admitted it to myself back when I started—or rarely even admit it now—but on stage, I really feel like "the luckiest man on the face of the earth." Every night when there's an audience to see me I am as grateful as Lou Gehrig was when he tragically was forced to express his feelings to the world as he retired.

I hate to admit it to you but I always felt more comfortable around strangers. I couldn't stand to make you or anyone else cry or unhappy anymore. At least not unintentionally. After you suddenly died, I freaked, and I guess I just needed to hear laughs. Lots and lots of laughs.

I was on a mission. Every day. For the rest of my life. It sounds stupid, Dad, but in a weird way for me I guess it really was true what they say, "the show must go on." I wish you could have been there. Just fucking once. It only took me about eight weeks to get up the nerve to go to a club but almost thirty years, and then not even to your face, to really tell you how I really felt around you.

The **Virgin** Richard

I might have been better off just masturbating my entire life. I recall before I ever even experienced an orgasm, my buddy, Phil, called during the dinner hour, sounding so euphoric and with such a sense of urgency in his tone that my folks, who didn't like me to leave the dinner table for calls, made an exception with the instruction to keep it short and call him back after the meal. When I picked up the phone, all my ten-year-old schoolmate had to say were the words, "Yank it!" before he hung up.

I didn't exactly put it together right away what Phil meant, and for weeks I yanked everything in my room except my penis: shades, switches, the sheets—everything. Until, one night, running out of things to yank, in a state of frustration, I yanked my penis. And I kept yanking it, and then something happened midway through the episode that signaled my brain to not let me stop. I didn't stop; and then it happened. I came! Holy, fuckin', son-of-a-fuckin', amazing, joy-to-the-world discovery! It might not have been a spiritual awakening but it sure got my attention. I had no idea life could feel so good. And I'm not sure it's ever felt as good since. In fact, after that first cum, even though I was still a virgin, there was no reason to ever come out of my room again. But for a number of reasons, like food and funerals, I was forced to leave my room over the years. Otherwise there's no telling what might have happened to me. Not long after that, with all due respect to the Virgin Mary, I began to feel that bearing that burdensome label "virgin" was a wretched curse, and that I too would need some sort of divine intervention myself to lose it for good and gain a real sense of my male identity.

And then it finally happened, although it didn't come from God but from a pal of mine. He'd lost his condom inside this high school junior, a buxom spitfire, then seemed to suffer a slight nervous breakdown over the mishap and I seized the moment, which delightfully turned into the beginning of the end of my virginity.

I was about sixteen and was primarily frightened that I'd never get accepted into a college. I was also paralyzed with fear that I would remain both zit-faced and hypochondriacal, and was scared shitless of going into New York for a hooker or making it with one of the school sluts and maybe getting a disease that might ruin my dick forever, even though the daily disgrace I felt over being a virgin was driving me insane. As far as sex went, I was striking out. I had the worst time finding a decent young woman who would mercifully make me feel like a man, and quite frankly, where or when this transformation might occur could have hardly mattered as long as I officially had penetration. I would have gladly settled for almost any scenario to get that monkey off my back and my penis into someone's nirvana. I was desperate! A sympathy lay was next on my agenda. I privately jotted down names of potential women who might be of service to me if I was able to come up with the proper frantic fairy tale. Basically, I was praying for any decent-looking chick to help me finally taste manhood and would have gladly settled for a surreptitious, unceremonious fuck in the janitor's closet, say after Folk Dancing club wound down its activities. Beggars can't be choosers when one's manhood is at stake.

It's a striking contrast when I realize that just a few years after this adolescent torment I would soon be in the middle of the "summer of love," and my penis would have such a full date book that it would (even without the aid of hallucinatory drugs) seem to beg me for sanctuary, or at least plead for time off for magnificently reckless behavior. Nevertheless, before things broke loose for me at college and I was still stuck being a sixteen-year-old virgin, I had to shamefully and simultaneously contend with a cool-looking older brother, who was sort of the Wally to my Beav, and a father who had the air of a William Holden. I felt that if I didn't get laid before getting out of high school I would implode, not only from feeling desperately uncomfortably boyish and inadequate around these two men, but from the sense that the longer I remained a virgin, the harder it would be to get the gold. The notion of wasting my penis left me feeling empty, impotent, and carrying around an important appendage for no apparent reason. Nevertheless, I was well on my way to setting the Englewood, New Jersey, Dwight Morrow High School masturbation record for anxious, sexually inexperienced Jews.

So when my buddy felt his life was over after allegedly screwing some girl from a rival high school, having his condom stay in her vagina long after he was gone, and ejaculating a potential child into this incredibly hot looking babe, I hardly felt badly for him. Rather, I was consumed with jealousy. I would have taken on his fear of impregnating someone in a flash if only I could have lost my virginity in the bargain. The drama began around 2 A.M. The party was over and once again I hadn't scored. A few guys from our high school were munching on chips while my friend was humping away in his bedroom. Each moan made me cringe with resentment. He finally emerged half naked and screaming for guidance. The girl in question, this siren of sirens, coolly called a cab, and got herself as far away from the frightened, neurotic, hysterical display by my shaken friend as possible. I kid the feminists, but even though this condom faux pas had the potential to become a major problem, I found myself focusing more on her vagina than on my buddy's paranoia and deteriorating mental state. I heard nothing as he pleaded with us indifferent, unsympathetic wise guys to get him out of this jam. My eyes were totally fixed upon the woman in question and I was

overwhelmed by her coolness and her sumptuous body. I was mas-
terminding as quickly as I could a way to meet this strange and
glorious-looking creature and shamelessly, clandestinely, cozy up to
her before she went outside to wait for her taxi. I was filled with
hope that we would exchange numbers, and that I might be one step
closer to knowing penetration and finally walking around with that
"gleam" in my eyes that I felt came as part of the package. My
friend's nervous wailing in the background somehow made my
unscrupulous pickup even more exciting, and the intensity I felt
must have registered when our eyes met; hers quickly hinted that
my long-awaited virginity might soon come to an explosive end.
Without having to say much, I soon held the Holy Grail. As I looked
down at her scribbled number, which she gave to me without so
much as a guilty twinkle in her eye (this immediately sent any blood
I had rushing helter-skelter to my cock), I saw light at the end of her
tunnel and the end of my enduring frustration. I would not be
denied, even if it meant totally fucking over my school bud and acting like a scumbag before I'd even get a chance to wear one.

I went home, a man with a mission to have his first legitimate
emission, and immediately called this curvaceous answer to my
dreams. An older woman answered so I hung up faster than I would
eventually cum once I actually got the chance to have intercourse.
(And trust me, that took some doing. It wasn't my fault or the girl's
but my cock just wouldn't be a team player). The next day I got the
girl at home and found out that her mother had answered the night
before. She went to some school in a neighboring town and, though
I rambled on and on about how guilty I felt hitting on her right after
she'd been with my friend, nonetheless it was still only days later
that I got the chance of my young lifetime.

She apparently wanted me, and from what I learned later, many
others (at any time, regardless of where or when). That hardly mattered to me at the outset, a whining virgin who had done everything
I could with a woman except feel what it was like to slip that "thing"
inside that mysterious other "thing" and I was beside myself with
glee. To make matters even better, my parents were planning to

leave town for the weekend. I had the whole bloody place to myself, to finally do the deed . . . or so I thought. She was smart and seemed to dig me and I was just in awe of her body and at the prospect of getting steady nooky throughout my senior year, then heading off upon acceptance to a university, feeling finally like I was a complete man. Little did I know the horror of what was about to occur. I didn't understand until almost thirty years later when my therapist told me that innocuous orgasms and applause from strangers seemed to be my only outlets for stress management. That was the last thing I could have known as a potential senior in high school on the verge of screwing myself into unconsciousness.

We planned a date and she seemed happy enough to just come over to the house and get to know each other. I avoided talking to my pal but through the grapevine I heard he was still bemoaning the fact that he might have gotten my new flame pregnant, and was carrying on like his life was over. I never mentioned this nor did I tell her that I hid about forty condoms under every conceivable hiding place in the house, just in case. I was so excited I even put a few Trojans in the refrigerator. What did I know? I thought we might wind up fucking in front of the fridge and I didn't want to have to excuse myself and locate my protection in another room, let alone a few feet away from the "act." God forbid she might lose interest, or worse yet, get pangs of guilt about my despondent friend and not only go back to him, but spill the beans before I could spill my seeds.

The next forty-seven and a half hours were intercourse hell! Cocky, I first sat by the fireplace for about eight seconds and held her hand before I tried, as romantically as possible, to rip her clothes off. I didn't have to. She ripped her own clothes off except her bra, which she (for some cruel, psychic reason) might have known I would struggle with, and I did so, until she groaned something that sounded like, "Jews are so bad with mechanical things," and undid the hooks or whatever they are until, there she was—stark naked. Instantly I had to think of a way to get us upstairs and into my bed, because even in the heat of the moment I couldn't help but think that if I ejaculated on anything in that living room, most of which probably came from my parents' parents, the very thought of having my cum on some antique from the Russian Revolution or on some Romanian ashtray left me shuddering with the thought of my inevitably insane explanation and its ultimate punishment. So with my pants down to my knees and my penis acting like a divining rod leading the way, she followed me as I pathetically hopped up the stairs to my bedroom like some half-crazed, Jewish Energizer Bunny, praying that I wouldn't lose steam after this childlike, pied piper approach to my bed. Well, by the time we got under the covers it was impossible for both of us not to notice the wallpaper, which had been there since I was a kid and evoked belittling laughter from her, followed by disdain from my erection. It's not easy maintaining an erection with cowboys and clowns staring at you. Feeling like the antilover (and, although I was a great kisser, having no game plan for foreplay), I immediately tried to jam my member inside of her. Obviously she'd had a shitload of experience and wasn't so much upset as startled; and found it rather humorless when the wind went out of my sails and my penis collapsed. It betrayed me, leaving me with the first of many hundreds (and well, let's leave it at that) of justifications that I'd conjure up through the years when my dick would go south and my ego had to grab the microphone and make up some sort of excuse. Much to my surprise she was sweet and tried to get me hard again and just when she had, once again, loverboy skipped over any sign of lovemaking ability and tried to immediately go for invasion. And just like clockwork, *Mr. Flaccid* ruled and I was again stuck with conjuring up some sort of excuse. I always stopped just short of saying that I was, at the most inopportune time, inexplicably summoning up images of the Holocaust as my sexually dysfunctional cop-out, but believe me, the pressure I felt to actually get laid for the first time led me down a bullshit path that came precariously close to not only fucking over my friend, but almost trying to trivialize the worst nightmare perhaps of all times.

After two days and nights of trying every bed, chair, couch, and room in the house, finally, without thinking what it might mean to me psychologically down the line, I got a great hard-on, and in the parlance of my own previrgin state of mind, "fucked her long and hard," but sadly did it in the bed where my folks were rumored to do it, and even though I lost my virginity, I couldn't shake the smell of my mother's perfume and the notion that her potion was the magic that put me over the hump, so to speak. This left me with a haunting, sickening knot in my libido and easy, entertaining fodder for many shrinks to liven up dull sessions with in later years.

But not that night!!!!!! Oh no, baby, I wouldn't take that event away from me regardless of how I smelled my mother when I came. My new girlfriend, at least from my glorious vantage point, was too young to mock me, and I was too happy to undermine what I thought was perhaps the single most important thing I had ever done.

The relationship didn't last long, though, and many years later I apologized to my buddy for stealing his lay. He seemed to understand, considering at the time of my amends he was already married and had a young baby and was perplexed as to why it had taken me decades to admit. He actually seemed quite pleased that he'd had a hand in helping me through that rite of passage and was more inclined to ask me just how many other friends had fucked him over. Of course I didn't know and now as I look back on myself as this horny teenager and try to figure out if there is much difference in me (thirty-five years later) in my evolution as a human being, sexually speaking, all I can think of is that I might be a better lover, that I can get an erection anywhere with almost any woman in almost any climate range, and yet, sadly, other than for that first time, somewhere along the line I've lost the concept that I can *still* enjoy myself without only caring about *how good* I perform. But far more important, I'm still aching for a good sexual run with one woman, when making love will have far more to do with feeling a deeper connection as a couple, rather than just an act, with nothing more to it than feeling like I had a great high school gym class.

Like I said, I might have been better off just masturbating my entire life. At least then I wouldn't have jerked anyone *else* around.

Jimi

Who knew that I'd go to college in the late sixties and be mostly sober and frightened of most drugs? I mean, if there ever was a time to get fucked up those were the years when it sort of made sense, at least historically speaking. I was pretty fucking straight, long hair and all. As alienated as I felt growing up I must have been happy enough by the time I got to college that I didn't have the need *at all* to wipe out my feelings or expand my mind as much as to discover who the fuck I was. I guess it was after I graduated—poor, scared, and feeling that I would amount to nothing—when every sidewalk became a red carpet to the nearest liquor store. Yet at school I had a ball and actually was mostly coherent for all of it. I mean, sure, I got high every now and then, but it never became a burning thing to do, or a must. New women and new rock albums and new books were plenty.

Without a doubt, my four years attending Ohio State were the most pleasurable times of my life. In fact, I'm sure of it. For one, I was away from home and far away from the scene of the emotional crime of making me feel invisible. I made friends who listened to me and admired my sense of humor. I'll always remember being out with a lot of pals, professors and artists at some Chinese restaurant, and I was in the middle of a riff when the waiter interrupted me and asked for orders. With all the people there it took about ten minutes. As soon as the waiter left, the guy sitting next to me turned and said very casually, "Now, where were you, Richard?" I was staggered. Not only did someone remember that I was talking, but he actually wanted to hear what I had to say. It was a stunning revelation. I haven't stopped talking since.

And what does any of this have to do with my future alcoholism? Well, I'm not exactly sure, and yet, ironically, given the newly dis-covered openness to drug experimentation and all that hippie shit going down (I think), absolutely nothing. In fact, it's striking to me that being so blessed to have experienced the carefree college years during an intellectual, breast-filled, penis-flapping, rock 'n' roll era, I didn't much think about getting loaded. I wanted to behave decently, study hard, and meet as many coeds as I could possibly juggle and be jiggled by, at the same time. Just waiting on line for the new Beatles album and standing on the stunning, colossal oval in the center of campus waiting to see if Eugene McCarthy was really going to show were such highs that getting loaded seemed superfluous. It wasn't even in my repertoire yet. Not to mention that I didn't smoke a lot of pot because I was too paranoid to begin with and strong grass made me think I was stalking myself.

I was just busy happily enjoying my freedom away from almost everyone I had ever known; meeting people who actually seemed to care about what I had to say; struggling with free love, and with my dismay at American involvement in Vietnam. That set the backdrop for my encounter with *the man*.

With the war on the tube every night provoking an insane amount of anxiety, I found myself (after a heated political discussion in some pseudointellectual bar) on the Ohio State campus wondering and wandering aimlessly, eventually to a friend's pad, while for the first time experimenting with opium. I was excited because the space cadet at the hippie saloon who I'd scored from told me it was pretty safe and that I would have beautiful dreams while walking home. I figured, since I was too afraid of LSD (thinking I'd kill myself unintentionally), pot was a bust, and beer didn't really interest me, that it seemed reasonable enough to give it a whirl. Being fed up with my recurring nightmares about not being able to find the classroom for my final exams, the prospect of having pleasant hallucinations while still awake seemed pretty damn cool.

The opium had no effect on me except it cost me money and gave me a craving to find a pickup basketball game and finger paint again. Well, okay, I guess that it had some effect but hey, I had wilder, more enlightening daydreams straight, and besides, I was living on a tight budget with money that my father sent me from back home in New

Jersey and it is very doubtful that he would have opened the coffers for recreational drug use . . .

"Hey, Dad."

"Richard?"

"Yeah."

"Wanna speak to your mom?"

"Sure . . . but . . ."

"Is everything all right?"

"Yeah, Mom . . . but I wanted to ask Dad something."

"What? You have secrets from me?"

"I'm sorry, you're right. Listen, can you ask Dad to send me an extra fifty bucks a month for opium?"

Like that conversation wouldn't have caused a double suicide.

The opium high a dud and feeling stone-cold sober, I still headed excitedly to my buddy's flat to cop a listen from this new rocker, Jimi Hendrix. My friend had heard the album that morning and had called me a million times saying over and over again, "My God, you won't believe this shit."

Now, when I got to his place, he let me in, said nothing, and handed me the *Are You Experienced?* album. He acted like he was the keeper of some dark secret. Displaying a rare twinkle in his eyes, he turned and retreated to his room. I gazed at the photo of this weird threesome on the album cover and then placed the LP on the turntable, anxious to hear what the big to-do was all about. I still get excited thinking that the time it took to place the needle down on the first track was all the time I had left to struggle through life without knowing that "Purple Haze" existed and would keep me company forevermore.

I was alone with the headphones on, lying on the dirty floor of his psychotically decorated living room, staring up at a Marx Brothers poster while my friend was either fucking someone in his bedroom or yelling at himself. He was a strange guy but it hardly registered with me for the next forty minutes or so.

Everything changed for me then. I mean really, really changed. I was only about eighteen or nineteen and I must have been inspired here and there before but I never was *so* grabbed by the lapels of my being and filled with some sort of quiet confidence; a hip shove towards some unforeseen passion, almost like a hit of subliminal hope that I would someday have to pursue something that meant more to me than anything else. Something that would be an extension of my being until they became one and the same. I didn't know it then but I think that was the moment I became a comedian because I was listening to someone who seemed to exist entirely for his music, much as I would soon have no choice but to survive largely through hearing laughter.

It saddens me to think that I must have felt so hollow inside that I needed to attach myself to something, some force that I could create from within to express to others, a "thing" that would embody what I felt best represented who I thought I was; and to do it to such a degree and with such a vengeance that there was no room to think about or attach myself to much else. Almost a quarter of a century later, after hearing a lot of laughs and drinking a lot of alcohol, I let God into my life. A God that would save my life. But before I needed a higher power, I needed hope on the ground. Hendrix played with such reckless, authentic, powerful purity, it shook me up in a way that—although I didn't understand at the time—ultimately gave me a faith in myself as an artist that I never thought I would have.

After I finished hearing the record I let myself out. In an almost trancelike fashion, I started walking back through the streets, trying to find my apartment, while in such a state of euphoria that I could've trudged on forever and it wouldn't have mattered. I had been shaken to my core. And hadn't even known that I had a core.

The music I heard that day sounded like nothing I had ever heard before or since. It was inconceivable that this guy and his two band members were making this strange sound and so much of it. It was indescribable. It was out of this world. In fact, I felt like I did when I fantasized walking in some field and actually seeing a flying saucer land, just standing there stunned as the aliens came down their gangplank to check me out. I'd be in a state of shock but mostly feeling amazed and blessed that *I* had the good fortune to be one of the few people on earth to actually know for real that there was more to the universe than just us little confused and conflicted earthlings.

Jimi Hendrix sounded like he came from outer space. I had never in my life heard anyone play as if he was put on the planet to do only this. Forget about different. This was it. Game over. Rock fans had their Messiah.

Finally, I had a private, ear-shattering sanctuary, a place I could go to and listen, for the rest of my life, for an energy and a touchstone that was so unusually forceful and full of love that I knew I could get happy no matter what.

Purple Haze was in my brain. For good.

Group **Therapy**

When I received the phone call from my brother that my father had died, it sort of made some kind of sickening artistic sense to me, considering that I was working as a librarian in the archives at the Museum of Modern Art. Listening to my brother's words through the receiver, I became mummified, frozen in time, just like the energized masters' paintings hanging on the walls. All my comedic painting was ahead of me, though, and I felt like an old, old man, after having only tiptoed into my early twenties, frightened that I'd never become a master at anything. And worse, if I did, the man I so desperately wanted to impress would now never know.

New York never sounded so silent as when I left the museum that day, heading into the subway to start my trek back to my crummy apartment in New Jersey to pack and then head down to Florida, where my folks had moved just a little over a year before the shocking tragedy. I felt so alone and frightened. I was forced to become the man that my father seemed to symbolize to me. He was such a big shot, and I was free-falling in a city filled with millions of people who seemed to know exactly where they were headed. The only thing I knew was that I needed tokens. On the train I sat there numb; not numb from booze or pills or dope, but from fear. I felt isolated, as if my father's death left me hanging onto a tether attached to nothing. I hadn't realized how dependent I was on the strength I felt knowing that my father was around; I guess somehow I'd always figured he would come through for me if I was on the verge of collapse. My worst-case scenario was that I didn't have enough of a self to make anything out of my life, and that somehow the King of Caterers would help me figure it out. But, the King was dead; that possibility was now history. I needed help. I didn't quite feel ready yet to be my own man.

I wasn't drinking heavily at this point in my life so I couldn't hide out from the pain; I really felt the feelings of shock and aloneness. I was petrified that without being a part of his life I was meaningless, and could no longer bask in his charisma or in the safety of his financial support, but instead had to develop my own. That was the whammy he had over me. Even though he didn't really support me financially after graduation, I had only been on my own for about a year and a half, and I perceived him, even as a twenty-three-year-old, just as I had when I was a small boy. With him gone, life seemed fragile and tentative.

I was a mess. In fact, I was sort of in a comatose state on the A train heading up to 175th Street to get a bus across the George Washington Bridge. But there I was met by a (now *former*) friend of mine who I had called from the museum to tell the news, figuring he'd help me get *my* shit together—as I had helped *him* a few years back when his father had died. He comforted me. He was a lifesaver. Many years later, after I became a celebrity and had lots of bread, he would beg me for thousands and thousands of dollars, saying he'd wind up in the streets otherwise, and I was alcoholic by that time and couldn't give it away fast enough. He of course never paid me back. Few people ever do when they beg. But somehow he was nicer as a younger man, and he helped me make my plans to get to Miami where he eventually paid his respects a few days later. My girlfriend at the time, who I had met at college, was, as usual, loving and loyal to my needs and would be my pillar of strength. It sounds so biblical, "pillar of strength," but when you lose someone who defines you, the way I thought my father defined me, you're left with such a hole in your gut that you need a tremendous amount of nurturing—or a mental institution. I opted for nurturing and sobbing, and a little bit of faith. Others close to my dad eventually wound up institutionalized or even in cults, but I was blessed with too much of a sense of humor to get that low, and was way too cynical to fraternize with mind-benders; and, besides, I was soon destined to find a group of neurotics to hang with in a group therapy situation to make me feel less isolated.

Therapy was the last thing I ever thought about even trying—until my life seemed so empty and I was absolutely scared shitless that not only wouldn't I find a real passion for living, but that even if I did, it would never seem real or fulfilling without my father around to validate it. Oh yeah, with feelings like that shrinkage is right around the bend or you can go mad. I knew I was depressed, but I had begun to fear losing my mind.

So I did eventually decide to seek therapy—for the first but certainly not the last time. First I spent a year as an outpatient in a Queens hospital, working with an intern from India who was gorgeous and Freudian and rarely spoke and had long legs and a beautiful turban and analyzed my dreams for a great price—a buck an hour. But I eventually felt more at home in a group founded by the Father of the Inferiority Complex, Alfred Adler. What a wonderful place to moan and groan. Imagine . . . eight or nine people, all fucked up, all anxious to be anxious in front of each other, tell their soap operas and then be hugged and even end the night with a few cookies and well wishes. What a safe haven for feeling like shit and eating junk food.

I mean here I was, a broke comedy writer with all sorts of odd jobs, barely holding on to a dream of maybe even being a comedian myself, struggling to understand how I could ever feel part of a loving relationship, suddenly without my Pop, having a mother who I could hardly communicate with, a sister in another state raising four young kids, and a brother on the loose in New York trying to find a niche for himself. But as the members of the group shared their miles and miles of misery it became almost festive. *I wasn't alone.* I wasn't the only one who felt like I had no shadow. I was surrounded by angst-ridden individuals who felt as shitty as I did. I loved these people! We were a human safety net for people who felt very unsafe. We were high-wire lunatics not afraid to fall anymore. We had each other. Well . . . it was a start anyway. We cried and fought and yelled and hugged and bitched and moaned—but mostly we felt as if we were part of the world again. Misery loves company and this was quite a bonanza! If we'd formed a softball team we would've won the league championship hands down, gone undefeated, since we would've made other teams feel too sorry for us to beat us.

We all would meet once a week with our therapist and then have this "after-group" gig at someone's apartment each night, after we'd eaten dinner at some diner near the doctor's office in Manhattan. This second, captainless session—this time without the shrink intervening with common sense and guidance—was like being in a clinic endorsed by the Marx Brothers. We usually ended near midnight, sometimes feeling better but *always* reinforcing the need to stay in therapy. We became dependent on people who had problems similar to our own.

I loved our little commune of confusion. I needed it. The only time I didn't dig it was when I felt good. That generally threatened the more unbalanced of the lot. Feeling good meant only one thing. I might be close to braving the city streets and love affairs without their help, and what gave me the right to have so much self-confidence? It really got tough to leave. I tried but they made it hard. And in the end I hung around for almost four years. That's a lot of permutations and variations on a lot of kvetching. Sure, there was a lot of love, too, but after a while our sessions seemed almost like contests to decide who was the most hopeless.

In 1976 I moved out to Los Angeles and for the first few weeks the group taped the sessions so I could keep up-to-date on everyone's problems. Then I'd tape my return problems and feedback on a cassette and mail it back to them. The problem with that was that by the time they got my tape I might have gone through thousands of other dilemmas and the dilemmas I'd sent them had either mutated or were dated.

Like clockwork, each week, the tape of the group's previous session would come in the mail to me at my hole-in-the-wall Hollywood apartment, and I would race up the rickety stairwell, take a seat at my ugly kitchen table, pour myself a little glass of cheap white wine, plug in the tape, and listen to my vulnerable New York buds whine and moan. I was so caught up in their tales of woe and missed them so. And, I must admit, for a time these tapes made me feel far less alone in Hollyweird.

Then a very bizarre thing occurred. Around the third week of the taping routine, one of the members, a very fragile, depressed female, who religiously broke down and wept when she shared, did so again. I poured myself another glass of shit wine, placed the tape recorder closer to my ear, eager to hear the outcome, hoping that the doctor and the group would help her. It was hard to understand her or hear how others in the group were responding to her through the theatrical weeping. It was making me crazy. Or rather, crazier. Then it happened. The well-intentioned therapist, knowing this session was being taped for their Hollywood escapee, cut her off midwhine.

"Could you please sob closer into the mike for Richard?"

That was the end of my group therapy career. I was stricken with unbelievable guilt that this poor woman had to start over relating her horrible relationship troubles and weeping again to provide better production values for me. Moreover, and I could be wrong, but I actually think I heard the shrink say, "Action!"

Within days I found a Hollywood therapist of my own and the intimacy of just sharing my wretchedness alone, with my own doctor and no one else (to the best of my knowledge) eavesdropping. After years of having to share my time with others, this was such a luxury and so exhilarating that I have never again felt an urge to have my therapy with a *studio audience* anymore. A good shrink is plenty.

Give me a decent couch, a great woman therapist who I can never fuck up by marrying, some Kleenex nearby, and I'm in heaven, baby.

Sunshine the Cat

As a kid, I thought Felix the Cat was just about the coolest character in the world. I wanted his bag of tricks in the biggest way. When my father died, Felix was a no-show at the funeral, and there were no tricks to help me get through it; but a mysterious cat ultimately named Sunshine stepped in and became perhaps the first miracle I ever experienced firsthand.

My dad had died suddenly and shockingly, after what the family had thought to be successful open-heart surgery. We wore his loss like some ugly shroud, our feelings all tangled up. No one in the family seemed able to confidently envision a future without him. In the years to follow, his death would continue to wreak havoc on the emotional state of our family, for some of us more than others.

I would soon have plenty of time to freak about myself, but right after I heard the news and went down to be with my mother in Florida, I was focused solely on how she, then in her midfifties, would carry on her life without our patriarch. Their colorful apartment in North Miami Beach overlooking a beautiful bay seemed all gray now, and the beautiful Floridian scenery lurking just outside appeared hellish.

I hadn't been to the condo very often. I was pretty broke, holding down many odd jobs back up in New York and New Jersey and just flirting with the notion of becoming a comedian. I couldn't afford casual trips down to visit. Right after the funeral, as soon as the mourning period began, the condo suddenly seemed like a place where my mother was hiding out like some old rock 'n' roller stumbling around in a funk in the legendary Chelsea Hotel, waiting for that sense of emptiness and dread to either lift or take her with it. Jam-packed with mourners, days grew into tortuous nights, and as time passed the more profound the sense of loss became. My mother seemed to be retreating more and more into an unknown state of mind. I couldn't shake the fact that sooner or later the mourners would have to get on with their own lives, and make their way back to their respective cities to grieve privately. My brother, sister, and I knew that we too would eventually leave, and it was almost unfathomable for me to comprehend how we could leave my mother in what I imagined would be a dreadful solitude. But on the second day after the funeral, with the house full of sorrow and in the grip of that overwhelming sadness that sucks all the air out of a place, a miraculous occurrence took place.

There was this sound . . . the purring of a cat from outside the only entrance to the condo. Someone opened the door and there he was. To those looking, it was a cat, and that fact was as obvious as its beautiful brown face, funny whiskers, and sneaky grin. But this was no ordinary cat. This was a cat that Felix himself would have traveled across the world to pay homage to. *This cat embodied my father's soul.*

As odd and weird as this sounds, I knew it instantly. It didn't take long for the *visitor* to enter and immediately find my brother, my sister, and me. In fact, there must have been at least seventy-five people there at the time, but this cat seemed to care very little about anything or anyone, other than rubbing itself up against a Lewis. It went from me, to my brother, to my sister (my mother was feigning some rest in the living room) and back and forth until I was so sure that my father had come back in some way, not only to do something to penetrate the gloom and doom that felt infinite, but inevitably to be company and comfort to my mother once everyone had said their last good-byes.

Initially he caused quite a commotion because it was logistically impossible for a pet to be there. Pets were strictly not allowed in my parents' condo community. My parents' place was on the third floor. Most people took the elevator to get to their homes and of course would never want to use the dark stairwell, which had heavy doors (always closed) on each level. The only way this cat could have even gotten to the front door was to take the elevator himself—quite a trick, even for the great one, Felix. That aside, there were hundreds of units and he would have had to inquire where the Lewis pad was—then manage to open the door on the first level, climb up the stairs, open the third-story door, meander over and then, of course— probably being unequipped with a small ladder that would make it possible to reach the doorbell or politely knock—he'd have to just purr his ass off for attention and admittance. Of course, he could have had an angelic co-conspirator. Stranger things have happened during miracles. Someone very mysterious and anonymous could have dropped him by the door and run—or perhaps flown—away.

My mother never liked animals. *This* animal she liked. She finally came in to the center of the action and watched with amazement as the cat licked and rubbed his head against her children, and no one else. Then stopped, seemed to look up at my mother, and dashed off.

The mood definitely lifted. There might even have been that first little bit of laughter since the news of Dad's death. A group of us went after the cat. It didn't take long to see the strangest sight I had ever seen. He was lying on my parents' bed, on my father's side. Somehow he seemed to be doing the best he could to place his front paws behind his little head. We all were silent. It was truly something out of this world. Then without much warning he bolted again. This time he went out on the little terrace and jumped right on the chair where my dad had spent hours and hours sunning himself.

The cat was drawing attention in such a way that there was no question he was coming from a very beautiful and mystical place. In a matter of moments my sister blurted out the name "Sunshine." And it was a keeper.

I recall there was a man there who I believe was a veterinarian or at least a huge "cat person," but even he had never seen anything quite like this. Many chose to be astounded over the mystery of how any animal could have gotten in the complex and into the condo, but that hardly mattered to me. It was still years before alcoholism and decades before I believed in God, but to me, back then, Sunshine embodied my father's soul and was only there to try to bring relief to the grief, in particular for his wife. I had no doubt then, and today I am convinced.

Daze later . . .

Sunshine slept with my mother and she didn't appear so alone. The condo was no longer a haven for crying, but a place where the four of us had to make sort of an initial closure to death, before going back to our lives to see how we'd do without him. That moment came when my mother wanted us to look through Dad's belongings and decide among us what we might want. I'm sure that this happens all the time but, perhaps because I was starting to feel the fear of growing up and discovering myself without a father, this activity somehow felt akin to cannibalism to me. I hated going through his stuff. I hated accepting he'd died. I hated feeling so afraid. I hated feeling so lost. I hated how scared I was. I paced back and forth while my brother and sister chose beloved memorabilia. I even started hating *them* for doing it. I was a mess in the making. Then a force somehow mellowed me out and pushed me toward his jewelry box, now under scrutiny. I had a scowl on my face and just wanted to be away from all the pain, these reminders of the loss of him. I wanted none of his stuff. I wanted his time and love and affection and understanding and nurturing and advice. His workaholic lifestyle and uninspiring parenting skills left me feeling angry and sad and resentful that this was all I could get from him forevermore. And yet, even as I wanted to move away from the box I felt this little push of encouragement to look inside. I had hardly talked for an hour, then suddenly I saw something that I had never remembered my father owning, and in a voice that came from the depths of my grief (I'm certain with a little help from the old man himself) I boomed out, "I want that!"

There was a stunned reaction from everyone. I had practically shrieked and it seemed so out of place and yet was so forceful and said with such conviction it was like no one would have dared not acquiesce to my demand. My father was with me. I just knew it. It wasn't wishful thinking. It really wasn't any of that psychobabble shit that could rationalize away what I felt was his sign to me. A sign that he felt my pain, that I deserved this piece of him to always remind me of my reluctance to take a dead father's stuff. I felt that he appreciated what I was going through and understood me deeply, and that this was our little memory that I should have. It made me feel special. Who knows, maybe he wanted me to. So I picked up the tiepin and everyone commented that they had never seen it before.

It was a little face of a cat. To me it wasn't, and still isn't, just some memento or memory of the father I lost. Because it seemed so new when I saw it, it represented some sort of psychic connection to the kind of father I might have had, had he lived longer. It was a little bit of sunshine that I could use as a touchstone for the rest of my life, that would not just be a reminder of the loss but of hope.

Sunshine the Cat stayed with my mother for a while after everyone had left her alone. Within weeks, she reverted back to her aversion to animals and made sure a good home was found for the magical cat. Two months later I went on stage for the first time as a comedian in Greenwich Village and although I didn't wear a tie, I knew that in a little box in a little drawer in a shitty little apartment in New Jersey was a little fashion accessory, meowing quietly to itself.

King of Caterers, Meet Your Prince of Pain

When my father passed away I was in a state of shock. Although his death catapulted me onto the stage to fill the emptiness and despair, I never thought I could become successful without his help. He was such a powerful figure in my life, a charismatic king of caterers to all the people who paid him to make their huge occasion one to remember. Yet for me, as a child, observing from the sidelines far down on the bench and eager to get in the same appreciation game myself (or at least understand just how he did it, how he made people love and respect him so much), I tended to idolize him. His early death left me clueless and without much understanding of why I was running on empty so early in life, and feeling so confused about who I was.

I had certainly inherited my father's drive, but also, sadly, his unwillingness to let people in. He never seemed to trust many people, and toward the end of his life his mistrust seemed valid as business dealings crumbled. Historically, I'm not sure about all the damage his alcoholic father did to him, or about the responsibility he was saddled with by being compelled to take on the role of man of the house, with a mother, five sisters, and a distant brother all looking to him for strength and money in his early teens. Forced to leave high school and help out, it seems that even with his glowing prowess as a baseball player he had to take most of the responsibility for the family; his older brother, an accountant from what vague pieces of information I've gathered, wasn't supportive at all in helping him pursue the prospects of becoming a professional ballplayer. He was stuck having to leave high school early, forgo his athletic dream, and start building a business—his success at which he would be enormously proud of. I don't know the true scenario, because my dad didn't speak much of his internal pain and observable melancholy, but instead carried them with him like quiet weights, closed off the outside world, and threw himself into his career with only rare, intermittent blasts of anger in front of the family. He thrived on success. He seemed nourished by accolades. In fact, accolades seemed to be the only thing that nurtured him. I should have seen it coming for myself.

My own mistrust of people was forever emblazoned on my psyche by the "vague" facts surrounding Dad's selling his part in the business. The word of mouth, at least on our side of the street, was that the much younger caterers who bought him out (after Dad was forced to retire after having many heart attacks) told him after the sale was completed that he should not come back—*ever*—and suit up in his tuxedo during the prime summer wedding season. This would have enabled my father to just get a taste of what he'd devoted his entire life to, and what on the surface seemed to give him a thirst for life. You have to know that he really was revered, almost like a Knute Rockne of the kosher catering business. But his presence must have intimidated the new guys. They probably thought he would steal their thunder.

My father rarely discussed the situation and kept it yet another dark secret. Although I recall that he acknowledged that he had to sell his part in the business for health reasons and be forced into retirement, he had always assumed he could fly up north once a year and show up like some famous ex–ball player suiting up for an old-timers' game. But no luck. He was shut out, blacklisted from the very company he helped create. The rug was pulled out from under him. He still looked mighty, but his heart was obviously broken, and he lived only about a year and a half after the news that he was unwelcome at the catering halls and functions forevermore.

Upon reflection, my dad's sudden fall from grace and his bad health remind me so much of how my silent hero, Buster Keaton, must have felt (although tragically he was much younger), when the studios took his toys away and he had nowhere to go with his genius. My father was always bigger than life to me, and to be cut off in his prime, then to apparently have his dignity fucked with, left me with this memory of a proud, hardworking guy—who in the end was left dazed, confused, and hopeless about what life had dealt him.

For months after the funeral I walked around pretty dazed myself. I was practically broke, living in dumps, scrounging for work, struggling with depression, and trying to keep a relationship with my college girlfriend afloat. I was full of fear. He had done so much to make my life comfortable; I'd never really given much thought to becoming anything, least of all a "nothing." Then suddenly he was gone; and with that, for an excruciating period of time, I couldn't shake the notion that he might come down from heaven, pick me up by my collar, and throw me into show business, without me having to figure out how.

No such luck. Dad couldn't do anything to help me. Except that his absence helped force me to believe solely in myself, and gave me a blind faith that without him around I could overcome my self-consciousness about my desire to make people laugh, and eventually allowed me even to dreamily contemplate (as insane as that felt) doing it for a living. It was that newfound need to believe in myself that helped me forge a career in show business, but also abetted me in thinking I could do anything on my own; even drink myself to death.

Club **Isolation**

I felt a strange energy churning somewhere very deep in my soul as I listened to John Lennon's first solo album. I was only about twenty-two when I heard and felt his amazingly beautiful moans with their primal, daggerlike finger-pointing, so gut-wrenchingly honest about such important shit and I knew at once that I was a billion miles away from having the balls to express myself like that, and that I had an overpowering need to do so. A need that I was way too embarrassed to admit to anyone yet, and was too scared to understand myself. Why did I need an audience so desperately, that I would risk busting out of the isolation of all my disgust with life, and share it? I felt like a twisted court jester without an audience.

My father had just died and I was mortified at having all of these unresolved feelings about his death—and most everything else. Most troubling to me, the little things in life, like who I was, what I wanted, what I'd do with myself, how I'd make a living, how to stay in the relationship with my college sweetheart without feeling like a fake, and, well, let's face it, I was a cafeteria of doom.

My bell-bottoms were the only sweet reminder of how blissful things had been just a year earlier when I was finishing up my glorious stint at Ohio State, and my dad still paid for everything. I made some lifelong friends there and I never had to think about death or what I had to do to function on the planet, except to be amusing to people, not litter, and get women to fall for me.

I found myself in one of a thousand different flats after college graduation, fairly broke, yet never broke enough to not gather up enough bread to buy anything by a former Beatle, especially Lennon. Somehow on this particular, soon-to-be-revelatory day, I was off from the many odd jobs I was doing at the time. My girlfriend was in school teaching her elementary kids and I was alone with John. As I think back now, it wasn't much different from the incredible rush I felt hearing Hendrix for the first time, in that this too was an extraordinary experience. With Jimi I was just blown to smithereens. With John I was frightened by the rigorous honesty and personal intensity. But as exhilarated as I was by the music and, in particular, the lyrics, I was also intimidated, because I knew I had so many similar feelings, and I knew also that, for me, it wasn't enough just to realize it. I felt the burden, immediately and in some powerful way, of trying to express all of this pain artistically somehow. Being a spectacular "class clown" made my sense of artistic direction easy, but I never realized how all-consuming it would be. *I was going to be a comedian.* Wow. I was going to be a comedian. I didn't become one for a while, but the seed was planted.

I walked around in a stupor for so long, before there was even a dim light ahead of me, but I smelled the blood of potential audiences listening to me moan and groan with the occasional punch lines thrown in. I had always felt trapped within myself; a man imprisoned and paralyzed by feelings of loneliness and completely clueless as to how to even begin to get out of this dungeon I found myself traveling in. My torture chamber was furnished with a tremendous amount of anger and neediness, and must have been built long before I knew I had the right to be myself.

But as soon as Lennon's music resonated in my head, I felt instantly free when for the first time I ever gave it a thought that little old me, Richard Lewis, could possibly say publicly how I felt, even if it might be harder to accomplish if you weren't a Beatle. Wild, man. Go public. Imagine? All the people. Go figure. What a strange idea. Who the fuck did I think I was anyway? I didn't really know, but somehow I had found a kind of inner strength that kept pushing me to fight back against my sense of crumbling, and into the building of self-confidence by admitting *all* my flaws, anxieties, and resentments. I thought if I could make light of how much I hated myself I would magically mend.

I had a need not just to work out my fears alone or with a shrink or even just with an overly sympathetic lover, but to work them out with absolute strangers. Paying customers no less. People who could hang me for my sheer audacity and self-centeredness. I needed to win over everyone who hadn't hurt me.

Street corners seemed too crazy and dangerous, plus I was afraid of the big moths that hung around those street lamps, so nightclubs seemed like a very cool alternative.

It was like I needed people to coddle me and tell me that I was okay for feeling so bad, so hurt and alone, and that everything would be all right. And somehow it made perfect sense that just as long as they laughed at me, I could be saved.

"You Got It"

It feels like an awfully long time ago, when a frighteningly hip, irreverent, eccentric, former comic turned nightclub owner, George Schultz—an early mentor to me and many others now sadly gone—took me outside after seeing me perform for the first time and said, *smiling*, "You got it." I took in this rare show of support in a big way because in the early days there didn't seem a chance in hell that I was going to make the slightest dent in "the business." But George was the legendary guy they called "the Ear," because he knew without a doubt who would make it and who probably wouldn't. He revealed only the former, and rarely. And, he was always right too . . . I'm proud to say. And not only just about talent, but as it turned out, about each and every joke.

Be that as it may, his *smile* left almost as quickly as it came, turning itself over to his gaze, which suddenly revealed a passionate kind of razor-sharp beam aimed directly into my own eyes, almost daring me to stay on my journey. This was a journey that I felt I had almost no right to be on. George changed all that. The intimidation of being with a real comedy mentor was softened a little because not only did we share many sensibilities but similar facial twitching as well.

Our stoop-shouldered shadows loomed impressively (for a change) as we stood on the docks overlooking the waters of Sheepshead Bay. We were right across the street from his comedy joint, Pips, when he suddenly said that sentence that rocked my being. It was shocking because all at once I knew it was true. It scared me half to death but the honesty freed me up and let me pursue being a comedian with a single-minded ferocity that to this day, in most all of my "creative" endeavors, keeps me company when nothing else will.

"You got it, man. But if you want to be a star you have to suck, fuck, and eat comedy. Or forget about it." He went on a little after that but I couldn't hear him because my hopes were rising so loudly. I had gotten a real endorsement, from someone who knew and was adored, to try to achieve something that most everyone else in my life would consider insane.

I felt validated. I got a taste of what it might feel like to really have an identity. He saw something in me that I desperately prayed would be there. I remember feeling guilty for a moment thinking what it would have been like if he had been my real father. To think how much easier it might have been growing up, feeling so much like an outsider, knowing that my own dad believed in me.

George mumbled some more positive shit about my future in comedy but he didn't have to. *I got it.* He should have known when to get off anyway. He was a genius about that kind of stuff. Anyway, you were right, Georgie, thanks. It nearly killed me, you fuck, *but I got it.* I love you. Once I tasted the confidence you gave me, it never left.

Somehow he knew how much I wanted it. He believed in me so

suddenly and with so much conviction it was dizzying! He made feeling twisted into something I could be proud of. To George, my problems were a gold mine for endless comedic premises, not just a black hole of self-pity. He made me feel like a survivor and not a victim. I've been on a comedy mission ever since. Almost like it was a calling. Really. I feel blessed. It was great to know so early that it wasn't supposed to be a cakewalk—ever. What a different look life has when something *becomes* your life, your *passion*. It takes the edge off. And I never felt like I had a job; it's just something I do, for almost thirty years now, all alone, mostly with a lot of encouragement from very few friends and God knows, without a wife. You see, to me, *relationships* seemed like a job and rarely one I was passionate about. They never quite felt like the real thing.

That's why I recently thought of George. About a year after he first saw me I bounced into the club one night to do a couple of sets. Appearing uncharacteristically happy, I cornered him a few minutes before I went on, to tell him how I'd found the woman of my dreams. I went on and on and on and on and on and on and on about how this young woman was (so I felt) the missing part of my soul that kept me, at twenty-six, feeling like I was on top of the world. It was such an obnoxious rant, and so full of shit that it forced George to contort that lovable, pliable, ancient face of his and say, "If you *really* loved her, you wouldn't have to tell me so much." That motherfucker. He was right. I was simply trying to convince myself and he knew it. I was running scared and didn't have a clue. He was right. You couldn't sneak too much bullshit by the Ear.

Nothing much has changed for me in the female department since then; almost three decades now. I threw myself into stand-up to run away from intimacy and into almost anything else to avoid it up until now. George taught me that there is no easy way of achieving anything worthwhile unless it's all-consuming. Right or wrong, that's how I live. And now I feel it's high time to *"suck, fuck, and eat"* a relationship. And I plan to. I just need someone right for the trial run. And this time around I won't have to blab about it either. And I hope neither will she. We'll just know, the two of us, and fuck everyone else. Let others judge us, we just won't care. And we won't look back either to try to figure anything out because there's no time to lose anymore. And if we don't spend that much time here on earth together that's cool too because who the hell knows, maybe we can float off into heaven together. We'll hang with George and we'll all have a big laugh. No cover charge. No minimum.

Santa Claus Has a Big Nose

and Is from Philadelphia

The reason I entered the world of comedy for a living was to feel like someone authentic, to express myself, and try to contribute to making people think; but mostly it was for attention. It never dawned on me that as soon as you get good at what you do a whole world of jealousy, greed, guilt-tripping, egomania, thievery, lying, manipulation, bullshit, sleaze, and intercourse without soul reveals itself at your doorstep. I've always fantasized some huge, stupid-ass holiday party with almost a thousand of these types lying and carousing and dealmaking and then suddenly, hearing this announcement:

"The asshole with a foreign luxury car is blocking the driveway and is in the process of being towed."

Suddenly I would be left alone with a group of bewildered caterers and my lifelong buddy in this business, David Brenner.

David Brenner is a star. He has been making millions of people laugh, in all kinds of venues, and all mediums, since the late sixties. He probably has done more TV appearances than any stand-up comedian ever. But that's the least of it. I trust him. He trusts me. It's weird to trust someone in this business. Trust me.

There are a handful of others but D.B. is special to me because while hanging out at the Improv bar in N.Y., he was the first famous comedian I met (prior to having the guts to go on) who I not only made laugh but who I also confessed to (with excruciating embarrassment) that I too wanted to be in this special world of comedy that he already belonged to, and he responded that he thought I was a natural. What!? A natural? This fucker must be kidding, I thought. But he wasn't kidding. He just laughed a lot at a lot of the shit I ad-libbed, and he just figured if I could make him laugh why not the rest of the country. *It was that simple to him.* His sharing his good opinion of my comedy was a rare, simple display of confidence in me without any strings attached. It was such an odd experience for me. He instantaneously became and has remained my true brother in this business.

With all the ups and downs everyone experiences over the course of a long career, David has always remained the single most important person to me because he constantly reminds me of the "gift" of being able to walk out anywhere, stare into a bright light, and make strangers laugh and applaud. Whenever that wasn't enough for me, he had that sneaky grin that communicated without saying it, "Wait until you need it again, pal." And I'll be damned if he wasn't always right. Whenever I would lose my passion for what I'd loved from such an early age, or would attempt to abandon it for other art forms that might not pan out into the different opportunities that I'd envisioned they should, that gleam would come back to Brenner's eyes and without him even saying it, I knew what he was thinking. "Stand-up, asshole. You're a comedian."

A few years ago over dinner, Lou Reed, who I like to call the John Cassavetes of rock lyricists, was sitting and listening to me whine about not getting enough dramatic acting chances after getting great notices playing a junkie in the independent film *Drunks.* Reed echoed Brenner's theory in his own inimitable style. He's a rock 'n' roll icon and maybe not the greatest impressionist but the spirit moved him and he tried to do "me" (which wasn't bad and looked a little like a cross between Edgar Allan Poe and Woody Woodpecker) and then told me that when all is said and done I will be remembered as a "neurotic comedian"—just as he, after almost thirty-five years and an amazing body of work, will probably just be remembered as the guy who sang, "And the colored girls go, Doo, da doo, da doo, Doo da doo . . ." You know the song. Everybody knows it. He sang a little from his classic, "Walk on the Wild Side," to make his point and I finished my pasta and knew he and David were right.

I could write endlessly on David's successes, encouragement, advice, friendship, courage, parenthood, coolness, charitableness, and on and on through the years and his tireless compassion for my obsessions and how he saw me through all sorts of bad relationships with women and career crises, but what I'd prefer to share is the single most astonishing thing that he did for me. And keep in mind that "me" is a creature who from my earliest memories felt most comfortable doubting himself and feeling undeserving of anything positive and, of course, always expecting the worst.

It was some time in the early seventies and I was holding down three odd jobs: freelance copywriting for a small ad agency, working in the Museum of Modern Art library, and a job in a sporting goods store trying to find, among other things, autographed Bobby Hull jockstraps for impatient customers with a lot of balls. I had to be living near the poverty level, even if when I grabbed a microphone, anywhere, I felt like a million bucks. Nevertheless I know I was scared. In my early twenties, I was usually broke, and as great as it was to have guys like Brenner encourage me, it seemed almost surreal at that point to think I could actually make a living at this one day and become a well-known comedian. Although my college girlfriend was very supportive, as were a smattering of family members and close friends—the latter of whom almost twenty years later, after I was wealthy and famous, *oh and an alcoholic,* would intervene to save my life—I'd always succumb to the opinion of those who doubted me and who thought I was about to go TKO in my bout with destiny.

Brenner not only believed in me but also I'm certain related to my insatiable drive and my need to score with audiences. One afternoon I met him at a deli near his Upper East Side, N.Y. bachelor pad. Although he was one of the few who I allowed to see some of the shitholes I lived in during the early days, since I trusted that he wouldn't judge me and just saw me as a pal and a comedian, on this

day I had a big favor to ask and was hoping that the energy of the
city and being out of the dump where I was living would give me the
courage.

I ordered nervously and Brenner, with the instincts of a streetwise cat burglar, cut to the chase. The conversation probably went
something like this . . .

"What do you want, nutcase?"

"What makes you think I want anything?"

"You're drooling."

"Oh. I'm sorry."

"Don't apologize every second. The whole world isn't your fault.
Just most of it."

It was pointless beating around the bush with this guy. Not only
did I have a feeling that he cared about me a great deal but he was so
fucking worldly and full of wonderful bravado (that I hoped would
rub off) and intuitive as hell, so I was just able to let my defenses
down and try to spit it out.

"I'm going crazy."

"You are crazy, my man. What else is new? What's wrong, pal?"

"I can't take doing all these motherfucking jobs and not being
able to really focus on stand-up."

"So? What are you trying to tell me?"

"Uhhhhhhhhhhhhhhhhhhhhhhhhhhhhh . . ."

Luckily the waiter came over but David waved him away.

"Come on, Lewis, tell me."

"Okay . . . I want to be a comedian . . . full time."

"Uh-huh."

"Yeah, and, uh, I can't—as long as I do all this other shit."

"I get it."

"You do?"

"Yeah."

"You're kidding me?"

"No. How can I help?"

"Well . . . look . . . uh . . . If I had a certain amount of money I could quit everything, roll the dice, and be a comedian full time without all this other bullshit getting in the way."

"What do you need?"

"A thousand bucks."

David whipped out a checkbook, wrote a check for a thousand dollars and handed it to me.

"You're a full-time comedian. Congratulations."

It was an act of such class and graciousness and confidence that it enabled me, maybe for the first time, to overcome the constant nagging of my self-loathing and really believe that I could just dive in with reckless abandon to do what I wanted to do. David's gift came from such a cool place; not out of charity but from a legit comedian to a struggling one who he thought had what it takes and who he was willing to bet on. His belief in me didn't make me less neurotic but did enable me to sustain the courage necessary to express my neurosis on public stages forevermore.

There aren't too many people in show business like this guy. Through the years we've continued to be support systems to one another but it's that deli lunch that was the boost I needed at just the right time, to be able to channel my inner strength and jump in and never look back.

Santa Claus has a big nose and is from Philadelphia.

Mrs. **Bruce** and Mrs. **Keaton**

Lenny Bruce and Buster Keaton had more impact on me than any other performing artists ever. Their work shaped my insatiable desire to carve out an identity of my own as a comedian. Through a twist of fate, both Lenny's mom and Buster's wife became my friends, late in their lives, and offered a sweet and memorable historic connection to both my profession and my zeal for comedy that still seems dreamlike.

Lenny and Buster both died in the sixties. Having seen Lenny perform live or hanging with an aging Keaton is something I can only fantasize about. At the time of their deaths I was just starting college and I was far from getting addicted on the art of stand-up. Rather, it was a time of real innocence for me, a time of searching for reasons to live my life in a meaningful and passionate way.

I first came upon Lenny Bruce when a close friend at Ohio State came into my cell-like apartment in Columbus holding an album, which was *Lenny, "Live" at Berkeley*. As I listened I just couldn't believe that I hadn't known more about this comedic prophet by then. Oh sure, I had read bits and pieces about his controversial legal battles but that was mostly it. When I heard this groundbreaking, gifted comedian wail, I was more than just blown away; I was speechless. I couldn't utter a word because upon hearing all Lenny had to say (and just on this one recording!) and the way he rapped, I just couldn't come close to articulating my fervor at discovering someone who sounded as if not only he spoke for me but was like a member of the family or a close friend I never had who could have the balls to express what he did. From that moment on, Lenny became the major stimulation to my still hidden, yet budding, comedic aspirations. Ironically, this stand-up comedian, who I would forevermore hold up as the bar of artistry and genius in the world I would enter years later, had already overdosed in Los Angeles. I was forced then to make this drug casualty my mentor without him ever knowing it. I was shocked to learn that he was dead but the stirring damage to me was very much alive. I became hooked on his legacy.

I was only about nineteen or so but I got it. Man, did I get this guy! He struck every nerve in my body. His language and style, spoken almost in jazzlike riffs, at once became my favorite musical. It was bold and truthful and hip and fearless and brilliant and provocative and unlike anything I had ever thought comedy could be. He instantly became an icon and I knew without a doubt that I had found my Hendrix of comedy. Almost thirty years later I would get a chance to not only spend time with Lenny's mom but do what I could (along with so many others) to keep her company, and also try to help raise money to get her through her last years as she fought a terminal illness.

Buster came into my life as I was on my last leg of a ten-week trek in Europe, a quarter shy of graduating from college. I wound up in London exhausted, and almost thirty pounds lighter than when I left, from schlepping around an insanely oversized, inappropriate suitcase from one train station to another, one shit hotel to the next, and walking what had to be hundreds of miles as I gobbled up every art museum and cultural highlight I could on my ten-dollar-a-day budget. I managed to find a room to live in in each city large enough to keep my suitcase hidden from all the European snickers while I did my sightseeing and brain-growing.

By the time I got to London I had about two weeks left of my vacation. It was the summer of the Manson killings, which left me in a scary, fragile state of mind that even the Beatles' new music couldn't rid me of. After about ten countries I was homesick, but still thankful that these new things called "ruptured hemorrhoids," that I probably got from schlepping that stupid suitcase around, didn't put a quick end to my travels early on, and thankful for a German doctor with a wooden leg and a magic pill! What a trio—van Gogh, Monet, and a mystical stool softener that enabled me to continue my journey without Edvard Munch–like screams every time I took a shit. Ironically enough, I guess I am forced to forevermore have a "soft spot" for Germany, as this physician saved my ass.

I was anxious about finishing up my studies at Ohio State and entering the real world, but mostly I was just dying to see my college girlfriend; because if I may boast, I'd had also ten weeks of complete sexual abstinence, and was convinced that no girl ever had such a loyal boyfriend travel through Europe, especially during the *summer of love*.

Well, okay, I did have one affair. I fell in love with Eleanor's husband.

Apparently, at about this time most of Keaton's films had been recently rediscovered and restored, and were finally being seen by a new generation. I had only seen little snippets of his stuff on those crummy compilation flicks and really didn't know much at all about the magnitude of this legendary, cinematic magician. But in London I fortuitously passed this movie theater hosting a two-week-long festival of Buster Keaton's films and shorts that would comprise almost all of his major works. I decided to check it out almost on a whim, having no idea of the impact I would feel after that first afternoon. I bought my ticket and was lucky to find a seat in the jam-packed cinema. They had this colossal, old-fashioned organ that played to each film live, like it would have been back in the old days when his films opened for real. The lights went out and I was very shortly in a trance. I was transported into a rarefied, comedic air. And it was heavenly. I was bowled over! I was enlightened! I was mesmerized! I was excited! I was astounded! He was simply the coolest, most creative, comedic cinematic performer I'd ever imagined could exist. I was in a Keaton haze. I staggered out after the first day and immediately bought tickets for the next thirteen. I saw a few other things of interest in London, but Keaton had me so awestruck by the throat that I think London itself was just icing on the cake. In future years, the uncontrollable laughter brought on by Laurel & Hardy, Berle and Benny and Caesar and Martin & Lewis, Mel and Carl and Winters, and Nichols & May and Berman and Leonard and Rickles, and Lenny and Saul and Woody and Renee Taylor and Joe Bologna's film *Made for Each Other* would reinforce the sensation that I *too* had to be in this world of comedy, but Keaton did it all without even talking, and I screamed. Of course I loved the magic of the movie world in which anything is possible, but far more moving was Buster's persona, that of someone unaffected by the worst possible scenarios, who would always emerge unscathed by the dangerous filmic premises he always placed himself smack in the middle of. Thinking back, as someone on the verge of being pulled not quite willingly into the adult world on my own, knowing I'd have to find a meaningful place for myself amidst all the insanity I perceived was waiting just outside the familiar comfort zone of college life, Keaton hit me in my funny bone at just the right time. I was enthralled and shocked at his hilarity, and at the huge body of work pouring out of this genius who, though he seemed so vulnerable, seemed also totally unafraid.

I wanted to feel that daring, too. Watching Buster flee from hundreds of cops, or escape being pummeled by zillions of rocks in a landslide, or be tossed around like a flea in the clutches of a hurricane, among other catastrophes, still being able moments later to brush himself off and flirt with a pretty woman, was the type of cool assurance I could only dream about.

I knew that I was clever but I didn't know if I had the strength to be on my own. I went from hiding behind a family that paid my way all through university and shielded me from the "suits" who seemed interested only in making money, war, and babies; to feeling naked, clad only in a cap and gown, and thrown suddenly with Keatonesque fury into near poverty and the horror of my father's death, without the training needed to feel confident that I could land on my feet.

But while I was levitating with joy in that darkened movie theater for fourteen days, I wasn't afraid of anything. I was gathering seeds of confidence for the eventful days that lay ahead. Seeing Buster was like the first time I'd heard Lenny Bruce. They were untouchables.

Never in my wildest crystal-ball notion of how my life would evolve did I foresee that, thirty years later, I would be in the position to both take the Great Stoneface's widow out for a luxurious dinner at the Beverly Hills Hotel, and to talk about his impact on me for a TV documentary about Keaton.

Decades and Decades Later

Sally Marr was dying but you wouldn't know it. In her late eighties, lying in a fifties-looking easy chair that enabled her to put her feet up, she held court in a tiny, borderline run-down, one-bedroom apartment in the middle of Hollywood, not far from where Lenny had OD'd. The main reason you could never know she was close to death was from her constant riffing, an endless stream of hilarious recollections of her show business–soaked life. She was almost like Bruce himself in drag, and what really struck me more than almost anything else was the constant reminder of just how supportive she had been of her son's career. I wasn't jealous that I didn't have the same dynamic with my own mother, but I was captivated by the notion of how it might have altered my own comedic journey.

I couldn't help but wish she was dying in a castle instead, given her comic royalty. But it made more sense for Lenny's mom to just be hanging out in any old place, because, like her son, it was the words, man—the words. She wore her language elegantly, in spite of the shape she was in. In fact, she might as well have been back in vaudeville; every moment when people were around seemed like a show to her.

Prominent filmmaker Robert Weide, who made an Oscar-nominated documentary about Lenny, let me know Sally was very ill and that it would mean a lot to her if I visited her from time to time. Many people loved her and stopped by, not just because she gave birth to such a legendary son, but because of her authenticity and her own amazing, show-business life. We had met a few times in the past, before she got ill, oftentimes with Lenny's daughter, Kitty, and they always made me feel, much to my delight, that I reminded them of "the man." They never told me just how, but I like to think I just smelled like him in all sorts of ways, and that was very cool. I mean, if anything, as self-effacing as my act always was and is, compared to Bruce's much broader, satiric, torrential overview on practically everything, I always set the bar as high as I could to be as revealing about myself as my guts would allow, much the way Lenny was always fearless about nailing society's hypocrisy. It's a great source of pride that Sally and Kitty dug my work and style and that they got a little scent of Lenny around me.

Years before she got ill, I'd sent Sally a signed poster from my Carnegie Hall concert, and eventually learned that she'd hung it up in her little pad right next to one of Lenny's concert posters. Through a friend I got a picture of that hallway, and hung the little Polaroid in my own home. I always felt fucked by never seeing him perform, never getting to hang with him and kibitz, and yet here was his mother, nearing ninety, and she got my shtick like she was my target audience. Imagine that shit! This was one fucking hip mother. This was not an old lady. If you tried to keep up with her you seemed elderly regardless of how much younger you were. She never made anyone feel sorry for her. Every story and every punch line was delivered with the same kind of heart as if she were doing a big gig at a great venue, filled with enthusiastic fans. She caressed her remembrances like a person born to perform, and it was clear that she would go out that way.

Although she was too sick to attend them, lots of comics did benefits to help raise bread for her mounting medical expenses. At one of these shows at the Hollywood Improv I remember sitting at the bar downing my now usual club sodas and lemon while waiting to go on, and rapping with Shelly Berman. I mean, I was sitting there talking to this giant of modern day stand-up comedy; it was a gas. We were moaning and groaning (and no one can grumble as artistically and hilariously as Mr. Berman) like struggling comics waiting to perform during those open-mike nights, complaining about how late the show started and about how the audience would be fucking burned out by the time we got on. We had a ball bad-mouthing which comics were abusing the amount of time they were supposed to do. I was bonding with yet another idol. It was too astonishing a moment to even begin to explain the thousands of flashbacks running through my head, like hearing Shelly's first breakthrough album as a teenager, or watching him on TV in the early sixties doing these amazing monologues, each so finely crafted and delivered like mini masterpieces. And now here I was, an old comedian as well, slumped over and made to feel like the time was over for me to continue to disbelieve in my success. And man, I don't mean to boast, but when Berman and Lewis whine simultaneously, happiness can be sucked out of a fucking carnival in Rio de Janeiro. More importantly, the show was a moneymaker, but sadly, Sally didn't have long to go.

The last time I saw Sally Marr was also one of the most defining moments of my life. It was at a screening of Weide's film at CAA, a premier Hollywood talent agency. I sat in the back row on the aisle (I always do whenever I can, because of claustrophobia and the unfortunate number of times imagined or not that I have to piss, and the painful excuse-making and apologizing necessary if I'm forced to walk out while seated somewhere in the middle of the row). However, this time I didn't sit on the aisle solely because of my aging bladder, but also because Sally was in a wheelchair being cared for by her aide, and looked so isolated. I wanted to sit in front of her so that from time to time I'd be able to unobtrusively get up and kiss her, or tell her I loved her. It was clear that she was gravely ill, and as cool as it was that she'd made the screening, her condition was really depressing.

She wouldn't have missed it for the world. The show must go on. And in Weide's documentary, Sally to some degree upstages her son, with countless interviews that intermittently pop on the screen and give life to the story of her deceased son's amazing, in-society's-face rise to comedic stardom, while most of the culture pissed on his First Amendment rights and abetted his ultimate drug-drenched martyrdom. The film is extraordinary but as it wound down I knew (having already seen it many times privately) that soon there would be a shot of a dead Lenny Bruce, naked, alone, and lying in his bathroom with his drug paraphernalia, then footage of the media circus that ensued, the police and the sleazy cameramen parading in and out. Society got their man, even though drugs did him in; the prosecutors enabled him as much as anyone else. The world of stand-up comedy has been flimsy at best ever since, with perhaps Richard Pryor as the only stunning exception, along with maybe a handful of others (the late Bill Hicks and Sam Kinison come to mind—comedians who pushed the envelope). Yet to me, no one ever came close to Bruce's overpowering genius, or command of the art form.

So, there I was, starting to get a panic attack thinking that Lenny's mom would have to actually sit through this and see that awful shot of her dead son that so poignantly illustrated just how Lenny was made a scapegoat for his honesty and artistry, and was exploited, fucked over, and abused to the very end. In my own panic about the upcoming sequence, I forgot that if you are Lenny Bruce's mother, you aren't exactly, for openers, a mom who would groove on a *Muppets Christmas Special* or exactly agree with how Donna Reed raised her kids on her TV show. It's clear that in this case, the womb came before the comedian. Forgetting momentarily just how maternally hip Sally was, I squarely got up and sat down by her feet. She started to stroke my hair and smile. I figured she knew that I did this to express in the only way I knew how my love, compassion, and sadness over her son going out so young, before her, and in such a tragic way.

Then the image came up. Lenny Bruce is dead. My comic hero was a goner, and her son was no more. I looked up at Sally and tried to smile, but it was forced, and although I meant well, it sort of died like a bad joke. Sally smiled back at me anyway, like she dug the effort. Her voice at this point in her life was pretty weak and she leaned down and whispered in my ear something that I'll never forget. And although she was of course Lenny's mom, it's still emblazoned *in my soul* just what it might have been like to have my immediate family be such a supportive part of my own torment and burning desire to express my anguish as a performer.

"So, baby?"

"What honey?" I replied pushing her damp hair back.

"Was I fuckin' funny or what?" she said.

Eleanor Keaton was cool, too, but in a much more distinguished, classic way. Still elegant in her seventies when we became friends, she'd been drop-dead beautiful in her heyday as an actress and dancer, and Buster had taken some time before finally mustering up the courage, in his middle age, to ask this "stunner" out for a date. The romance blossomed, and seemed to keep going even after Buster died, as Eleanor never remarried and seemed to keep her aging beauty and dignity even more intense by always being the woman of his dreams, and he the man of hers.

As hip and scattered as Sally was, that's how single-minded and outspoken Eleanor was. Once an actress, always an actress. I met Eleanor at a party given by the producers of an A&E biography of

Buster. We sat down and chatted and I asked her out, with as much embarrassment and blushing as some kid out of Tom Sawyer's neighborhood. I thought it would be cool to take her out to dinner and perhaps show her around my house, which is sort of a museum of rock art, rock photos, an immense collection of work by New York painter Carl Titolo, and hundreds of photos of so many artists who sort of became my silent family growing up when I felt cut off of life support during my own creative journey. Buster, along with Lenny, was certainly at the head of the class of my personal heroes.

I can't remember exactly why but months went by after that, maybe even a few years, before I finally felt confident enough to give Eleanor a call. She shrugged off my apology for the lengthy time between my suggestion and my call like it was a forty-years-ago audition, and she hadn't gotten the part, and had long ago moved on.

"So Eleanor, you live in the valley, so I mean, we could go somewhere nearby you."

"Why?"

"Uh . . . no real reason. Then, how about a dinner at the Beverly Hills Hotel?"

"Sounds great."

"You sure it wouldn't be better to go to a place closer to you?"

"No. You said the Beverly Hills Hotel and that sounds great."

"It's a date."

I was suddenly thrown into a panic. I was going to be alone with Buster's widow for hours and hours and I freaked. I mean, holy shit! What the fuck was I going to talk about besides the millions of queries I had about how it was to be with him, and what did she know about every possible question I had about my silent hero? To avoid my nervousness I faxed the maître d' at the Polo Lounge and the general manager of the hotel, and told them I was coming in with this extraordinary woman. Although I told them it was an important dinner for me they didn't know why, except that I was a comedian they liked, Buster was an idol of mine, and this was his renowned widow who I wanted to be treated like gold. Ironically, this hotel was just a few hundred yards from a mansion where Keaton once unhappily lived as a young filmic god, in a miserable marriage, drinking away his feelings. Little did he know that years later he'd meet the very woman I was intent on giving the perfect dinner to, a woman who would make his life full again, even without the glitz and fame. This was a woman who in the twilight of her husband's life, many years after the "talkies," jealous studio heads, and alcohol had doused his legendary heat in Hollywood, would escort the sometimes cranky old film visionary she loved from film festival to film festival all over the world, to collect the many overdue honors in his name, that somehow seemed to give his artistic journey the kind of closure it deserved. Less embarrassing and more enjoyable for Buster was doing what they loved most . . . just playing cards in their humble abode, raising their dogs, or taking occasional side trips together for little TV gigs and commercials before he died. I put pressure on myself to have this night out somehow be as perfect as possible to help symbolize and celebrate how this woman had dedicated herself to help my hero live out his life in a way that made all his fans joyful. Even better was that she had not by most accounts just been some caretaker of a former film god but part of a very, very cool marriage.

I had arranged for roses to be sent to the table at the most propitious time during our evening. I trusted the instincts of one of the most famous restaurants in the world to do what was right. They were perfect from soup to nuts. (I being the nut.)

Man oh man, we had THE TABLE, and everyone treated her like a goddess. Mrs. Keaton this . . . Mrs. Keaton that . . . Mrs. Keaton what an honor. Whew! I was so grateful—until I had to talk. Let it be known that I can be at a loss for words. I became my own silent movie! I choked. Most kids dream of winning a World Series with a home run; for me, glory was having the chance to ask famous people in the world of comedy anything on my mind. I briefly blew the audition. At least Buster occasionally had a script or a story idea to work from. I just had steak and fear. I was a wreck. I felt out of sorts, her husband meant so much to me, and yet at the same time I wanted so much for her to have fun. This golden opportunity left me speechless and without a shred of the entertainment value Buster effortlessly displayed on film. I sort of inadvertently paid homage to him by copying his constant deadpan eye in the midst of my hurricane of emotions over dinner, freezing like Buster's great stone face, tongue-tied and not knowing at all what direction to take an already silent conversation.

Eleanor made it easy. She intuitively felt my love for Buster and was immediately open to my slightest curiosity. Whereas Sally would riff, Eleanor gave stirring lectures on the history of old Hollywood, on both the husband she'd loved and her understanding of the superstar he was, even though she had been too young to fully appreciate the power of that moment when he burst on the scene and changed so much about combining the use of a camera with the soul of a persona. She had an amazing presence about her that let me know how formidable she must have been half a century earlier, when men were left gasping for breath by her beauty. She seemed not only to enjoy the attention, but to feel very much at ease with it. It wasn't the disgusting type of egotism that many actresses display, but one of tremendous self-confidence; of a sense of her place in history. More than anything about her that I loved—Keaton groupie that I unashamedly am—was her total dedication to making sure that Buster knew before he died just what an icon he really was, even when he might have had reason to think that no one cared who he was anymore nor remembered anything about his amazing body of work.

Lenny, sadly, didn't care to stop drugs from killing him. Buster, although an alcoholic, led a wonderful life with Eleanor and apparently was able in his later years to nurture a glass of beer every now and then without ever spinning out of control again. I asked her about this. I told her that my own drinking days were over but she just gracefully smiled and made it seem that it was hardly her business. Still, I wanted to know how Buster was able to enjoy his life after he'd stopped falling all over himself (and *not* with magnificent cinematic stunts), once he, like Lenny, got shafted by the system and lost control of his work. Lenny couldn't get a nightclub stage to perform on; Buster wasn't allowed to make his own films anymore, and was soon demoted from a King of Comedy to a gag writer and boozehound.

Eleanor spoke very freely and with a great sense of pride about how much Buster enjoyed his life creatively, well after he was out of the Hollywood mansions and the limelight, be it with little TV appearances or even commercials, which were not only fun paydays but enabled him to show flashes of his immense authenticity and originality. She flashed a quick grin when reminding me just how much fun they had together, living modestly and yet appreciating their time together, sharing their love of dogs and enjoying a gang of great friends who were always around to add merriment to their lives. I also learned from her that Buster wasn't tortured late in life by not doing more, but actually loved doing less. And she would know.

These two kings of comedy both died in the same year and one tragically didn't have to. And yet their legacies remain intact, and as much as I wish Lenny had found his Eleanor, he had a Sally, a mother who early on pushed her son to be an earth-shattering humorist, continuing to nudge him as far as his guts and brain and balls would let him *cook*. And although she wasn't responsible for his tragic overdose, she is regarded primarily as a kooky yet sublime catalyst for his emergence as the most articulate hipster of all time. And to think that both these women were friends of mine. Wow! Mind-blowing!

Now if I can only manage to figure out a way to take Gena Rowlands out for tea, I'd be a happy man.

It Was a Blast Before I Got **Hooked**

Let's see, it must have been sometime around 1973. Watergate was a happening thing, and as for me, I didn't mind being poor, drinking, smoking weed, and obsessing about nothing except how that night's set in New York City would go, or the prospect of meeting new women. Oh baby, what a blast to care only about stand-up and women. Man, how I dug my early twenties. Family wasn't driving me crazy (I mean, at least I had some logistical space), I had great friends, and I was on a comedic mission. All I had to do was take care of myself. It's a piece of cake when you're happy—or at least think you are.

I was so jazzed by the daily experience of actually being accepted as a comedian by my peers, not to mention by the parade of well-known comics from my childhood who now watched me perform. The same twisted quipsters who were once just images on a TV screen making my life easier to stomach as a kid now were actually telling me, *live and in person*, that I made them laugh. It really was a dream come true.

Had I stopped for even a second to worry about my future in such a capricious, self-centered, and cruel business, I might have shrieked and hid like a coward for the remainder of my life, and done nothing but dream about doing the thing that mattered to me. But at that point in my life some undeniable force drove me to find some kind of authenticity. Luckily I didn't have a realistic bone in my body and had also felt so alone and misunderstood for seemingly forever that I had no trouble diving into a business where most fail. In fact, failing as a comedian never entered my mind. I was in a cocoon, living day to day without much thought about doing anything else, ever again. I was having the time of my life. I was on my own, forging an identity I'd had such a hard time figuring out during my adolescence, and answering only to what audiences seemed to like. I could then go home without being accountable to anyone for anything else afterwards.

As a recovering alcoholic looking back, I'm sort of jealous of this former me, because I did all of this high-wire, taking-a-shot-at-the-dream stuff while still being able to drink like, I guess, normal people do. You lucky bastards! It's a shame H. G. Wells isn't around now and open for business so I could rent his time machine and try to nip my disease in the bud before it got me. No dice. Shit, alcohol is really tricky. But as with Tricky Dick, the cover-up can last just so long if you are destined to be taken down. Yet booze didn't control me then. It wasn't even my friend. It was more like a cool acquaintance who hung around just to enjoy my goings-on, and didn't ask for a damn thing in return. It was a setup.

I drank and occasionally smoked a joint when I was back in the sack in my numerous shacks (they were hardly apartments) with, believe it or not, struggling comic groupies. Hmmmmmmm. "Step right up and watch me hump and if you fake your orgasm good enough I'll even throw in a few new monologues afterwards."

It was a real pleasure to get a nice buzz on while actually *nurturing* a few glasses of wine (*nurture*—what an impossible thought now) and to be in a head space where I felt so loose and self-confident that I actually might have been legitimately relaxed and happy. In *those* good old days when I drank, I was rarely if ever sloppy or mean-spirited. I even think I stopped to worry about driving my car if I was too high. Given where I've been since, by comparison, I was a picture-perfect drinker in those days.

My idea of what a drunkard was, at that time in my life, was based on gossip I'd heard about alcoholic relatives I rarely saw or who were out cold when I was visiting, or on painful-to-watch films where guys like Ray Milland and Jack Lemmon could make you taste their own puke, or on tales about legendary artists who drank themselves into oblivion. I never saw myself in any of those scenarios.

This "normal" type of drinking and fucking around stayed pretty stable for me until I was about thirty—when I suddenly started to worry about everything. But why think about that now? I miss back then. It was excruciatingly delightful when Nixon was about to be impeached and I was on stage almost every night along with the likes of Leno, Kaufman, Brenner, Klein, Landesberg, Walker, Boo-sler, Belzer, David, and everyone who was working the club scene in N.Y. It was for me the place I felt most at home in, almost at peace, and yet, perhaps hidden way down deep in my subconscious, even when I was getting accolades as a rising star, I still nurtured a tiny lit-tle seed of belief (I'm pretty certain now) that I was a fraud.

It was perhaps that little feeling of insecurity, which I couldn't deal with or have much insight about, that I began to douse with what I thought was a normal consumption of alcohol. This was a frightful harbinger of bottles and bottles and bottles of champagne to come in the not-too-distant future, a future filled with so many great nights and ultimately many alcoholic escapades, until at last I realized that my greatest accomplishment would not be having the clout and artistry to sell out Carnegie Hall, but having the balls to one day finally admit that I was a drunkard.

It's easy to know when you're funny, but much harder to know when you're fucked up. I mean, how can you know? You're fucked up. So eventually I was no longer just watching old movies about alcoholics, I was living my own.

"Good Night, Everybody!"

That's how Jackie Gleason used to end most of his TV shows.

But before he went off the air, and before I had to go to sleep, was maybe the closest I've ever felt to having a real family I connected with. All the Lewises would be sprawled out on my parents' bed, screaming and laughing. We were a team. We had home field advan-tage. I felt so safe, even sound, for the time the show was on. I was a little boy and I wouldn't have known how to utter the words, "I think I need to see a shrink," so I had to take what I could for surrogate sustenance and Jackie provided it, especially in *The Honeymooners*. Watching *The Honeymooners* made me think that, just maybe, my family could one day coalesce in other areas besides just worshiping a celebrity together. It was like a little holiday for me away from feeling so shitty, always sensing that I really wasn't part of any close-knit household. As long as Gleason was on I felt connected. But only now do I see that what I was feeling connected to was the creative power he possessed, not to the family who just for that hour experienced something together.

It was uncanny. We would all be in bed, in our pajamas, watching *The Honeymooners*, and scream and laugh until it felt like we would burst. It was only during times like those that there seemed to be some greater force at work than our own need to feel bad. It felt almost as if Gleason was a pied piper leading us out of our heads, allowing us a few precious moments to feel what a real family might *really* feel like. As we all sat in awe of Gleason, we laughed like people who not only loved each other for all the right reasons but loved ourselves as well.

God did we laugh! We fucking laughed our asses off! All of us. Together . . . Lovingly . . . And more than most families I ever saw. But when *The Honeymooners* was over the honeymoon was over, and the bullshit would begin again like it had never even had a breather.

The *high* I felt watching my family laugh together before we went our separate ways and isolated ourselves in our own worlds would quickly evaporate. And since Gleason was only on once a week, we were in trouble. Maybe if we'd lived in his TV studio my family might have had an opportunity to experience more joy together and have it be more of an everyday thing, rather than some rare, shooting star of sanity that left as quickly as it appeared. Gleason and his genius had the magic power to make us all, and especially me, forget how much we needed and longed for some sort of connection.

Comedy in black and white, on a very small screen, from legendary comedians like Gleason the Great One, and Caesar and Martin & Lewis and Berle and Silver gave me such a rush, such an escape from my own sense of emotional distance and solitariness, that it makes perfect sense to me now how I chose the comedic path to help guide me out from under a growing stack of adult problems. By making light of my anxieties, I'd have a career of making others forget theirs.

Fast forward twenty years.

I was an up-and-coming professional comedian working in a tough nightclub in Florida. The place was jammed to see the Temptations, certainly not this unknown opening-act comedian with his subtle Hebraic stylings. Moments before the show Gleason stumbled in with two blondes, and was escorted to a table right in front, just a few feet from where I was about to go on. I didn't know whether to burst out of my skin with excitement or quit right then and there. Suddenly my life was a slow-motion playback. For what seemed an eternity, I thought back and recalled vividly just how much impact this colossal talent now wending his way through the crowd to cheers and applause had actually had on my psyche as a small boy. How would I ever be able to suck it up and actually entertain him? This comedy god! Impossible. No one in the sold-out room seemed to matter. It was just me and Jackie and I didn't stand a chance. How I felt about *me* depended now completely on how *he* felt about me, just as it had depended on how other authority figures felt about me. Although I wasn't a kid anymore, I sure felt like one, and next to him, for sure, as a comedian I felt like a newborn. I hadn't yet developed enough confidence to really command the stage and I was a jellyfish inside when the manager shoved me back to life and barked, "You're on."

I bombed so fast and so decisively I probably made a whole host of legendary dead comics turn over in *and* heckle me from their graves; almost as if my performance dramatized how little I thought I deserved his recognition. My funny bone just vanished. Then, to make matters worse, for whatever reasons swirling inside of Mr. Gleason's head that night, he thought it appropriate to come up onstage. Rod Serling couldn't have scripted a more surreal, tortuous moment for a relatively new comedian in the business. The place went wild but of course not one shred of the excitement was for me. I actually got a slight laugh by introducing him as my singer on the bill, but that quickly subsided into the almost incredulous sight of Gleason trying to grab *my* microphone. It was after all *my* gig. We played a brief little improv game, using the mike as if it was a baseball bat, placing our closed fists one upon the other, creating a very unfunny premise that whomever was on top last would perform.

I felt like a pebble standing at the foot of Mount Vesuvius, and the audience was waiting for the wrong act to deliver the punch. The irony of it all. Here was the icon who had given me so much strength while I floundered in the midst of a family that provided more questions than answers. Here was the guy who gave us our weekly dose of togetherness. Now he was taking away my stage and, in effect, making it nearly impossible for me to get the crowd on my side. And I never did. In fact, after what felt like an eternity for me, Gleason finally left the stage and took his seat, to booming adulation, and left me out to dry. I then resorted to doing what I did often very early in my career when I lost an audience. Rather than try and get them back, and give them the attention they paid to feel, I immediately resented them. Eventually I tried to win them back on my own terms, by showing my disdain for them while delivering my most esoteric material. This was a comedic death wish. It was like saying, "Hate me, but hate me for *me.*"

God knows Gleason's legendary drinking might have contributed to his behavior, for he was not just stealing my thunder but sucking up the entire club into his divine presence, leaving me no chance in hell to perform well. Curiously, I also thought at one point, giving him a huge benefit of the doubt, that he was actually trying to help me. You know, famous comedian giving young comedian some credibility by joining him on stage. But I soon had no doubt that he wasn't too concerned with how I went over. The first words he cockily spoke into the mike—during this *Twilight Zone* comedic nightmare—in his ever familiar, grandiose, hysterical fashion, were, "Here's how you do it, my boy!"

I finished my set, and broke into the four-minute mile on my way back to my motel room, a block away from the stage. I had so much flop sweat it was as if I had showered on the way back to the flophouse the club put me up in.

While lying on my rickety bed I flicked on the TV. It would've been a nice parallel if a repeat of *The Honeymooners* had been on, but it wasn't. I had the strangest sensation just lying there on my back, staring at the walls with their few pathetic flamingos painted randomly on them to remind the occupant that this was a cheap, Florida motel room and not a cell in some state penitentiary. It was a strange sensation for me because it was uncommonly positive. Shockingly, I didn't even give a shit that I was lousy that night on stage. I felt down but far from out. Generally, knowing me now and certainly back then, it would have made perfect sense if I had started beating myself to a bloody pulp for having bombed in front of one of my idols, but just the reverse happened. I felt badly for *him*.

I wasn't a big drinker myself yet, but somehow I just had to think that somewhere down deep he knew that what he'd done to that young comic starting out was pretty rotten. I mean, if I had been a junior member of the Rat Pack it might have been cool, but I wasn't, and what he did sucked. Even stranger, instead of thinking about what he might have been thinking about me and how critical he probably was, I thought about how cool it was that I had actually gotten far enough in my young career to even find myself in such a surreal circumstance. It seemed like progress to me in some happy, masochistic way. There I was, in some dingy motel paying my dues, just like Gleason had done forty years before. And who knows, maybe Al Jolson got him a little shaky one night at some cabaret.

I couldn't believe it! I was in the same business as Jackie Gleason. I was in the same business as Jackie Gleason. I was in the same business as Jackie Gleason. I just kept saying that over and over to myself until I fell asleep in my clothes.

I had a good show the next night. Gleason wasn't there, thank God. I wasn't ready to perform in front of more royalty yet. I knew that. I also didn't fall asleep in my clothes again. But trust me, there would be many nights for that to happen, down the road.

Fast forward another fifteen years. I'm watching one of my comedy specials premiering one evening on TV, at a party thrown in my honor, at my manager's house. It is a huge success. As soon as the show is over I check my answering machine at home to see who might have called, wanting to suck up as much adulation as I can. The first call is from a very famous, older actress I met on a TV show a while back. We had exchanged numbers, me thinking it would be an honor to maybe take her out for a dinner one evening and tell her how much she meant to me through the years. Sadly I had never followed through on the meal, although I did call her from time to time to see how she was. I recall when we met the first time she was very flattering, so of course true to form, I had a hard time letting it in. I've always had an easier time focusing on the negative. Still do. Anyway, I was blown away that she had called. And was the first person to do so, too!

Audrey Meadows was a fan. Bless her soul. Imagine, Alice Kramden dug my act. Pretty fuckin' cool, huh? I felt like she and I *were* "The Honeymooners" that night she called to congratulate me. She told me that she had laughed and laughed and laughed.

Mr. Gleason, I hope you weren't upset that your legendary, gorgeous Alice loved my comedy special. And anyway, you and I had a history. We were the worst act ever. Remember that ragged set I did that night in Florida? Man, did I suck! I'm sure the people in the audience will never forget seeing you in person. I sure as hell will never forget. Anyway, Audrey's call made me feel like a million bucks! Just the way she probably used to make you feel. If she were near me that night, I might've hugged her and said, "Baby, you're the greatest."

I just have a feeling that you would have understood my jubilation and been happy for me, from one comedian to another, the second time around. I sure as hell paid my dues, and I know you would have respected that and seen the difference in my performance twenty-two years later. And, big guy, I might have even made *you* laugh too. I got funny eventually. And please, do me a favor, send my love to Audrey, if you don't mind.

Anyway, save me a seat up there at the bar, that I'm sure by now you have made famous. Oh, and by the way, when I get there, just order me a club soda with a twist of lemon. I don't drink anymore. And much to my surprise, I'm funnier that way. Plus, I wouldn't want to take the chance of making it a habit of bombing in front of you. I wouldn't want to put you, or us, through that again, man. Once is enough.

I know my limitations. Finally.

And awaaaaay I go.

Thanks, Vin

My first love in life, I'm pretty sure, was the Brooklyn Dodgers. From about five years old on, I was completely consumed with that team. The Yankees were authority figures, the Giants unpredictable, but the Dodgers had it all—except of course validation. I couldn't bear how great those amazing talented "bums" were, and how crushed they must have felt every fall, until 1955, about never having won a World Series. And this wasn't just about a franchise never winning, like the hapless Cubs, but a long-standing group of future Hall of Famers, year in and year out, thrilling everyone, but always coming up short. It makes sense to me now that while, as a kid, I slowly started to feel lost in this world, I would identify with the Dodgers, who even though they lost clearly still had the greatness of world champs. Even though it was always "Wait 'til Next Year," they would come back in spring training looking stronger than ever. When they were losing all the time I loved them even more, because I knew they'd show up again in the spring and try harder. Their tenacity left a permanent imprint on my being. (I didn't know, of course, being a small boy, that they had no choice but to show up. But why ruin a good story for yourself?)

Even more consistent than the Dodgers losing World Series championships to the Yankees was one of their broadcasters, who soon would become their "voice," and a heavenly escape for me. Vin Scully's voice and perceptions have sometimes taken up more space in my head than my own thoughts, which has been a great thing when my thoughts are making me miserable. I never missed a game on radio or TV while the Dodgers were in Brooklyn unless school interfered. When the "Brooklyn Bums" abandoned us for tacos and palm trees, it meant an unbearably long, resentful twenty years of not hearing Vin on a regular basis. And one of the only cool things about moving away from New York to seek fortune and alcoholism in Hollywood was that Vinny had moved out there too, continuing to create his historic legacy, now with the "Showbiz Bums" and those lucky-ass listeners out west.

When I moved to L.A. and got to my new Hollywood dump of an apartment and started to unpack, I immediately put on the radio, and there he was. The Dodgers had left Brooklyn but Scully had not left the Dodgers, and his voice was as crisp and eloquent as ever, even . . . biblical sounding. My God, he had gotten better at his craft! How could he get *better*? On TV he is great, but on radio, for my money, he is the master image-maker of this great sport for all time.

All my fears and doubts and concerns about being in a strange city pursuing my dream were at once washed out by my memories of the "Boys of Summer," and I floated back in time and started to visualize the Dodgers, just as I had as a little boy when this same evocative artist painted his word-pictures with such effortless verbal brushstrokes. I remembered how much I'd loved Jackie Robinson because of how amazing his heroics were as an African-American in such a racist country, and how Gil Hodges had been my idol, and always seemed sort of Paul Bunyan–esque to me with his mammoth hands and cool hip muscles; and how I'd tried to mimic the way "The Duke" trotted around the base paths after hitting the ball out of the park into Flatbush Avenue. I remembered the dazed confusion I had felt when I was forced to realize that Roy Campanella couldn't stand up again. And now, twenty-five years old, two decades later, unpacking in my shithole apartment, I noticed while listening to Vinny call the game that my recollection of Carl Furillo was not just about his shotgun arm or his clutch-hitting but how much I thought he resembled Lenny Bruce.

The Dodgers weren't the "bums" anymore. They weren't Brooklyn's anymore. That sucked in '58 and it sucked in '75 and it sucks now. But, selfishly, I'm glad I was in the place they moved to after their owner chose to abandon the greatest, most forgiving fans of the most insane little borough of any city in the world, because *that voice was back* and could keep me company on my journey as I contemplated either becoming a famous comedian or hiding out forever. Plagued as I was with low self-esteem, self-loathing, and sadly edging ever closer to a disease that would derail me for many years from ever achieving anything close to serenity within myself, *his voice* created an instantaneous harbor of happiness for me at that scary juncture in my life.

I was in this little, run-down apartment that had big bay windows from floor to ceiling and not much else. As I recall, the hippest description of this little "pad from hell" came from Jay Leno. He too came west to chase the same dream I was chasing, but luckily for him a simultaneous career as a psychotherapy patient wasn't on his agenda. He once drove by to pick me up, honked the horn from the street while waiting in his car, looked up, and would later comment about my mammoth windows, which looked so out of place in my diminutive pad, "Jesus, Lewis, I could see your feet from the street!"

The apartment house was right next door to some motel that doubled as a whorehouse. Fifty years earlier, only a few hundred yards away, Charlie Chaplin had been making his movies. Now I was making the best of it.

I put my hands behind my head, lay back, forgot about goals, fears, money, *everything*, because Vin Scully was back on the radio, and that was good enough for me. I wasn't happy, but he'd made me forget that.

The Dodgers are playing the Mets tonight as I write in my house in the Hollywood Hills, only a few miles from where it all began out here for me. I just put on the TV and plan to relax again and forget about everything, if only for a couple of innings. Because even more than the game, I just have to hear someone else's voice in my head. And that voice would have to be Vin Scully's. Thanks, Vin.

Nina

Daydreams can come true. About five years before the magic actually happened, I was sitting in a New York theater with my girlfriend and another couple watching Robert Altman's *The Long Goodbye*. As much I dug the director's style and thought the film was cool as shit, the thing I remembered most about it after the house lights came back up was one of its stars, Baroness Nina van Pallandt, the most stunning, sensual, earthy-looking woman that I had ever seen.

The only thing I knew of this actress was her rashly unwarranted guilt by association with Clifford Irving, the would-be biographer of the then notoriously secluded Howard Hughes, which led to her appearing on the cover of *Life* magazine in 1972. She'd been in Ibiza, where she usually spent her summers, and happened to meet a writer claiming to be writing a book about the most infamous recluse of the twentieth century. At the time, both Nina and Irving were no longer married, and they dated a few times. That's all it was. Then Irving, this unprincipled, self-centered imposter, ruthlessly dropped a bomb that left her emotionally distraught, while he got fifteen minutes of ultra fame. This so-called writer claimed that Nina had actually accompanied him to an interview in Vegas with Hughes—which of course never took place—and then asked her to falsely validate this lie to the press.

Nina's virtuous character would never allow her to be part of a scam—certainly not one to authenticate an unprincipled author. Yet a journalistic circus ensued and Nina was forced to testify in court against her media-created and alleged "boyfriend." Her beauty and honesty were somehow twisted by the press, so she was not only raked over the coals for not standing by "her man," but ultimately deemed responsible for busting up the guy's marriage. What a farce! A couple of dates with a single man and having some integrity were enough to cast her as some diva, and he as a poor writer being fucked over by his powerful publishing house. It was all a crock of shit except for the pain that Nina had to endure. The press, especially in Europe, had a feeding frenzy, ripping her apart, without a shred of truth or humanity to the story.

It was a dreadful nightmare for her. For a while, this stupid ruse made Irving some sort of momentary big shot, a *folk hero* of sorts, while the principled Baroness van Pallandt was labeled a *scumbagette*. The only true thing about the whole affair was that Nina was used and manipulated and ultimately crucified, as the press sided with the bullshit artist and got their rocks off at the expense of her decency and exquisite nature. Nina retreated to Europe for almost a year to care for her children while being persecuted by the tabloids.

But of course, back in that New York theater, I was still very much in New York and very much in my head. While watching the film, my mind wandered incessantly to the question of how I'd ever act around a woman who looked like Nina if the inconceivable opportunity arose.

That fantasy aside, I mean, there I was, fresh out of college, trying to get over my father's death, figure a way out from under my newfound poverty, up to my ass in couples' therapy with my college sweetheart who had moved to New Jersey to teach, and in a daze from having just started doing stand-up. I was frightened as a motherfucker about my show business career obsession, and that I might be exactly what a family member had called me . . . "a dreamer." Nevertheless—maybe even *because* I was so lost and unsure of myself—I couldn't get that cool, beautiful, self-assured Danish actress out of my head for many hours after the movie ended.

Five years later, after I had moved to Los Angeles, the ultimate shocker happened—Nina and I not only met but fell madly in love. I experienced almost four years of bliss with a woman who was so loving, beautiful, and supportive that I finally felt—at least for a while—rescued from all my doubts and fears about being loved and being able to love.

We met at the Improv where I was performing, working on material for an upcoming shot with Carson on *The Tonight Show*. I'd had a great set, and afterwards came out from behind stage to hang at the bar with everyone, have a few cocktails, and see what life had in store for me, especially on the female side of things. I hadn't even started to get a buzz on before there was a great commotion. I looked around and, though the joint was hopping, I could see that many of my pals all seemed to be frozen, mouths agape, inordinately amazed. Within seconds my mouth dropped too. Holy shit! There she was! She appeared a little too classy and out of place standing there as her acting agent held court near the entrance to the club. I knew the agent but, more importantly, I knew that Nina had just seen my show. I was bursting with uncharacteristic self-reliance. I immediately flashed back to that night in the cinema when I'd watched this same woman on the silver screen, and became determined to make an effort to try to meet her. I didn't even stop to think whether or not she was already with someone; I was too dazzled by the prospect of kismet. Downing my drink, I found myself in sort of a huddle with my pals that gave the appearance of a circle-jerk more than anything else. When I announced my bold plan to ask her out I was ridiculed almost as much as the Hunchback of Notre Dame. But, though my posture was already as bad, a libidinous little angel was sitting on my shoulder. Somehow fueled by all the mocking, I made my way to the baroness.

Immediately I was introduced by her agent, our eyes locked, my heart pounded, my penis was frantic and my tongue tied. My guardian angel was working overtime, and the agent, fortuitously, began to work the room, leaving the two of us alone. I glanced over just for a second to see my friends' astonished expressions, and then Nina broke the ice.

"I laughed so much. You're very funny. Even when I didn't get it, it was funny."

"*I* don't even get it," I probably shot back, or something to that effect, knowing I was working under the gun, and trying desperately to figure out a way to tell her that I wanted to meet her outside this madhouse without looking like some star-fucker on the make. I mean, I didn't feel like a star-fucker; I just felt smitten with her, with how sexual and elegant she was. But why the fuck should she want to go out with me? Then her smile and her laughter gave me a kind of courage that I'm certain was a gift in return for something charitable I'd done in a former lifetime.

"Listen, Nina. Can I call you Nina?"

"I think so."

"Look . . . uh . . . listen . . . uh . . . look . . . a long time ago . . ."

Oh my God. I wasn't going to bury myself with the movie theater story was I? It seemed I was but thank God I saw her agent finish her rap and begin to head our way. I panicked into a stupidity of legendary proportions that turned into a most productive pickup line.

"I'd love to be able to see you away from this place."

"Uh-huh."

"Oh . . . and . . . well, if it is cool with you, I'll give you my number and you can call me if you're free and I'll . . . treat you to a tuna fish sandwich anywhere in town."

I was looking down when I finished the sentence and hated myself through and through until I heard Nina's laugh.

"Sure."

I wasn't certain she'd said that, yet quickly gave her the number to my hole-in-the-wall flat, and much to my surprise, she gave me hers. Moments later she left and I was feeling too high even to boast. I'd been in a zone that night on stage, and I felt as if my luck was going to change.

For our first night together, we chose to meet midway between her apartment and mine, in the parking lot of some store in Beverly Hills that we knew would be closed. I got there a little late and there she was, in a T-shirt and jeans, looking like a very tall mermaid, and, like myself, very happy. We decided to follow each other to the beach in Santa Monica where we walked for a few hours. We laughed almost constantly, and I was really afraid to do anything even remotely passionate but soon we were holding hands and I just knew, in a flight of imagination, that this was going to be a long sweet ride. I later followed her to her place and gave her a tentative good-night kiss; the next day I called, and then didn't stop seeing her for almost three and a half years. We were inseparable. I loved her. I was faithful. Even more momentous to me than that, I was able to be myself with her. I cared for her kids. I even had the luxury of putting her in *Diary of a Young Comic*—a film I cowrote and starred in for *Saturday Night Live*—in which she played herself and I played—what else—a struggling comic.

A few things ultimately got in the way of this dream come true and kept it from actually becoming an enduring affair. I was almost fourteen years younger than her; she was long divorced with children; and somehow I never, down deep, felt capable of raising her three young kids if we married because I felt like such a baby myself. I had almost no money. Her marriage and eventual divorce from a baron of course made her a *baroness*, while I, self-effacing jokester that I am, quickly assumed the title of her *nothingness*. And I basically came to the conclusion that however much I loved her I would feel hamstrung in pursuing my career by additional responsibilities like a looming marriage and sudden stepfatherhood, and I felt that I had to bail as early and as cleanly as possible to give her a chance to find someone with all his marbles in place, someone who might offer her and her children a more stable future. I know it sounds like such a cop-out, saying I left the relationship to ultimately free her up to meet the right man, but I knew in my heart of hearts, back then, that I really was incapable of settling into a drama-free, nurturing instant family. I had this constant, massive urge to first establish myself as a successful comedian, feeling that only *that* would define me as a man, and that until that time I had no right getting in the way of another person's journey. Although I was building a great reputation as a comedian, I had no money to show for it and no real monetary crystal ball to know whether I ever would. Who does? No one. Yet I ultimately felt that I should struggle alone and not be loved while I was agonizing over my future. This, of course, was the logic of a moron. I didn't know how to juggle my intense career drive with acceptance of this warm, luxurious love and affection coming from Nina and her family, just for me, Richard Lewis, the person.

Ours was about as glorious and cool and unconditional a relationship as I could ever have dreamed of. Here was this loving, intelligent, charitable, worldly, glamorous creature: a cover girl and cover woman for most of her life, a famous singer for decades worldwide (both solo and with her now deceased ex-husband), and, mainly due to Robert Altman's consistent belief in her, also a budding film star. Yet, perplexingly enough, she was head over heels in love with me, a loving yet off-the-wall, frazzled twenty-nine-year-old relatively unknown comedian (albeit with a growing, neurotic cult following) living in a hellhole studio apartment next to a very well-known "whorehouse motel." Go figure. She totally accepted me, and that was somehow totally unacceptable to me and my sense of self.

So I eventually chose to leave the relationship. But until that time it seemed beautifully surreal. Too beautiful for me. Nina's daily love, acceptance, and compassion cultivated the fantasy into a reality that I ultimately couldn't feel worthy of. Our breakup was maybe the most torturous loss I've ever had—if only because I intentionally gave up something that was solid and good.

Nina and I did not remain real close. Our split was so painful, almost as if two lovebirds foolishly flew away from each other, that it was just too hard to keep any real friendship meaningful. We've stayed in touch occasionally through the years, and I have of late communicated with her grown children, many of whom now have broods of their own—and finally have started some sort of a loving communication, if only by fax, after almost a decade of silence during which I kept away from them thinking that I would be intruding on Nina's apparent desire for sanctuary from me. I know that it was me who left, regardless of how I rationalized my reasons at the time and no matter that I felt my decision was probably in Nina's best interests—especially given that, when we parted, I was already on my way to becoming an alcoholic. I will always understand her reluctance to continue a relationship anything short of what we had and what we could've had. It's one of those excruciating separations where you can't figure out what to be if you can't go back to how great it was. I just know she knows how much I love her, and I know she loves me.

One night several years ago I heard from a mutual friend that she was in town, and yet she didn't call me except after apparently catching my first real dramatic feature role in the movie *Drunks*. The phone rang, but I had the answering machine on and by the time I recognized her voice and practically dove for the receiver, she'd already left her message and hung up. The message was: "You finally got your role." I felt so sad that we couldn't have a discussion, since it was clear by her not leaving her L.A. phone number that it wasn't meant to be, and yet I quietly felt her love again. I just knew, or at least I wanted to think, that she had the need to reach out and express her satisfaction at the pride I must have felt in finally scoring in a film so far afield from my stand-up persona. I was beyond grateful that I could still feel her love for me.

The greatest thing for me in loving Nina, aside from the joy we brought to each other, was that I actually found out at a fairly young age that a man emotionally warped and scared of surrendering to intimacy with a woman could change. And even though I ultimately ran from it, I intuitively knew that it could happen again.

PMS Diaries

PMS! What a horror show! What else can make a woman, for no apparent reason, choose to speak in tongues? Arguments arise with as much unpredictability as that kooky, nutty monster in *Alien!* And after all these years, I still feel sucker-punched. I wouldn't be surprised if throughout the course of history, dictators began wars the day after their honey, out of the blue, went *bonkers*. For a guy, this isn't about not getting laid. It's about getting *screwed*. Once a month. No questions asked. No reasonable explanations. And if you want to stay in the relationship, you have to accept it. *Period.*

Thousands of black days come to mind . . .

At the time of this incident, PMS CASE STUDY #67,980—*Fashion Model*, I *was* a few days from hitting the big 3-oh. Maybe that had something to do with my bleak state of mind. Things were a little scary back then. The biggest concern for me, and definitely not a small one, was that I thought that maybe I was wasting my life, and that my obsession with becoming a successful comedian would turn into one big joke, with me as the *punch line from hell.*

Historically, when all else fails to bring me pleasure, I usually find solace in the company of beautiful women. So finding myself feeling like shit, I was hoping to be bailed out, yet again, by another female "prize." Career problems aside, I still was the same guy inside when it came to women, a man brimming with superficiality and lacking any real courage to find out what kind of heart and soul might really be behind the attraction of surface great looks.

There was this old girlfriend of mine—well, actually she wasn't your *traditional* girlfriend, and was really not that old, come to think of it. Still, *Amoral* (her modeling name) had by all accounts the streetwise sense and aplomb of a very learned woman, much older than her nineteen-plus years would suggest.

Nevertheless, naturally taking Mother Nature's lead, she surprised the shit out of me by blurting out, "Your mother sucks cocks in hell" (that Linda Blair *oldie but goodie)* at a prebirthday celebration dinner in front of a gang of my closest friends.

Although I hardly feel that I deserved to suffer such an assault on that once-in-a-lifetime occasion, I might have set myself up perhaps, by including *The Exorcist, March of the Wooden Soldiers,* and scores of others in a collection of videos I insisted she see because they were some of my favorites and I felt uncomfortable that she hadn't experienced them. And *this* was right on the heels of me submitting my favorite fifty novels for her to slowly but surely digest. I'm *so* easy to get to know.

Sure, she was not entirely without cause in showing early signs of hostility towards my being a control-freak (even though I had assured her I didn't want to become "her Rasputin," as she put it) and having a "sickening feeling" that I seemed a little self-conscious around other people when she talked. I admit that I felt a tad embarrassed when she fell short of holding up her end of a conversation with *anybody*, even a ten-year-old fan of mine who stopped me for an autograph and then suddenly, for no real reason, started grilling Amoral on American history. I never should have used the phrase "educational and cultural makeover," even in jest, the night before. Though I was going for the laugh, she (rightfully so) got offended and started to weep uncontrollably while we were in line to buy her nightly sno-cone before we bedded down.

I know this all sounds very incriminating. It does, doesn't it? Well, in my defense . . . I don't have one. The problem was that not only was I well into my pattern of trying to get impressionable younger women to fall in love with me but I was also, simultaneously, going through a fairly deep depression, and irrationally looking for her to get me out of it.

To her credit, Amoral was really something else and in a class by herself. And whatever that something else was I would never find out. Prior to her heading into that "mysterious fourth week," we spent torrid days that bled into lust-filled nights, enjoying sexual pleasures I never thought I deserved or that my trick knees would endure.

We had first met in the waiting room of our mutual psychologist, a doctor whose intelligence was outdone only by her sensuality. My soon-to-be new flame was not only early for her scheduled session (her presence shocked me, because it was inconceivable that my shrink would ever enable socializing among her disturbed roster) but, much to her chagrin, it turned out she'd come the wrong day as well. Her earth-shattering beauty momentarily rendered me deaf to the fit she threw. In the attempt to achieve a real dynamic love, I have always been slightly more clueless than a village idiot. This explains how I could coolly dismiss her cursing and screeching and carrying on as if her calendar faux pas was clearly my doing. Even with her irrational, childish tirades resounding in my skull, I still managed not only to charm this lovely *trauma queen*, but shamelessly ask her out. This classic, horny display of my overpowering neediness for a beautiful woman was made even more pathetic by the fact that my sleazy pickup attempt occurred well within earshot of our psychologist, who, at the time, I was trying to make jealous. (I would never date my shrink but I wasn't healthy enough yet to think it was impossible to titillate her.)

But back to the babe.

My overlooking her blatant rudeness (which, in retrospect, might've been one scary precursor to her *period*) during our shocking first encounter was quite a wise investment at first, since the next three weeks were not only amazingly sensual but tranquil. Of course, what goes around comes around, and when we reached her next soon-to-be-infamous premenstrual syndrome, the honeymoon period abruptly came to a senseless, screaming halt.

None of this would have occurred if I hadn't been well on my way to developing an obsession I like to guiltlessly label "consensual womanizing." Which is, as I like to justify it, my easygoing readiness to detach myself from any responsibility or emotional impact I might have on the lives of these women. In return, they can fall in love with a man who they can feel safe with, me, given that I in all certainty won't ever bother them with the worry or the hassle of planning a wedding.

It generally works like a charm for both of us. It's flawless, in fact, just as long as none of these ladyloves asks me any questions that lead to a dredging up of who else might concurrently be a heartthrob. Or worse yet, don't adhere to my rule of thumb that they shouldn't have any misgivings, or hold me accountable, for anything that I might affectionately spurt out (verbally) while humping. These parameters, I would imagine, are similarly enforced and the implied philosophy espoused by a vast majority of the male species in the animal kingdom. Why should I feel that I have the God-given right to be any more special or responsible than any of his *other* creatures?

And I have to add (even though it might appear that I'm blowing my own horn for a change) that Amoral would have been the first to admit that she had no problem with our lovemaking. In fact, I can proudly report that she even put it ahead of watching her beloved *Eight Is Enough*, in syndication, and simply had a goddamn ball with me until nature fucked us up. Not unlike some verbal meteorite heading straight for my balls, she had that satanic outburst that put our heat in an instantaneous deep-freeze.

Believe it or not, I actually have a videotape of that very moment. Actually, I had nothing to do with it—the video, that is. One of my buddies, a blithering JFK assassination conspiracy freak (his vanity license plate reads "GRASYNL") and a psychologist by trade, said he just "had a feeling" that this latest girlfriend was primed to murder a nice moment for me and that he felt compelled to document it. So, in the tradition of his much-loved Zapruder Film, he arranged to shoot it, forever capturing on video, in slow motion no less, one of my typically poor choices in women.

My buddy died years ago trying to photograph Bigfoot. And Amoral is a man now, living in Paris—it's a successful primal scream therapist. I'm single and still have the videotape.

Had I been a filthy-rich asshole, back then, and looking for that elusive woman of my dreams to cocreate the imaginary child needed to keep my father's name alive for no sound reason before the clock struck the wrong side of forty, I would have, in the blink of a desperate eye, commissioned the famed conceptual artist Christo to cover each and every one of my ex-girlfriends, during their *time of the month*, with a custom-made, relationship-saving, soundproof *Kotex*.

Hey, man, whatever it takes. I'm desperate. It might sound like a cop-out but I'm convinced that PMS has been responsible for starting arguments that ended every decent relationship that I have ever had.

I still live alone. Surprise, surprise. Still, when I do experiment in being part of a couple, I at least try to take responsibility for any of my illogical, inappropriate, loudmouthed, or insensitive tirades. And much to my credit I'm no milquetoast, either, when it comes to shouldering the blame for communication problems.

Yet there is just *no way* that a well-intentioned guy in a relation-ship should be held accountable if everything crumbles under the horrid influence of an unexplainable and totally groundless monthly harangue!

If I'm ever to get married, my future fantasy wife's crowning and mandatory characteristic has to be—it becomes rather obvious—*Hot flashes.*

Mr. First-Class Big Shot

Somewhere in the very early eighties, with a handful of successful Letterman appearances under my belt, I found myself in First Class, flying back to New York with more belts of champagne under my belt than most normal people could even dream of consuming in days, much less before takeoff. Although, to make bullshit excuses for myself in retrospect, we *were* on the tarmac waiting for our run-way longer than usual, and as I vaguely recall, I just so happened to board first, so I had more time than anyone to chill before we split. Not to mention, I wasn't driving, didn't have a show to do that night, and the stewardess kept asking me if I wanted another drink, so all seemed very sane and right with the world. My world. Wel-come to Blur Land.

Or maybe I drank too much because of nerves. It was, after all, my standard way of unwinding. Back then the thought never occurred to me that I was ill. I felt instead invincible and excited about my budding career but the startling number of show business stars in the cabin was so astounding to me that I just didn't know how to be myself—whoever that was—let alone feel comfortable without the bubbly numbing my senses in order to deal with all the nonexistent pressure I was putting on myself to feel like I fit in. Sadly, I didn't have to exert much real talent to eventually steal the show from this VIP-filled cabin.

I wasn't really drunk so much as excited during the first hour of the flight. I had a little buzz from the early glasses of champagne, but was mainly wound up about being surrounded by a remarkable array of celebs and power brokers. I was on my way to a show that was clearly the biggest break I'd ever gotten as a comedian. I felt prepared to do the appearance; and filled with excitement to be heading to New York and the wide-open opportunity to meet new women and score on network television again; but I was also petrified—petrified more than anything else by my assumption that being a celebrity among celebrities meant that I had to do something more than just sit there in my cushy seat. I just didn't think being myself was enough. So I drank heavily, unconsciously reasoning that the quicker I could loosen up, the sooner I'd be able to be myself in such a star-studded, celestial environment.

By the time the seat belt lights were turned off and we'd reached a comfortable cruising altitude I was cruising a great deal higher as well. I had papers full of thousands of jokes and new premises stuffed into the roomy pouch in the seat in front of me, which I'd usually pore over during long flights, but on this day I felt too distracted to concentrate. The nonstop drinking became synchronized with the nonstop flight. I didn't always get *sloshed* on a plane, or anywhere for that matter, when I drank. However, on this particular flight, I was feeling so out of place (even after getting my fair share of "hellos" and nods before we took off) that my drinking was on automatic pilot. I was going down, even if the plane wasn't.

Always overly obsessed with my weight, particularly when I had to do shows on TV, I rarely ate when I drank. It never dawned on me how many calories I was drinking but somehow I ate so little that even the booze didn't make me gain much weight so much as it made me look bloated. But how I looked should hardly have been my biggest concern. It's pretty crazy, looking back now, to think that I cared more what the scale said than what I said.

As I sat looking at my jokes with one eye (careful not to inadvertently spill my glass of champagne and bring any sort of foolish attention to myself) and ogling the rich and the famous with the other, I soon felt the need to work the room.

I had the need. I can't say enough just how selfish one can become when mixing showbiz and alcohol. The glamour, the hype, and the pressure combine with drink to make one hell of a cocktail. The feeling that *all that matters is you* becomes paramount. And paradoxically, at the core of all of this self-centered madness, you really don't think you matter at all.

On this flight I wanted to matter *so much*. And I seemed to be getting the attention I so craved. Every acknowledgment of my presence seemed to be an indication of my growing success in show business, and the drunker I got, the further away from reality I slipped. Once the seat belt sign was turned off, I started countless jaunts to the lavatory. When I drank a lot I had to whiz like every five minutes or I thought I would wet my pants. It strikes me as funny now, but even then, when I was blitzed out of my mind, I was always paranoid that other passengers thought that I was going into the bathroom to do blow. I mean, I was a human pissing machine and getting drunk enough to do somersaults down the fuckin' aisle singing operettas like some goofball, but God forbid they thought I was a cokehead! I knew where to draw the line back then. Sure, I liked to drink, but I wasn't much of a druggie and I didn't want my reputation sullied by any of these people thinking otherwise. Christ, was I a jerk!

So, here's the scene. I'm drinking constantly, nibbling the endless flow of the finest of airline delicacies, idiotically waving to people and every few minutes or so walking back to the john to take piss. What a blast I was having. A few hours into the flight I felt no pain. Exactly where I wanted to be.

Plus, I felt accepted. I got the courage to talk to a lot of people who, though they would engage with me very politely, had this odd look in their eyes. And again, these were really prominent people in the industry. I was amazed at the attention I was getting. I kept going back to my seat and calling my manager to harangue him for not realizing just how popular I was and berating him for not making bolder moves with my career. I must have called him at least five times, repeating the exact same message with increasing incoherence. To me, I had absolutely no doubt that I was *way* more famous than I'd realized, more famous than my agents and manager comprehended; and as irritated I was that my reps weren't doing their job for me, nevertheless, all of this attention felt too good to be true.

On my way down the aisle for the umpteenth time, I stopped and grabbed some cheese and crackers, snacked and smiled, and once again took note of all the glances made my way by fellow flyers. Full of cholesterol, alcohol, and urine I made it safely back to the toilet, once again. This last parade down the aisle brought so much recognition that I decided to have a heart-to-heart with myself in the bathroom mirror (which makes you look a little warped) giving myself a kind of rehearsal of what I might say to my manager when I got back to my seat and called him yet again. And this time I would really let him have it for how little he appreciated my "heat" in the industry and tell him he'd better shape up or our relationship was on rocky ground. As I looked down at my zipper I became startled and humiliated. The champagne seemed to leave my bloodstream faster than I put it in. My fly was open and the tail of my shirt was sticking through, almost a foot of it. I had been walking around looking like a character from *One Flew Over the Cuckoo's Nest*. At once I understood the ramifications of all those smiles, the bizarre gleam in the eyes of all those powerful people, all probably doing their best to signal me that I was unconscious.

I no longer felt like a big shot. But the saddest part of this tale is that it would take me almost twelve years after this circus act I put on to finally admit that I was an alcoholic.

What a pisser.

Doing Stand-Up

While Feeling Like **Falling Down**

One night I fell off of a nightclub stage and landed on my head. Although I got a laugh and the few people there at 1 A.M. found it amusing, I could've killed myself. It was one of those nights when I hadn't planned on performing, and therefore felt free to drink as I pleased, but for some ungodly reason, perhaps because I was too drunk to have better sense, decided to go up to get some adulation. And as we all know, whatever goes up must come down, especially when one is in a liquored-up state and thinks the stage is bigger than it actually is.

I survived the incident and blamed it on the shape of the stage and poor lighting. I didn't once think about how crazy it was to be that intoxicated and still go on stage and present myself as a comedian when being a comedian had become the single most important thing in my life. Clearly, even in that early stage of my disease, I was out to destroy my love for my work just as I had destroyed other relationships that might have given me a sense of self-worth. I got the laughs and almost cut my life short in the process.

As the years progressed and my success grew I did remain devoted to being the best and most honest stand-up comedian I could. In my heart of hearts I believe I accomplished that. Even after alcohol became a very close friend of mine, I did try to keep away from him as much as I could when I had to perform. But the more successful I got, the more convinced I felt that I could become even more successful if I had a few more drinks before I performed. Long story short, ultimately I became a pretty great, functioning, alcoholic comedian. I didn't think at all about how my performance—my timing and memory in particular—would be sabotaged.

Most of the time I would choose the most unimportant venues

and gigs in which to drink much more than I usually would. I'd sometimes risk getting loaded if I were playing a nightclub in the middle of nowhere, for example, whereas I'd have at most, maybe, a little wine to calm my nerves before doing talk shows and prestigious venues. Although, sadly, I remember being on fire for well over two and a half hours at Carnegie Hall, I drank so much afterwards that the next day I hardly remembered how successful I'd been, or how great it felt.

As my disease progressed, and even TV shots and gigs at important spots couldn't compete with my desire to drink, I quit stand-up altogether, somehow forgetting that it was the thing I was best at and most passionate about, and tried to make money doing things that would enable me to isolate myself and spend more time alone or with other carousers.

There's no doubt that many shows I did while drinking could've been better. Beyond better. On the other hand I perhaps didn't fuck up enough, early enough, to perhaps bottom out sooner. But that's the past. Fuck it. So many addicts die or lose everything. I was lucky.

During my recovery my acting and performing and writing have all been better than they were when I drank. And as honest as I have to try to be just in day-to-day living, I apply that principle to my work and discover that being sober has helped me creatively in ways I could never have dreamed of. It's really cool to know that if I ever get a standing ovation from an audience, it will be purely for me. If I suck and they walk out, that too is cool. It's cool because if they don't "get" me, I know that it's not because I was slurring my words, or because I fell off stage and cracked my skull and lay there unconscious with blood pouring out on the front-row patrons who paid a lot of bread to see something a little more entertaining.

I know who I am now, and for better or for worse so does everyone else who watches me perform. For most of my career, I couldn't truthfully say that. Now, to tell you the truth, I'm one of the few people in the business who actually think that there is such a thing as a *bad audience*. I know the bullshit about how it's the performer's responsibility to make people satisfied, but now that I'm sober and giving it everything I've got and being everything that I am out there, if they don't like me . . . well I'm not thrilled, trust me. It blows seeing people scratch their heads and start squirming in their seats; but now I sometimes know that it wasn't my fault because I was truly being me and doing my best. If they think I sucked as a comedian, I accept it, but I also think they sucked as an audience. I allow myself, being sober, to have enough self-assurance to know that I just might have been performing in front of the wrong people.

What a relief, finally, to always know that what people are getting from me, be it an audience at a comedy club or an audience with the Pope (fat chance), is Richard Lewis the way I'm supposed to be.

It isn't easy being me but it was a hell of a lot harder making excuses.

Intervention #1

When the doorbell rang I was trying to take a little nap after a few weeks on the road that had left me feeling on the verge of nervous exhaustion. At least that's how I would have described it then. I didn't think that I was on the verge of dying. The four or five guys (I sort of forget now) who were ringing my doorbell came over to surprise me—uninvited of course—with the news that they had seen enough, heard enough, and were scared enough about my wellbeing to tell me that they were convinced that I had a "drinking problem," and that something had to be done about it or I would lose everything.

Their attempt was not an immediate success but it got the ball rolling. The problem with an intervention is that if it isn't hardhitting enough and doesn't contain an immediate follow-up plan to go along with it, it usually doesn't work—at least not right away. Since I lived rather reclusively and drank to excess most of the time privately, I don't think these bold guys really and truly knew the depths of my illness, how cunning it was and the denial I was still entrenched in. Even so, it's pretty hair-raising when the bell rings and you're expecting no one and even perhaps thinking about getting a drink, and then find at your front door a group of grown-ups confronting you with the very thing that somewhere deep down you are most afraid of—the truth.

Their heroics, and those of others like them who do this for their loved ones or others they want to help, never really fail, even if the alcoholic doesn't do anything right away to help himself. The event is so dramatic that it leaves a sober scar that you are always aware of the very next time you start to get shit-faced again, and the time after that, and when you wake up one morning not too clear about what you did and where you did it the night before.

Thanks, guys. It eventually sunk in.

I remember listening to them as they graciously looked me in the face and shared with me each in his own uncomfortable manner their feelings about how my drinking had "gotten out of hand" and was ultimately going to bring me down. It's really scary hearing that about yourself, particularly when you have no intention of doing anything about it. I certainly didn't, although I told them otherwise.

As everyone was leaving, thinking their mission was accomplished, I called back into my house the man I felt most comfortable with and who had probably seen me drink most often. I looked into my buddy's eyes and fell to my knees, there in my own home, the place I was so proud of myself for buying with money made from a dream-come-true career as a comedian, frightened out of my skull and sobbing uncontrollably, and I shamelessly lied to him and I swore on my life that I would address my problem. But consider the source. Me. What a joke. How many drunks do you know who you can trust, even after they swear?

The oddest part about my dishonest, Oscar-caliber, tearful speech is that I wasn't being a sleazeball so much as that *I really didn't know what to do about changing my behavior*. I also felt, as incredible as it seems to me now, that I could actually concoct a way to deal with this alleged drinking problem by simply cutting back on my consumption. That way I'd never get drunk again, but instead just enjoy my wine or champagne like a regular person. No one ever told me that it was near impossible to go back and drink normally after I'd crossed the line and had the disease of alcoholism. But hey, it sure sounded like a cool plan. A day at a time, I would never get drunk. But I wouldn't have to stop. This seemed reasonable. Anything at that point seemed reasonable, so long as I didn't have to give up alcohol.

Think about it. Here were people who were very close to me, and had been for years and years, who made it a point to plan a surprise attack on me in my own private abode because they had witnessed behavior that so alarmed them they felt that they had no choice but to say, "You are throwing your life away." And yet I didn't buy any of it. It's astonishing to me, even to this day (although I understand it a little better now, being in recovery almost seven years now) how such huge clues about the disease are so invisible to the eyes of the alcoholic. Denial is so profound, and requires so much self-deception and lying, that drinking becomes a full-time job. In fact, once you've hit that addictive stage it becomes a new career. And I had hit that addictive stage, the stage you can't get off of, but I wasn't ready to surrender and call it quits. No way. No how. Drinks were still on the house, even if I had to have a lot of them alone or clandestinely. The only resolution I made was that I sure as hell would never drink around those guys again. I'd show them!

By the time intervention number two happened, I was truly lucky even to be alive.

After you're fingered in such a dramatic way, the disease really kicks into high gear, with shame riding shotgun and self-deception its chief defense mechanism, and you're like some adolescent punk doing all he can to fuck up and rebel against his parents at any cost. But really, it's more like you're rebelling against the person that used to be you—*the real you* . . . the person who is afraid to come out anymore. It's incredible how low one has to get before it sinks in that *nothing* has become more important or has more meaning to you than getting high. I mean I cried like a baby when these men tried to help me. I *did* need their love. I *did* need their concern. And I *was* screaming for assistance. I had probably been asking for it, in one way or another, for over a decade. But when the cavalry finally came and at long last split, all I wanted to do was celebrate. After all, I was still only a few blocks from my favorite liquor store and now, with my glorious new plan to control my drinking, I still, as insane as it sounds to me now, felt invincible—even after hearing that I was going to "lose everything." Unless you really want to do something right then and there to stop drinking and get help, warnings that you really have a serious problem only serve as a wake-up call to get loaded as quickly as possible in order to bury the thought that you can't ever get loaded again.

I had maybe a solid year and a half left of some of my most serious drinking ever, before a second group of caring people delivered another intervention. This time it was over three thousand miles away, in a hotel suite in New York City. This one made the first intervention finally kick in, and made me finally come to terms with what I had already known when I lied to my friends at my house.

I was a sick motherfucker and I needed help.

Fuck Stand-Up Comedy

I turned my back for almost three years on the real true love of my life, stand-up comedy, in order to concentrate on drinking. It is an incredibly scary thought to me now that I would ever have allowed my passion for comedy to take a backseat to booze. But I did it and rationalized every second, without a care in the world, until I almost died. It was so sneaky, too, how this willingness to annihilate myself grew inside me with every swallow of booze. I mean I have some of the fastest segues in the business while on stage as a comedian, but my cleverness pales by comparison to how satanically clever this disease is as it begins to dictate one's path to destruction.

Being obsessive as well as an alcoholic, I first worked every minute at my craft, and then, eventually, spent just as much energy working on when I was going to be able to drink. Not having a family made it very easy to fully live the life of an artist without much concern for anything else. When you have little else, including faith, it leaves a huge hole for alcoholism to run through; as if the great offensive line from the Green Bay Packers in the sixties were just mowing down their defensive opponents and letting their great running backs run to daylight. Of course, in the alcoholic's case, what you're running toward is darkness and inevitable oblivion.

Looking back—something I probably will not do much more of after finishing this book—it seems that the height of my denial was when I tried every which way to rationalize not performing live anymore, suggesting to everyone in my corner that if I was to make gains as an actor I had to detach from the very world in which I'd made my name. It saddens me that at the height of my popularity I was so uncomfortable with success that I opted to shy away from really enjoying it and pushing my art form to its limit, and chose instead to retreat, to be alone with my insecure feelings about myself and to medicate them as fast as I could, and to stay as far away from the movers and shakers as possible.

And I did pretty well for as long as I could, until the arrogance and relentless urging of the disease kicked my self-loathing into such a high gear that I must have looked to put myself in drunken situations that were nothing more than muted cries for help. In fact, I recall once sitting at a very chic Hollywood restaurant, totally buzzed on champagne and gesturing to a very famous acquaintance of mine at a nearby table who I never would have labeled an alcoholic (which he surely seemed to be) since his drinking behavior seemed too uncomfortably like mine and certainly *I* was not an alcoholic, but instead, wrote a little message on a napkin and gave a stupid, grandiose, gargantuan tip to some waiter to deliver it to my drinking mate across the way. He got the note and looked up, spotted me, and laughed uproariously. The note said, "I'm crying out for help." I knew he was a fan and I also knew down deep that he probably understood my cry and that I wasn't able to express it to anyone who actually could help me. It's wild how two people with the same disease can turn denial into a form of amusement. That night it was a piece of cake for us two comedians.

Thinking I was outsmarting the disease by staying off stage and thus avoiding not being the best comedian I could be, I also avoided the sauce as much as possible when a few acting gigs came up, just as I did when I worked regularly on TV. Yet, even if I wasn't performing as an actor or comedian, there were still times when I found myself in the company of prominent people in the industry and no doubt displayed varying degrees of intoxicated bad behavior, and of course couldn't have been sending a great message to any producers or directors who might have thought to hire me. And even though these occurrences were few and far between, the important thing for me to always remember is how much denial I was in, how lost I was, and how I was uncontrollably being brought to my knees by this love affair I had with alcohol.

My life was at stake. Fuck stand-up comedy—that was just becoming an afterthought. Success and love and depression and fear and health and hopes and dreams were slowly becoming a blur, rather than sources for material. Alcoholism had me by the throat and my punch lines were willingly put in mothballs. All the stories I had heard growing up in the business about so many of my idols who were destroyed and died young seemed but a distant echo; their warning was made insignificant by my apparent thirst to blot out feelings, real feelings, good or bad, wonderful or painful, with booze.

So it went for a few years. I stayed away from my first true love and actually thought I was living life by my own design. How crazy too, considering this was soon after I had finished four seasons costarring with Ms. Jamie Lee Curtis in the television series *Anything But Love,* which clearly was the biggest break of my career, and helped put me on covers of magazines, headlining concert halls, and on the minds of probably over a hundred million people. Sure I was depressed when we were cancelled, but rather than using the opportunity to capitalize on my stardom and go back on the road and perform live and work through the disappointment creatively and make money to boot, I withdrew into my disease, rationalizing the decision to myself by saying that I needed to stay off the comedy stage so that industry movers and shakers would think of me only as a serious actor.

A few years before I bottomed, I was invited to the premiere of a big movie. I of course went, as I would see friends, maybe meet some women, do a little PR, network . . . Of course, I stopped at a bar about an hour before and put down a few glasses of wine so I'd be a little looser at this "Who's Who in Show Business" gala. I felt pretty together when I got to the theater and found a seat in the front row. But as soon as the lights dimmed and the titles came on, I fell asleep. I awoke to applause. Not for me, of course. The movie was over. It dawned on me in this horrific moment that I in fact had slept through the whole fuckin' film and although I didn't think that I was even *that* loaded (who does?) so much as tired from the drinking, I was also filled with paranoia (perhaps a healthy dose for a change) that *everyone* knew. I was determined to leave that theater and look as sober as I could. I thought I did. I even stopped in front of a few TV cameras and blatantly lied about how much I enjoyed the film and the performances.

What I didn't know for sure was how I might have been behaving before I fell asleep. I found out a few hours later when a comedy friend of mine, who was also there, called me. And although we weren't, and never became the best of friends, still, he had the kindness that night to wake me out of my second sound sleep and scare the shit out of me. He basically told me that I was obviously loaded and that I acted like a jerk, and that if I thought people didn't know it I was crazy. He went further than that. He told me that I would lose my career, my house, and my life if I didn't stop. After he hung up, we hardly spoke much until I had been sober for a few years. I called once to leave him a thank-you message on his answering machine. He never returned my call, but I hope he knows how much I appreciated his concern—not that I did at the time. I know now that it is these early warning shots that make recovery easier because it's not such a shock to the system when you finally quit, but rather makes it simpler to just give up the alcohol, rather than give up everything in its place.

Sadly, almost eight years later, I found myself at the house of the director whose picture I had passed out at so many years ago. Turned out that this talented person was a hurting addict. This time I was wide awake and tried to help spread the word (as best I could) that getting sober was the biggest break I'd ever gotten in this town. I even told the humiliating story about falling asleep at the premiere. It didn't seem to make a difference. It might one day. It was the very least I could do. It's what I have to do. Helping other addicts is not only essential for me now in my effort to stay sober but a way of life. It's essential because when I don't get a visual reminder of how others are so out-of-control—like I used to be—with this disease, it's just a matter of time until I begin to get complacent and believe that I have my alcoholism under control—and that is a surefire recipe for disaster. When I'm not helping other addicts and alcoholics try to get turned around I know that my own disease is starting to get dressed for a night on the town. How *quickly* I would like to forget that I can't drink anymore.

I don't. I tell jokes instead. I love stand-up comedy.

Good Morning, Mr. President,

I'm on My Way to Rehab

Well, I didn't *really* tell him, it didn't seem appropriate. But there I was, man, an invited guest to the Oval Office—a symbolic gesture of thanks, I guess, for all the work I was trying to do and had done for the Clinton-Gore ticket since the day then-Governor Clinton announced his candidacy—even as I was on my way to being a paying guest at a rehab.

It was early in 1994 and I was in horrible shape both emotionally and physically when several close pals, my then-current *squeeze* (and I say that in the strictest feminist sense), and a close family member surprised me in my New York hotel room in person and via conference call to tell me in no uncertain terms that enough was enough, and that they couldn't sit around and watch me die a slow death. They insisted that I visit an alcohol and substance abuse specialist in the city immediately, and he had the delightful task of telling me that I had to go to some rehabilitation facility or risk losing my connection with these people who loved me and with life itself.

"But shit! The President expects to see me!"

That hardly mattered to them, as it turned out. They had a plan and were playing hardball. I ultimately vowed to follow their plans, as insane and confused and tormented as I felt, just as long as I didn't miss an opportunity to meet with the President. My girlfriend, who had sort of thrust herself into the role of an affectionate bodyguard by that point, said she would accompany me to the treatment center. My friends, although not trusting anything I said I would do anymore in regards to sobering up, didn't have much of a choice, having their own lives to lead; and I guess in their own way, just prayed I would follow through. After all, they had all heard my Bloody Mary chants about cleaning up before, when I of course hadn't had any real intention of doing anything about it. I had lied shamelessly to everyone. But somehow this time, they convinced me that something had to be desperately wrong with me, because I was adversely affecting everything and everyone in my life. I was spiritually bankrupt, and didn't even know it.

Still, I also felt how pointless life would seem, hanging out at a bar with friends or eating amazing delicacies at some spectacular restaurant, if I couldn't unwind with a drink. In truth, more times than not, I didn't so much unwind as unravel. And what would happen to all my bartender, waiter, and waitress pals, who were always on the receiving end of my inebriation-induced crazily generous tipping habits, and who had treated me like some sort of king through the years? None of them, I suspect, realized that I was destroying myself. I was clever. I generally behaved well in my favorite places and only granted myself the dumb-ass luxury of making a fool of myself in places I usually never went back to. When I was really focused on drinking, if I ever found myself in another country or even in a city where no one from the "business" was, I might as well have been transported back to the wild, wild West. My thirst knew no boundaries.

I also drank alone a lot or with lovers in my house, so I was one smart, alcoholic cookie. I burned very few bridges at outstanding bars. Few drunks do. I was always welcome and tipped with as much grandiosity as an alcoholic could. What a man! What a drunk! What an icon!

What a lost soul.

So this was the D-Day of my life all right. I'd also figured one day I'd just hit all the old haunts, have a few diet Cokes and tip like 9,000 percent to make up for my new cheaper bills. I was making a zillion dumb promises to myself just to keep myself from focusing on the fact that I couldn't pick up another drink, and that I was shitting on everyone's love and the preciousness of existence itself.

I mean, alcoholism is sort of a cool disease if you have to have one. You have to give it to yourself. Or you don't. I *was* giving it to myself, and I had to stop. Yet up to that point, and short of such a forceful, supportive intervention from a group of people who just couldn't take seeing me throw my life away anymore, I don't think I would have stopped.

I was beaming as I entered the White House. Jim Beaming. Well, not quite. That was sort of a joke, but the real joke was that, though I was stone cold sober on that one proud day in Washington, D.C., I had, up until a few days before my visit, been drinking with such empty passion and recklessness that I'm lucky I even had enough willpower to show up to see the President, without drinking beforehand. What an amazingly painful experience it was to be so elated, to be invited to such a special place, while knowing that as soon as I left I was facing the hardest battle of my life. If I could have stayed at the White House forever I would have. Anything but having to deal with what was really going on.

And I was treated so well while I was there. So many of the staff were fans and before I got into the Oval Office, accompanied by the woman I was dating, I was made to feel like the "real Richard Lewis," the one they knew and dug and appreciated through my art and my efforts in helping the administration. They, of course, to the best of my knowledge, had no idea that I was an alcoholic, a few days away from rehab, and feeling as if I was in some sort of straight stupor. One of the President's main speechwriters took me aside into a private room and with a huge grin said, "Man, I idolize you." He idolized me? My well-being and self-confidence were so diluted from all those many years of heavy drinking, and now a frightening day of reckoning was looming ahead of me, so I only faintly heard what he said. Yet even in the shape I was in, some little part of it sunk in. I was sober, at least this one day, so some spiritual seeds were being planted. I inexplicably felt that there was so much more to me than this fear I was having about not drinking, ever again.

My woman and I were led into the Oval Office with the other visitors. I tried to keep smiling to hide the fear that somehow I might crazily blurt out how much trouble I was in personally. Fortunately I didn't embarrass myself, and President Clinton was amazingly cordial, and thankful for all I was doing to help his political agenda.

Then the Oval Office was suddenly empty except for the President, my girlfriend, and me. We talked a little about how he'd seen me the night before doing color commentary during a basketball game between the Knicks and the then–Washington Bullets, and what a kick he had gotten out of it. We were just sort of like bullshitting like old pals. What a trip. What a sober trip.

With the country and the world waiting for his decisions it was suddenly time to take a photo and be scooted out of there. Although I don't recall now whether my girlfriend had a clue yet about how scared I was about making any sort of real commitment to her—I seemed destined to be headed into the then-horrifying world of sobriety and I couldn't imagine being committed to anything ever again—I still joked to the President, before they took the shot of the three of us, that he should sort of squeeze closer to me, because I was sure I was going to break up with this woman as I had with everyone in my past, and it would ruin the photo, which I knew I would covet. Well, he laughed and she, as hip as she was, joined in. Still, not only did I eventually break up with her (what else is new?) but the picture sucked, because I leaned so close to President Clinton I looked like I was growing out of his body.

A few years later, I got to meet the President in person again. This time I got a much cooler photo, and although still an alcoholic, I was proudly in recovery, and doubly proud to be introducing him and the Vice President to tens of thousands of students and faculty on the oval at my alma mater, the Ohio State University, where I was also to be grand marshal for homecoming that very weekend. I was really beaming that day too, just as I had been years before in the Oval Office. But back then, my smiles weren't so much a reflection of my pride at being commended by my country's president as they were an attempt to disguise my confusion and dread at knowing I was hours away from heading toward what I'd conjured up to be "sobriety hell." Now I was, simply, happy.

And even though it was raining like a motherfucker on campus and I was getting drenched, I didn't feel a drop. I was too grateful.

Before You Can Say the Word **"Rehab"** . . .

I raced out of the rehab like a madman looking for a slice of insanity. The hundreds of phone calls and the intervention and the hopes of loved ones meant nothing. I was feeling frightened and threatened and still, incredulously, bigheaded. I was not trying in the slightest to understand what got me to this fearful precipice. I was scared, obviously still in denial, and obviously still wanted to do it my way.

Yes, I split from the famous recovery facility, Hazelden, like a panicked hare after staying for just about eighteen hours. In a funk and halfheartedly trying to do the right thing, I went instead to a self-help program back in Los Angeles that I had known about for years, where I planned finally, after years of torment, to surrender to the fact that I was totally powerless over alcohol and had to stop drinking. I felt scared bolting from Hazelden but at the time it seemed less imposing to deal with my drinking problem back home with sober friends waiting to help me, rather than to stay at a "rehab" place where strangers recognized me, leaving me feeling humiliated more than desirous of help. I was too fucked up to give up, and if it hadn't been embarrassment or shame I would probably have said the beds were uncomfortable and left anyway. I was too paranoid and my disease was too cunning.

Now, of course, with almost seven years of sobriety, I look back and wish that I had stayed at Hazelden and left with a better understanding of what had gotten me there in the first place. Yet even though I bolted I'm certain that I wouldn't be sober today had I not spent at least that one night and morning, a hopeless drunk, feeling humiliated and out of control in an actual rehabilitation facility. My disease had finally taken me into a place where in my wildest dreams or drunken stupors (of course) I would never have thought I belonged. I might have been in a state of shock but I also, thank God, knew then that I was not superhuman. More importantly, it was clear that I was teetering on the brink of my demise, and to prevent falling I had to admit I was an alcoholic.

Who knew that acknowledging it was a far cry from making a change? It wasn't until a little over three months later that I finally hit my real bottom (this was probably the real reason I left rehab—I wasn't done trying to die). Since then, one day at a time, I've remained sober.

Unlike the first intervention, when my friends had the greatest intentions but no useful plan of attack, *this* intervention had everything going for it except my unwillingness to go along for the joyless ride. But the laughable part is that my fear that it would be a joyless ride was based on my inability to imagine giving up the taste of booze forevermore, not that the "taste" actually mattered after a while. What I really found so delicious was the deadening of my real feelings.

My memory of how I got to rehab is as blurry as my life had become, but those involved have filled me in on how it happened. The woman I was dating back then fortuitously blew the whistle on me to many of my old friends, telling them that I was drinking with such reckless abandon that I was spiraling out of control. None of these people were surprised. They went into action. I was long overdue for another intervention and unbeknownst to me, these lifelong friends of mine, particularly my friends Gail and Jon, had been thinking about doing an intervention for quite a while.

I guess there is often a final, mortifying, or near-death event in an addict's life that really sets these kinds of high-drama interventions into action. I had already had my share of these sickening occurrences, and it was just a matter of time until my friends involved decided to put their friendships on the line and take this "tough-love" stance. They decided to act when they heard I was coming to New York, since many of them lived there and knew my sister was just an hour away by plane in Maryland. Knowing I was coming to town, they met beforehand with a psychologist who specialized in alcohol and drug abuse and who would eventually become one of the most important and inspirational people I would ever have the good fortune to meet. This doctor soon became a point guard, with other people at the ready to fly in from other parts of the country and assist if need be to gang up on me and, no matter what kind of fight I put up, get me to this doctor. He would perform a formal medical evaluation and make arrangements for me to go into rehab.

While the intervention was in the works, my own personal Pearl Harbor was about to take place. Already in New York, I humiliated myself by being wildly shit-faced in the presence of two pals at a Knicks-Nets game. To this day I forget whether the game was played in New York or New Jersey. At that point in my drinking life it hardly mattered. My behavior that day in front of my pals made it fairly obvious that I was flirting with an abyss of my own making. Word spread fast among my friends behind the scenes, behind my hazy, alcoholic, tortured back. All the people on "Team Save RL" were contacted and a makeshift intervention took place faster than expected. Gail and Jon couldn't get to my hotel room that day but, knowing the gravity of the situation, arranged to have my girlfriend conference call them at my hotel room. They also arranged to have my sister fly up immediately. They decided it couldn't wait any longer, even if this meant that a few of the buddies who would've been willing to fly in couldn't be there. My behavior was so whacked out that they knew they had to get me into the doctor's office *ASAP*. It's both heartbreaking and courageous for anyone to step in like this and, in effect, play God. And, of course, ultimately only God could save me. But without the love of these people I might have been dead before I gave God a chance. I was being cornered by a lot of loving people and it was one of the most traumatic and moving moments I'd ever had.

Arranging my sister's presence was an especially great strategic move because she had rarely, if ever, seen me in the kind of intoxicated state that the others had; and because she was family, would shake me up in a way I might not have been shaken without her. She reconnected me to my past, and to the lost little boy I'd been and still, in a way, was, and made me feel more human and less just "a drunk."

The jig was up: The flask with vodka at a football game. The amazingly sweet combination of champagne and fresh peach juice. The tender loving gifts of airline-size booze bottles from stewardesses. The after-dinner drink after breakfast. All of these drunken tap dances around clarity would have to come to a sudden halt or I would lose everyone and everything.

I immediately tried to figure out why these people were involved and certain others weren't. Since some people who cared for me *weren't* taking part in this humbling occasion, I tried to tell myself this was a sure endorsement that I was still cool, these other people were wrong about me; I wasn't going to die a sloppy death, and I deserved yet another reprieve from the unthinkable hell they seemed to want to condemn me to: an endless sobriety.

(I know now that others knew I was sick and cared but they had their own shit to overcome. Many people—I've come to learn—

don't like to place themselves in a position to tell another person what to do. I've also come to learn that a lot of people, who themselves are addicted to one thing or another, may feel uncomfortable with this intervention process.)

As it was, the hotel room seemed no bigger than a shoebox. I felt desperate to run, or just stay there and cry forever, or endlessly vomit my bad memories and guts out. There was more than enough hard-core love in that room for me. The walls were stinking with the stench of alarm. It was loud and clear that they were mad as hell and wouldn't take it anymore. One of my friends said, "I can't stand by and watch you kill yourself. You are going to die and I can't watch it anymore!"

But their love for me was *conditional love*. If it hadn't been, their intervention never would have been successful. The condition was that if I didn't follow through this time and stop drinking, and go immediately to the addiction specialist they found for me and follow his mandate, our relationships would be severed. It was pretty clear that they had had enough of my alcoholic behavior and that this would be their final act of love towards me, unless I decided to change.

They got me to the doctor—let's call him Austin—who sat serenely in his chair and looked across at me, almost as if he knew that every fiber in my body was screaming to me to *run out of there*. He knew he would somehow beat me to the door. The office was very peaceful and unassuming and in some bizarre way, acted like an antidote to the sinister stirrings I had rushing through me. Austin's expression was compassionate, yet stern. I was *very* alone and he struck me as being very, intimidatingly, together. What I didn't know for quite a while was that he too was an addict. An addict, but a recovering one, on a day-to-day basis, closing in on a quarter of a century of sobriety. This former drunk knew whence I came. During the session, I felt like a caged animal. I wanted to pounce out of my skin into a new body that no one recognized; so I could magically not let those who tried so hard to help me feel shattered by their failed effort, and so I'd have a new disguise in which I could just drink and drink and drink without feeling so fucking bad about it!

And yet, this goddamn, hip, brilliant (even self-effacing at times) angel was in my way, from the moment we met. And to this day, he still makes it difficult to throw my life away. From the outset, it was clear that he had a tough chore in front of him in me, and yet he still had a gleam in his eye. Somehow this reminded me of the flame I once felt in my gut as a young boy while feeling both alienated from my family yet hopeful that I might someday find my true self. This doctor somehow managed in a few short hours to rekindle the "candle" that had come so precariously close to being snuffed out. Nevertheless, I resented the shit out of him, the people who cared enough to find this guy for me, and mostly the frightening lifesaving situation I found myself in. But, at least for one day, my friends had succeeded in making me aware that to go and get a glass of wine would be tantamount to a self-inflicted Armageddon.

My recollection of the next few days is hazy. Several options were given to me and all of them involved going into a rehabilitation facility. I was to do this immediately, everyone agreed, I'd be washed up, lose everything, and sooner or later be either a living joke or a dead man. I started to feel that they were right, but I still wanted to drink. And when I knew I wanted to drink, even in the face of the crystal clear evidence my friends presented to me that I was in very grave danger, I knew that I was sick. Thank God I at least admitted that I was sick. It was this little dent into my denial that started to pave the way to my recovery.

I started to see that for the first quarter of a century of my life I had never liked myself regardless of who did. I had relieved the pain with laughs. That helped. Then I started to get adulation. That helped even more. Then I actually started to get money for making people happy. That was too good to be true. The only problem was that I still felt like shit, and had spent decades drinking away my feelings, and now I'd wound up in Austin's office listening to him tell me that if I didn't pull the curtain down on this show and go way off Broadway for a while and clean up and get a new perspective everything would come to an end. I believed him. Thank God, I believed him.

Then came some negotiating. I insisted that I be able to keep my date to visit President Clinton at the White House. I had worked tirelessly for Clinton from day one. There was no way I wasn't going to get my up-front and personal thank you and handshake. It took a lot of doing to convince everyone to postpone rehab for this occasion, but finally, given that my girlfriend would go with me and we'd stay with my sister and her husband in Maryland, the deal was struck. So, yeah, I made it to the White House and I was sober the hour I was there, but unbeknownst to the President, the forty-eight hours before our meeting and the few days after it were terrifying.

At my sister's I snuck out and drank as much as I could. Since my drinking days "in theory" were numbered, I convinced my girlfriend and older nephew to take me to places where I wouldn't be under the scrutiny of my sister and her husband, allow me my last day or so to go out "my way." I was so scared and yet so obviously determined to finally put an end to the madness that they were sympathetic, even given the manipulative pressure I put on them. *Needless to say, I wound up going to a record number of local restaurants.* I wanted to make sure that before I entered the prison of rehab, in almost a dyslexic homage to my past insanity, I would do as much damage to my liver as I could. I drank on the plane as if I were on death row and a few friendly prison guards had taken pity on my condemned ass and allowed me unlimited booze. I drank when we landed, too, as if I were already dead and it was quite a chore for my girlfriend to get me into a rental car and make the drive to our destination. I forced her to let me get out along the way and drink some more. She couldn't stop me. I think she was positive that I would run away if she refused to go along with my last blitzed-mile condition. She was probably right. And yet she also trusted that I would eventually check in. And she was right again.

To me it was simple. If this was the end of my drinking days, I wanted to feel as fucked up as I could. So there I was, a day or so after I proudly, and soberly, left the Oval Office, allowing my woman tearfully to help me stagger drunk and bloated into Hazelden. She would go back to Minneapolis to stay with friends and, I imagine, to pray for me. But as I watched her—my last link with the outside world—walk out the door, I freaked.

I knew I was there for one reason only and that was to detox and learn how to live a different life. It was clear to everyone who worked there that the deadly game would be over for me if I just shut up and took direction, and they made me feel that if I didn't, I might as well just put a gun in my mouth and pull the trigger. They didn't fuck around because they knew people like me. Thousands upon thousands of people like me. You can't bullshit a bullshitter and I learned very fast that you can't bullshit people in the recovery game either. It was their business to strip me of all my babbling, drunken, self-justifying bullshit and start the rebuilding process. I hated it. From the second I went in and was shown to this little room (which appeared to be a bustling area dedicated to detoxing drunks like me) I resented it. I hated everything about it, but not as much, obviously, as I hated myself.

After a sleepless night and a myriad of tests, I was given an endless list of instructions, from janitorial-like chores I was supposed to perform to, most importantly, workshops and support groups I was supposed to attend. My time was no longer mine. I had squandered enough of it boozing, I suppose, and so the powers that be at Hazelden meant to set the rules, to refuse to tolerate any of them being broken, and to lump me in with hundreds of other addicts just like me who couldn't find their way out of their own hell either. On paper, intellectually, it made sense, but to my alcoholic brain I was ready to dig a tunnel out to freedom and dealing with this problem my way—on my own terms. Wrong! I flipped out from fear and felt a loneliness that I never want to feel again. I thought, once again, that I had the answer and that I had to leave and try to get sober my way. *My way.* How absurd! I was too out of it to realize that doing things my way had gotten me to Hazelden in the first place.

I bit my tongue and played along as I was given a hospital-type wristband and asked what name I wanted to be called. Although I was highly recognizable, I still crazily suggested to the "Head of

Some Department" that my name was Holden Heller. Or was it
Joseph Caulfield? In any event, my pseudonym was both a private
little tip of the hat to J. D. Salinger and Joseph Heller and a key to
the reason I had to run away. Most everyone knew who I was and I
couldn't bear it. I couldn't stand that people who I didn't know, even
if they were addicts like me, were looking down at me rather than
up to me like I was used to. Or at least that's what I crazily imagined.
I didn't know then that they were just trying to be nice. I was so
ashamed of myself. I was so scared that I would be judged by everyone there as "that comedian" who is fucked up. I couldn't stand the
pressure. Though in reality there was no pressure. That's the joke. I
just wanted to stay a drunk.

I didn't stay at Hazelden long enough to get what I know now
would have been great insight and training for the rest of my life. I
would have been given the tools to recovery that I ended up getting
only sometime later. Instead I told my girlfriend that I had an alternative game plan. She was in a tough position, having to announce
my decision to so many people who loved me and who were probably dead certain that I would be dead sooner than later if I left
Hazelden. But I had a plan, and even though it took another three
months to sink in, this time it was God's plan, not my own. Even
without knowing the words or knowing the tools to recovery, I did
have the desire to get sober; and I knew that I couldn't do it alone
and that there were sober friends in Los Angeles who would try to
help me learn how to live.

My girlfriend wanted me to stay at Hazelden but neither she nor
anyone else could force me. My friends in New York were disgusted
and scared. Who could blame them? I'd lied to them for years. Even I
knew that I was still running away from help. Why should anyone
trust that I'd actually follow through on my alternative plan? Why
should they believe anything I said anymore? They shouldn't. And
yet, somewhere down deep I trusted myself enough to know that I
couldn't trust myself anymore. I knew I would at least feel more comfortable with my recovering friends back home. They, too, felt I should
stay put, but if I opted to come home they said they knew they could
help me if and only if I would just follow their directions without

question. They said if I did anything less I'd most likely be a lost cause. It came across loud and clear that I couldn't get sober alone.

It was a motherfucker leaving because they don't fuck around at Hazelden. They are in the business of putting people on the right track, not in making it easy for an alcoholic to think he has the answers anymore. Two doctors there did their best to let me know that if I walked out I was walking out on everybody who loved me and most of all on living itself. They couldn't really know that I was serious about getting help in what I thought would be less of a "fishbowl." *I was serious.* But they had been in the recovery field too long to buy any horseshit. It's easy to see now that they were prophetic and I was pathetic, putting my celebrity and ego ahead of the disease I had. I was ashamed of being known not just as a drunk but as a famous drunk. I know now of course how stupid that is and yet I do wish I could have been totally anonymous. I bet I might have stayed if I'd been someplace far, far away from American network television. *Is there such a place?* If Hazelden had a place near the Arctic I would've been on the next plane. (Who am I kidding? I just wasn't ready to commit.)

Even today, though I feel so blessed with my sobriety, I still wish I had stayed at Hazelden. But I guess I had more bottoming out to do. I was lucky that I didn't end up doing it at the bottom of a grave.

After fleeing I did stay true to my promise. I went home to Los Angeles and entered a program of recovery on my own, with the help of my sober friends and daily phone sessions with the doctor from New York. I was a good student and listened and slowly lost my craving to drink and started to have spiritual awakenings I never thought possible for such a skeptical, drunken agnostic. When I actually said for the first time, in a room full of other alcoholics, "I'm Richard and I'm an alcoholic," I had finally started a real journey to achieve a sober lifestyle.

But I will always tremble with the dread when I recall the initial, seemingly insurmountable prospect of getting through even a few minutes without an escape enabled by alcohol. I had grown delightfully comfortable being numb. Alcohol made me feel like I was living in a documentary about myself without having to be the real person. Until I entered that rehab, I really had felt invincible, in what I know now was an imaginary suit of armor, steeled against anything that would force me to deal straight on with reality.

Even though drinking had made my life miserable, it was never obvious to me. I denied it. That's what denial is. It *was* frightfully clear to people close to me that I was on a one-way trip to hell. And even after all the thousands of hours of unconsciousness and scores of humiliating experiences and hurting others, I still wasn't convinced I had to change until I actually allowed myself to walk through the doors of that rehab. Even though I wasn't exactly ready yet for the big commitment, my going there in the first place was the first time I demonstrated to myself and everyone else that I was ready to change, although still, as it turns out, halfheartedly. But at least I was trying and, most important, I was doing this for myself—which is the only way it works. Although I was feeling like a lunatic and craved a drink, at least I knew I was safer with other alcoholics on a premises with trained people who wanted to help. At this point in my life anything was better than to be left to my own devices. I had tried to stop drinking so many different types of ways, and yet things always wound up getting worse. Alcoholism wants to bury you—not treasure you.

Although I didn't even stay at the rehab long enough to sober up, I knew I was at a crossroads. Finally, I felt I had no other choice but to totally be honest. And as it turned out, lying and drinking was a billion times harder than just saying you had a problem, though in these early days it was hard to recognize. I ultimately learned that admitting that I was an alcoholic and powerless over alcohol was *the* necessary first step to embrace in order to be able to walk away from the bar *without* a drink yet without feeling that life was meaningless, boring, and empty.

And yet, four months after I returned to L.A. and acquired a whole set of new "tools for recovery," I still had the need to hole up in my house for a few days and do so much cocaine that I was pushed to the ultimate moment of truth. After starting to hallucinate, I called two friends to get me to an ER.

Lying on that gurney, I noticed that most of the nurses and doctors and their patients recognized me. I remembered my paranoia about being "recognized" at Hazelden and how uncomfortable it made me. But this time, as I finally hit rock bottom, I smiled to myself. This wasn't about shame or show business. It was only about my readiness to stop drinking and admit I was licked. And so I finally lost the battle of trying to lose my life, and won an opportunity to find myself again. I knew for sure that I was a true alcoholic. Now that I finally realized it, I was proud to give myself a chance to live.

The torturous days before I entered Hazelden and heard the tough, no-bullshit lectures from the experts at that facility—none of it was wasted. After being body punched round after round, sooner or later you wind up on the mat. You either get up and take more punishment or surrender. *I finally surrendered.*

The doctor in the ER looked at me and asked me what I had done to get into this condition. Now it was easy to admit without shame. Drugs. And when he asked why I was doing this to myself, it was easy to say that I didn't know. And when he asked me what I was going to do about it, it was, finally, easy to say one word that I had lost along the line somewhere.

"Live."

There Are No Accidents, Just Bad Drivers

I was once taught, or read somewhere, or somehow became familiar with the notion that *there are no accidents* in life. But I didn't understand what this meant for a long time, until I looked at my reflection (or what I thought was my reflection) intersected by the lines of cocaine on an antique mirror. My reflection in the mirror (although I was hallucinating) seemed to register some sort of concern for myself.

I was in the second-floor office of my seventy-five-year-old, three-story house, which was nestled in the Hollywood Hills (Me?

Living in the Hollywood Hills? No way. Had to be a dream) and faced a spectacular view of the Pacific Ocean, none of which I cared about since I was near to caving in to self-induced insanity and hopelessness. Giving up seemed the charitable thing to do. I was *at the end of my rope* as they say. Most people who get there are lucky to get there again—take my word for it.

At this juncture in my life, and at the end of *this* rope, everything that was good in my life didn't register and everything that was driving me crazy I graciously acknowledged and magnified to monumental proportions. Having very little skill at rolling with the punches, I wanted to forget all the bad, become unconscious, and like they also say, *throw the baby out with the bath water.* I was close to dying.

My social life was in disarray mainly because I didn't know what I wanted, who I wanted, or if I wanted anyone. My indecisiveness hurt women in my life who I thought loved me, though some of those who I'd thought loved me, I was beginning to suspect didn't. Never having really loved myself, it was easy to feel like a victim. I was semi-involved with someone and although it was rocky I didn't know how to extricate myself from it in a sensible way and perhaps be alone and ponder the universe without always thinking I needed company. In truth, the only company that I really wanted at that point was alcohol and drugs.

My career was in suspended animation. Nothing worthwhile was going on and I was too depressed and too addicted to booze by this point to make things happen on my own, the way I always used to. Some people in my business life at the time, though they may have been trying, weren't doing the job as far as I was concerned, which just made it easier for me to get into a funk and pile more blame on others for the disease that was strangling me. Also, after so many years of having devoted my life to the arts and struggling so hard to achieve fame and great creative situations, and never giving money a second thought, I had begun to fear that, once having had the bread for almost anything I ever wanted, I might now lose it all.

Yet even though I might have been confused in my love life and in a down time with my career, it was really my alcoholism, and not these "normal life situations," that made me feel impotent as a person and close to having a nervous breakdown. I was bottoming out, and the days and minutes and seconds of being hooked on drowning my feelings were coming to an end, although I didn't know it. I didn't know anything anymore. Nothing made sense. I felt like I was disappearing into some void that I deserved to be in. It was as if I became an invisible adult, unworthy of a good and happy existence, just as I had felt in my childhood and adolescence like an invisible boy, misunderstood and hung out to dry and forced to fend for myself. But I couldn't do it by myself anymore. I couldn't do much of anything. There was nothing but darkness in my soul and a craving for booze in my throat and the newfound love of cocaine up my nose. I rubbed that blow on my gums with such a vengeance, as if to signify that I wanted every part of me numb to real feelings. I felt more than just hopeless—I felt like I was going to die right there in my house that I had bought with the financial fruit of my perseverance over the years and my respect for the craft of stand-up and my acting and writing. Yet as bad luck would have it, I had lost any respect for my own well-being.

Feeling despondent, I manipulated some young, sweet model acquaintance of mine into believing that even though I had stopped drinking, it was cool, on occasion, for me to have some cocaine around for recreational use. I was so whacked and dejected at that point I actually believed my own bullshit. After all, it was alcohol that I really loved and this new high was not a step backwards to me but more of a sidestep while staying sober. The logic of a madman. The logic of an addict. The logic of a pretty decent human being who had no idea how to be good to himself. I scored about four grams and had no need for anything else.

I stayed home for days, doing coke, and didn't reach out to anyone who could help me. I lost about ten pounds, and rarely left my couch. And after finishing the four grams, instantly obsessed with how to get more, I fortunately made it up to my bed and stared at myself in the mirror that is behind my headboard. I *thought* I saw myself in the mirror but I didn't recognize me. I saw me as a stranger.

Worse, I started to hallucinate and my heart started pounding like it was begging to leapfrog out of my chest into that of a saner man. I do remember thinking clearly enough for long enough to recall all the people in my life who I was sure loved me. I knew for certain that I didn't love myself. Praying wasn't even an option.

I did know, somewhere inside, about the possibility of sobriety. I had been sober a few months, and this was my second "slip" back into the quagmire of my disease. The first slip had been a teeny-weeny line of blow, which I had instantly hated myself for, and I'd thrown the shit down the toilet and believed I could stay the path again. I did, but not for long. Once you pronounce yourself an addict or alcoholic, any slip that happens, after you know that you have the luxury beforehand to reach out for help and prevent catastrophe, is simply an indication that you just don't believe yet, like I didn't, that you are powerless over this disease. I still felt invincible even though I was just a shell of a man.

Through the grace of God, on this night, my overwhelming feeling after this sickening drug experience was that it would be pathetic to die in my own house without trying to save myself. That's when I called a friend, a sober friend, two in fact, who came over and we all plowed into one of their cars and they were able to get me to a hospital. It was there where I would once again pray to God—shocked that he was still there for me and sensing that he was always there and might have prevented this deathly drama had I had the brains to hit my knees a few days earlier and ask for guidance.

Both of my friends were bad drivers, and the erratic ride to the ER mirrored the traumatic situation. It's odd, though. I was so high that, although I sensed that the driving was rocky, strangely the more stuntlike it became, the calmer I began to feel. I intuitively knew that I was blessed to still be on a path, albeit more like the last lap at Indy, to finding out who I was—or rather, who I used to be— or maybe, who I might yet become.

By the time they miraculously got to the hospital they both

looked even worse than me after our harrowing trip. They knew that I was at a crossroads and they could have cared less about stop signs. They cared more about me. I'm eternally grateful.

And we didn't even have an accident getting there. There was a much bigger wreck in the backseat.

As I said before, I'm pretty certain that *there are no accidents* in life anyway; otherwise I wouldn't be here living to write about it.

The Show Must Go On

Early recovery is better than no recovery but it's a bitch. When it dawns on you some days that you have to pass every liquor store *orderless*, sit at every restaurant washing down the pasta with bottled water, and "just say no" at every party for the rest of your life to even one drop of alcohol, suddenly the fear of living forever sober grips you like the hand of some strangler on the loose in a murky passageway, and getting through even the simplest tasks can seem monumental and overwhelming.

Early on in my sobriety I often opted to stay in bed and daydream rather than to fake living like I was content, because when I privately projected staying sober for the rest of my life, at a time when faith was just hanging on by its fingernails and I was full of fear, it felt safer to not do anything, see anyone, or even attempt to get out from under the covers. Those were the days when I forgot that prayer was essential. Instead, I'd daydream.

One such morning, when I was filled with irrational terror at the prospect of popping out of bed and celebrating life without a drink, I sought solace from my usual happiness-deprivation with the help of yet another daydream . . .

It was about four in the morning. I was standing on the Brooklyn Bridge contemplating suicide at the thought of how miserable it was going to be staying sober, when miraculously, some of my idols turned up and tried to talk me out of it. Robert De Niro, Mel Brooks as the "2000-Year-Old Man," Don

Rickles, Woody Allen, Marlon Brando, and Jackie Mason (who was, just by chance, looking for stragglers on whom to try out some new material) all huddled a few yards away as I teetered over the railing, doing the best they could to (hypothetically) stop me, given how sleepy, put-upon, and potentially narcissistic they were so early in the morning—icons that they are.

Unbeknownst to them, these guys had instilled in me, both historically and in person, the belief that I could be exactly who I am. But now they pondered the question whether, given that exactly who I am was an alcoholic mess, I was worth saving.

Fortunately, through the grace of God, no matter how depressed I've ever gotten in my life, suicide has never been an option, just a punch line. But a guy can daydream, right? And on this particularly dark day of depression and near insanity I got a little help from my friends.

Rickles

You think this is funny? Huh? Really? Do you realize that I might miss the Today Show *for this horseshit? Seriously? You want attention, Lewis? Why don't you just take your dingleberry out, lunchtime, at the Carnegie Deli and leave us alone. No one cares if you die. I mean, you're a nice kid, but really, your life has had no effect on anyone, mainly yourself.*

Lewis

I totally agree, Don. And don't mock me! Although many strangers have come up to me and told me they loved my act, I just wish I could love myself a little more. Plus, I'm not sure if I can get through another day without a drink and well—oh what's the use, I'm fucked either way. I don't believe it when people say they love me and if I start to drink again I'll be a dead man. I think death might be a tremendous compromise.

Brando

Jesus Christ, you're fuckin' nuts! Drink, take it up the ass, have illegitimate kids, nothing will matter in fifty years anyway. You know, I'm a compassionate human being when it comes to society and the underdog but if you can't help yourself out of these constant depressions just because you're allergic to booze who gives a rat's ass. And besides, I'm hungry and cold and all your self-pity is so self-centered. I have no time for that. Maybe if you got out of yourself and started to live rather than think so much you'd be better off and I could be in Tahiti, at a diner, or at least getting a blow job somewhere.

Allen
Marlon, with all due respect, and I think you have had some of the best moments, creatively, of all of us here—really—although I'm not quite sure what made you do a hundred and eleven rotten films in a row at one point, but when you seemed to care about your craft, I mean, you know, forget · Bergman, Fellini, uh, even Engelbert Humperdinck in his prime, you are truly one of a kind, but in this case I think you might be underestimating the humiliation of plummeting to your death so close to the morning rush hour. I don't have a drinking problem like he does but, believe me, I think about death routinely and I think we should at least consider how we'll be affected if he dies, even though I've never been especially wild about his work. Although I did like some of his attempts at dramatic acting.

De Niro
Uhh . . .

Rickles
That's enough Bobby. Really. You don't want to overexpose your vocabulary.

De Niro
Yeah . . .

Mason
What gives us the right to even think we know what Richard Lewis wants is so wrong. Personally, I hardly know him and could care less if I get another chance to get to know someone I could care less about in the first place. Is anyone listening to me?

De Niro
Maybe . . .

Mason

Who's asking you, Mister Mobster in every movie? As far as I'm concerned, you did a few good pictures and you should have quit. I'm sick and tired of schlepping and walking and traveling and caring and worrying and waiting and paying and caring about your next movie. There are more important things in life than just how important you think you are. And Richard, why do you think that just because you're in recovery we have to care? We don't and why should we? Your carousing and dark thoughts mean nothing to people like us. We're too busy having our own to spend even a second caring about you being dead. Do you understand me? I'm talkin' to you, mister.

Brando

Shut up, you piece of shit. Don't you know that the Native Americans continue to be shafted and, I dunno, it's all so fuckin' bleak. Even the additives these cock-sucking, capitalist pigs continue to put in our foods make a mockery of civilization. Nothing really has much importance.

Allen

Absolutely. And, if I may take it one step further, not only does nothing matter, but it doesn't matter pointlessly enough as far as I'm concerned, and I've thought about how meaningless everything is from practically every viewpoint and I'm convinced that from my . . . albeit relevant vantage point, the only thing that matters is reconsidering the possibility for Pete Rose being inducted into the Hall of Fame. As far as Richard Lewis wanting to die, in my heart of hearts I feel his therapist should be the one to make the call.

Brooks

Hold on here. Let's just take a breath. Time out. Stop the music. I've taken over four hundred billion breaths in my two thousand years of living and every one is precious and adorable and for us not to try and come up with some reason for Richard Lewis—who is a cutey, although granted, a nutcase—to try and have a reason to live would make it very, very difficult for me to get a good night's sleep, not to mention I'd like to use him in my next movie.

Rickles

Are you clowns done? I'm not kidding. It's not like if the kid dies the world's going to shut down and there'll be a funeral at Arlington Cemetery. Life will go on. Even better! And I have a massage in ten minutes back at the Waldorf plus I hate to be a party pooper, and I don't know if you've noticed, but Larry King isn't even here . . . so really, who cares whether he jumps or not? How important could it be without CNN?

De Niro

It's important to me because . . .

Brando

Been there, done that, fucked that, ate that, blew that, reamed that, and sucked that comment.

Lewis

Mr. Brando, I'm a little intimidated.

Brando

That's good. Then let's go eat. I'll treat. You like venison?

Lewis

No thanks, my cholesterol was over 8,000 last month and I'm taking drugs for it and besides, my cardiologist told me that I'm not supposed to eat anything I see on the Discovery Channel. But thanks, anyway. Marlon . . . can I call you Marlon?

Brando

Sure, you can call me Marlon. But if you don't kill yourself, it goes back to Mr. Brando or I'll be very troubled by your audacity. But brainchild, what's in a fuckin' name anyway? We're nothing but specks floating aimlessly around in a godless universe that couldn't give a shit about us.

Lewis

I know. I know. Particularly about me. Don't you get it. I get it. I'm nothing. I'm a hoax. I'm less than a speck. I was dying from drinking and I think

*that's precisely what I wanted until some friends and family made me feel
like I was worthwhile. And yet, all I want to do is drink.*

Brando

*It's a little early but I'll buy you one if we can get the fuck out of here. If you
think that if you drink that would be as bad as what is going on with the
black youth in this hypocritical democracy then maybe you should fuckin'
jump.*

Allen

*Marlon, have you ever considered some anger management, coupled with,
you know, maybe a low-fat diet?*

Brando

*Hey, blow me, Woodman. You married your ex-girlfriend's adopted daugh-
ter.*

Allen

*Love is as strong as the need to drink. I think Richard needs us and even
though I can't stay I think most of you are being very selfish.*

Lewis

Thanks, Woody. You really don't think I'm funny?

Brooks

*Funny, shmunny! Funny is Sid Caesar. That's it! Fini. Period! Over! Done!
You're cute, Lewis, and you have crazy, bouncy hair, and the rest of you have
had your moments but Sid is the king and as far as you jumping to your
death it's in God's hands. And I know what I'm talking about because God
and I are very, very tight and have played cards and shared secrets and he is
so smart and wise and, trust me, if you jump it's not because you are
depressed, it's because God wants you to. I hate to demoralize you even more
but I've been around and the truth is, other than all the women I had the
honor to ball the last two thousand years, nothing means a goddamn thing.
Brando is right for once. Well, except a good potato latke. Hot on the inside
with a little sour cream, oy yoy yoy—what else could there be. Well, I mean,*

I'd take a little tumble with Sophia Loren over a latke but how easy is she to find?

De Niro

If you don't shut up you'll die first. Hey, that was a joke. How come no one laughs when I tell a joke?

Allen

Don't take this the wrong way but your primary thrust as an artist is hardly in getting guffaws. In fact, and again, I mean this with the utmost respect for your craft, but even if your life depended upon it, you couldn't be funny if there was a hand grenade up your ass.

Rickles

Oh, this is great. I'm missing a TV shot, Lewis is trying to stop drinking, and you two perverts are discussing the art of comedy. Why don't you two yo-yos jump?

Mason

If you think I'm going to stand out here for one more excruciating minute pretending that you people are even in the business, you got to be out of your mind. Richard Lewis jumping into that water would make a bigger splash than anything any one of you have done in the last ten years. And Mel, if I hear that routine one more time I'm going to jump! Now me, I'm a phenomenon. Every night, new lines, new this, new hookers, new slacks. I know how to improve myself and just because I came from a family of rabbis doesn't make me better, you understand me? I hope somebody does, because I don't. And between you and me, the fact that Mr. Lewis is a Jew hardly means a thing because I have a feeling that he feels so persecuted anyway by every single, stupid, foolish, obsessive thing that's happened to him that the entire history of the Jews would be a cakewalk *by comparison. But that's not the point. What is the point? You see what I mean, you egomaniacs got me so confused. You all talk just to hear yourselves talk whereas I talk only to hear me because let's face it, what you have to say, I could care less about, and if he takes his life what's the difference because it's his choice and if he's an alco-*

holic it's his own fault like every other dumb career move he's made and what you say on this bridge won't mean dickshit anyway because only he has to figure out in his own cockamamy head whether he wants to live or not and I could care less because even though I'm not an alcoholic I'm old and could die a million different ways so I could care less about his selfish addiction and if he jumps he'll be dead but I'll still be here, and there will be a lot of traffic and it'll be virtually impossible to get a taxi. You follow me?

De Niro

Yeah, I'll follow you. Where do you want to go?

Allen

If I may, I know we are trying to save someone's life and to some people that might be a nice thing; even though it might not mean much later today but I'd be remiss if I didn't tell you that there seems to be a rather ominous figure heading in our direction and not that I'm a pussy, and I rarely use that word without feeling a little bit of remorse because I've been to the Vineyard with some major feminists, but I'm not armed and considering that this could be a serial killer or some madman with an uncontrollable urge to wipe out talent on famous landmarks, I say we split.

Brando

You self-absorbed, inhumane piece of shit . . . Okay, let's go.

De Niro

I don't know. You think that's the thing to do? Just go? Do you? Do we? Do us? All right. If that's what we all want. Then fine, that's what we want. Bye, Lewis. And for what it's worth, I disagree with Woody, I thought you were funny.

Mason

He's funny!? What? Did you fall on your head, Mr. Raging Bull? I'm the only one here who is funny and besides, I could care less what you want. What makes you think that what you want makes any difference to me or to Lewis? Personally, this stranger heading our way is more important to me *than the possibility of Richard Lewis jumping off that bridge. And the only reason I say that is not only because I'd rather hear myself talk than anyone else here but because quite simply, what you have to say . . . Oh my God, look who it is? Kid,* jump.

Rickles
Oh whoopee, Rodney came too. Now I want to jump.

Dangerfield
Hey, you're funny, Don, huh? You got a good act—but it worked better during the Civil War.

De Niro
How did you know my next film takes place in the Civil War?

Brando
Get over yourself, Bozo. Christ almighty, I gotta get some breakfast. I'm famished. I could eat a cow. I can't believe you pig-fuckers! This planet sucks!

Dangerfield
No kidding. And Richard, let me tell you, I heard the news and I came right down. That's the kind of guy I am, you know? Trust me, it's no big deal. Forget about it. What you're going through is nothing. Believe me. You think you got problems? In my family, suicide is considered a step in the right direction.

It was just about then that everyone laughed and started to walk back to Manhattan. I didn't laugh but I was dying to. Rodney was pissed and seemed offended that I didn't give him his due.

Dangerfield
What's the matter with you? That line's a killer! I was going to do it on the Tonight Show *tomorrow and now you got me all fuckin' paranoid.*

Lewis

Rodney, I don't think you understand. This is serious. I feel like shit.

Dangerfield

Hey, you're halfway there.

Encores

I was an alcoholic for the better part of two decades. During that time, during the vast majority of days and nights, I didn't drink. This is sometimes hard for nonalcoholics to comprehend, but even though I was better than some at controlling my drinking some of the time, and functioned pretty well and with some amazing successes, I was still an alcoholic, and suffered all the emotional pain and confusion that goes along with not understanding yourself. And my alcoholism progressed, as alcoholism always does. Towards the end of my drinking, nothing else was as important as chasing that high, which really was not a high so much as being blinded in a blizzard of unconsciousness and nonliving. But I do remind myself and others that I wasn't *always* wasted, because if I remember only the rotten times then it would seem that I was out of it every second of every day and that just wasn't true. I was fortunate to experience some magnificent times and wonderful people, even while I was drinking, and there is something to be said for being a little kinder and gentler to oneself after sobering up.

But it's also just as important to remember horror stories—both to share with you how bad things can get and to always remind myself that as far as I've come, I can very quickly go back to a living hell.

For example: Vacations are supposed to be a way of enjoying yourself, but when I was a full-blown alcoholic, vacations were not only an excuse to drink a lot more than usual but special occasions for feeling sorry for myself. In Europe once, many moons and bottles ago, I vacationed with a great woman. I loved her, but I didn't know how to express it to her. I was also conflicted about whether she was the "right one"—although I know now that in the condition I was in, I was the one who could never have been the right one. My girlfriend was sleeping after yet another night of no sex from me, mainly because I couldn't enjoy myself with her out of fear that she might think my enjoyment meant that I was sure I loved her. This has been quite an ongoing ritual of mine through the years with great women who treated me well—to pull back sexually, thinking that doing so was more honest, when mostly what I was doing was putting up a wall against intimacy. The whole bloody dynamic of dating is so fucking controlling and your thought processes are so preposterous when you are alcoholic. It never dawned on me that maybe some of these women would have felt just fine just fucking without receiving a marriage proposal soon after the orgasm (like that's the most romantic time) and that some of them might have turned me down if I *had* proposed, which would have been the intelligent move given my state of mind. But anyway, there I was, in Paris, the city I was so mesmerized by as a college kid after devouring so many of Truffaut's films, a beautiful woman in my bed and me, drunk, naked, the bathroom window open to the lights and sights of this sensual metropolis, sitting on the toilet, trying to get a hard-on and masturbate as if cumming would be some sort of affirmation that I was still alive.

Panicked, I snuck down to the bar and pleaded with someone to allow me to make a long-distance call and bill it to my room. I called a buddy in New York and sat there on the bar stool, crying and trying to make sense out of my frustration.

Years later, I was at a famous Hollywood restaurant with very famous people and my not-too-famous-but-drop-dead-beautiful-and-half-my-age girlfriend, who, although she liked me a lot more sober, had no problem with me experimenting with drugs since she thought drugs were "enlightening." Well, she was very young. For me, drugs were just a sideshow to get me in the mood to drink. The entire evening, which might have been fun, turned into a nightmare of embarrassment. First I hounded this young woman to make sure that before we went out she called her friend who lived an hour away to get her dealer to come up to meet us at the restaurant with enough crystal meth to keep us both sleepless for a long time. Then, once we were at the restaurant, though she was happy just sitting with these Hollywood icons, the novelty of having this gorgeous trophy by my side soon wore off and all I could think about was getting blasted. This was around the time, a few years before I bottomed out, that I began to sort of enjoy drugs because I thought they would enable me to go out in public more often and still be blasted but not look like a drunk. What a self-delusion! It's inconceivable to me now and sickening and heartbreaking to see myself so out of control and yet so sure that I was always right. The connection finally showed, and I greedily got the dope and disappeared for the entire dinner. The entire dinner! I stayed in the bathroom getting ripped, and didn't give a fuck about my date, my friends, the restaurant's reputation, my chance of being busted. Needless to say, the night was a catastrophe. When I finally returned I had succeeded in alienating everyone there except, of course, my date, who had managed to get her own "shit" to snort, was quite content without me, and actually got us home safely where we could continue our drugging.

One of the people at that party was a friend of mine, a world-class musician and an artist, who years later I made amends to for my behavior that night. Then I had the thrill of attending a show he gave as a sober and a different man. I also wound up going back to the same highbrow restaurant years later, and made sure the owner and maître d' saw the new, sober me as well.

I have made, rather than drunk, a lot of those kinds of rounds since 1994. For years I gave a lot of wasted public appearances. After I began recovering from alcoholism, I made a conscious effort to give a lot of sober encores.

I Fell on **Good Times**

So *what happened to me?* Hmm. I was born and felt alienated very early on in childhood. I know I was raised but yet felt so low in the process so early on it was hard to get a true sense of myself. It was beyond challenging to connect with my family, who each had their own path to travel and didn't place communication or understanding high on their list of priorities. I felt that my opinions were meaningless, and began to feel like the invisible boy. I retreated into my head and slowly started to mistrust people. I never felt good enough. I never felt I deserved good things because I never felt good about myself. I gravitated toward thinking that bad shit was all that I should expect. I took on stand-up comedy as a way to escape from this inner turmoil and have my feelings validated. The laughs and the accolades didn't fix the damaged person inside, but helped me put off really examining why I needed so much attention. The struggle was both exciting and torturous, and alcohol eventually became the best way I could find to avoid feeling or examining anything.

Then I fell on good times. I became one of the fortunate comedians in this country who was actually considered authentic and successful. I made lots of money and became famous. I drank more and more because I was the same old damaged goods inside and I knew it and I couldn't stomach or even conceive the thought of my sickness being exposed as I gained more popularity and respectability as an artist. The more I accomplished the more fraudulent I felt. It's not surprising that as soon as there was a brief lull in my career and I suffered creative setbacks and frustrations, only the bottle was left as a place of refuge from fear.

Then my life started to spin out of control. I still think that I was at the core more or less a decent man, who then more than ever continued to live not just to enjoy myself or to find inner peace, but to continually prove myself and please others at all costs. And it almost cost me my life. Yet, when you hardly feel worthy of anything, losing your life has very little meaning. Soon my existence was basically centered around getting high, with no thought about spirituality. In order to fill up my hollow self-image, I had an open-ended need for approval. Solace was nowhere in sight. Bars were everywhere. Worse yet, I had the unfortunate mind-set that nothing I achieved could ever be enough, or could happen soon enough; that I needed what I wanted when I wanted it, or I felt only despair. I was like a passenger on a motionless train looking out the window, watching as beautiful cities and exquisite moments passed me by.

Yeah, I fell on good times and it only made times worse. What a horrible place to be. Until I sobered up I just felt like I didn't matter *and* that I was *all* that mattered. I think a Hendrix song has a line in it, something like, "I used to live in a room full of mirrors—all I could see was me," and that was pretty much how I felt as an alcoholic. When I finally saw the drunken image of a man in emotional ruin, I somehow or other ran out of excuses to continue drinking. Fortunately, I lived to see the crossroads, and with that opportunity came faith enough to get outside of the torment and look into that mirror with a new perspective.

Now, thankfully, the image reflects a man who sees life as it really is and not just how I want it to be or through a drunken, distorted lens. I ran out of hiding places. My next stop was an early casket, jail, or a mental institution, and I took a pass. So now I'm alive and sober *but still play nightclubs.* And trust me, some nightclubs are worse than death.

I'll live with it.

PART 2: The Middle

One Down, **a Zillion to Go**

I wish I could tell you that it was great being sober. Okay, it's great being sober—but it sucks being addicted, even in sobriety, to what feels like everything that could fuck me up and not much that could bring me peace. The truth is, when I stopped drinking, I still had no clue how to live, or even who I was. From so early on in my adult life I had the need to be accepted and become someone with a "voice" that was appreciated, and couldn't stand being disliked for any reason. As glorious as the struggle to make it in the arts was, and as exciting a life as I've lived, eventually the thrill of hiding from my feelings behind the progressive need to drink away my fears and hide from my successes left me a sober man with a lot of new living to do. I hardly recognized myself when I saw my reflection in the mirror. And why should I know who the fuck I am? If you live most of your life feeling that you are mostly wrong, then take on a profession where you have to please everyone, including some of the most shameless and vulgar people you can imagine, then once you stop your self-destruction of choice, you are left with an outline of a being that seems to resemble you, but your insides are pretty empty. I have been in the process of getting back to the Richard Lewis I am. Not the celebrity, not the people-pleaser, not the occasional out-of-control drunk, not the functioning alcoholic, not the, not the, not the, not the—not the zillion things that I have become and still have a need to be even sober; I have to change and learn a new way of living in my skin and let life take care of the rest.

It's a bitch, believe me. I take my fucking hat off to anyone who has been ruled by addictions, any one of the endless variety, and has been close to being destroyed by them, in the process hurting many loved ones and wiping out lots of chances to have a decent shot at life, and then starts out again, a recovering hitchhiker on a new road without road signs, without much to say to any benevolent driver who picks him up and asks, "So, who are you?"

Who am I? I'm not sure. I get feedback from friends, enemies, read reviews of how I am professionally, get some awards, some nominations for this or that, but for the first time I really have a chance to define myself in a way that isn't blocked by booze or the need to put on airs. I figure I can just be myself now and see what happens. I'm not married but I'm sort of looking at life now with that same vow, "For better or for worse."

I think I work a good program for myself in my recovery: stay sober, have a nice support group, and do whatever it takes to accept people for who they are, be loving to those in my life who love me for the right reasons, try to keep my self-loathing to a workable level so I can still feel funny and be able to perform, and pray a lot. I pray that I never forget where I came from, and that regardless of how fucked up things can get I can know that it'll pass, just like the good shit will pass and that I can keep the zillion other addictions that are potentially as powerful and destructive as alcohol locked away in a cage where they belong, so I don't fall prey once again to something else that controls me or makes my life spin out of control.

It's amazing how many addictions come out of the woodwork as soon as you think you have your big one under control. "Do not pass go—go directly to the addict." They are waiting patiently. It's quite a rude awakening when you sober up and realize just how enticing it is to do any number of other things that will take your mind off of positive behavior, and begin again the same sort of love affair with fear and self-centeredness. Addiction will go out of its way to come through for you whenever you're not sure you want to live life in a happier and healthier fashion.

Trying to calm down for the first time in my life really is stressful.

Trying to eat properly is a new experience. Trying not to fuck around on a girlfriend seems like a pipe dream considering that it represents trusting someone very strange . . . Me. Those are just the appetizers, man. Getting out of depression is a frightfully difficult trip. Ongoing fears of career doldrums and financial insecurity always tuck me in at night. Waking up with free-floating anxiety that can oftentimes leave me wanting to stay under the covers until I stop breathing isn't exactly a holiday. And the thing is, I've had these feelings for quite some time, but when I was drinking I had an easy way to nip them in the bud and forget about them until I'd wake up, sometimes in the same clothes with a headache that pounded a gavel of guilt, pain, shame, and avoidance.

Not anymore! I feel strong. I'm in the ring and am taking all comers. I sort of feel fearless. You can't lose after you lick a disease. Lick a disease. How fortunate to be able to actually kick the shit out of the disease that was kicking the shit out of you. I never have to drink again. Wow, how cool is that?! The downside is that I have to stand up to all the new vices and addictions that have waited their turn. I'm up for the struggle. I've been down for the count for the last time. Every time my life gets fucked by some event or person, I swear to God, as long as I handle the situation without drinking myself through it, it always, and I mean always, works out better than it would have had I tried to deal with it unconsciously. That might sound very obvious to the nonaddict but, believe me, a zillion things have happened to me that I used to experience before sobering up and not one of them hasn't had a better outcome. That's really proof enough for me.

I have had friends think they could go back out there and do more research in the world of alcohol and drug abuse and give it a second or third or fifteenth shot, and many have tombstones to show for their effort. Others may still be living, but are either in prison, insane, or hurting more people than they ever imagined possible once upon a time. So, yeah, I have a ton of cravings waiting to control me, and it's not easy, but when all is said and done I'd rather down a quart of ice cream, or irresponsibly neck with a woman who isn't my girlfriend, and then try to cope with just how badly I feel about myself the next day, if not the next moment, and work on those and other hard-to-control passions, than go back to drinking and kidding myself that I have a chance in hell not to live in hell.

I'll drink to that. Maybe I'll head down to the health food bar and toast with their frozen lettuce, carrot, cranberry, prune, super-duper protein shake. I can't wait to puke my guts out and be a better person.

I'm not kidding though. I'd rather get sick from that shit than two bottles of champagne. At least I drive home and have a better chance of not killing anybody.

When these zillions of yearnings that seem poised to take over my life strike me, I have a new game plan and it seems to be a cool plan. I heard someone talk about this once and I tried it out and my life has improved a great deal. It hasn't always worked but it certainly has helped. Say I have this overwhelming desire to drown my sorrows and self-pity with an entire chocolate cake. I visualize the drive to the store, buying it, getting home and eating it or chewing it and spitting it out or whatever. I think about how I'll feel afterwards. I think about how it won't change a fuckin' thing that was getting me depressed or fearful in the first place, and how badly I'll feel for having done it, which will make me want to do even more damage to my system. By the time I work through this scenario, and actually see myself gorging on this dessert for twelve people, more times than not I don't act on it and feel fantastic afterwards. Sure, I'm stuck with what life dealt me—the incredibly strong urge to find ways not to deal with something difficult—but I do now deal with it faster and with much more self-respect and with fewer calories.

I sound so healthy. You should only be aware that if the truth be known, right at this moment, I could eat about a thousand spareribs.

Buddy, can you spare an egg roll?

An Addict's State of **Mind**

It blows. Even though I have given myself the chance of a lifetime to reevaluate my past and try to make amends for whatever smashed ruins I might have left in my drunken wake, and though I now live each day sober and full of gratitude, life is still replete with so many minefields of pain it sometimes feels senseless, comfortless, and even more insane than when drinking was at the center of my existence. Today has been, so far, an example of me living the life of an ungrateful addict in recovery. I didn't thank my God for anything. I didn't take any time before I started my day to count my blessings. (Ha! "Count my blessings." What a wimpy phrase. At least it always seemed that way to me until I became *and* admitted to being an alcoholic. It was the kind of shit I always seemed to hear in some inane Christmas flick or screamed about in a tent full of fearful believers by some money-grubbing pulpit-thumper.) I didn't think about others less fortunate. I didn't call any fellow recovering addicts like I was advised to do, when I was feeling like shit and shaky, from day one. Instead, I isolated and allowed myself to feel that the rest of my life was passing me by, and that there was nothing I could do to make myself feel better. It takes a long time to fill the empty glass with spirituality when alcohol is out of the question.

Apparently, even sober, when I don't get what I want when I want it, and, in particular, don't run after women the way I used to after spotting someone that leaves me thunderstruck, I get amazingly depressed. Women, one of my many major, co-headlining addictions, came leaping into my life faster than a speeding pussy once I gave up alcohol. And, apologies to the feminists, when I mean pussy I mean pussy. Pussy to me is not the woman the potential sexual act is attached to, but the word and how it's really a way to demean myself. You don't make love to "pussy," you fuck pussy; and as long as addicts fuck themselves up they will never be able to have true love and really know the feeling of making real love to a real woman on more than just the animal level. And so the real pussy is the man.

As far as I know, female sex addicts or women with intimacy problems don't have any corresponding or similarly disturbing slang for their men. It's about time they came up with some, though, because there are just as many women who are real cockhounds as there are pussyhounds—although a very intoxicated woman once spent several hours in a crowded bar trying to convince me that women were only "powerhounds" and that cocks had very little to do with much of anything. Her companion, dressed in a tight foil dress, with perfectly cut-out holes for her nipples to take in the sights and sounds, chimed in occasional moans of agreement when she wasn't caressing her smashed date's body.

Anyway. This morning started out like shit because I couldn't help thinking obsessively about all the things I hadn't done, so I decided to run out of my house to buy a CD, to try to let some good music drown out my pointless thoughts. Then the "disease" struck. I spotted a woman so beautiful and so striking that I forgot momentarily that I was in a relationship. I was at once conflicted, the old me competing with the new and improved sober me who was trying to live life with more principles and dignity and not to act out every desire. But man, it's like being in a goddamn vise. It's actually easy now for me to go back to bars and just relax and have a few diet sodas and have fun or write without igniting in myself any interest in drinking, but this pussy thing is a motherfucker. If only I didn't continue to enable myself in addictions other than drinking, life could be a breeze; but I do, and it's torture. Acting out with a woman while I'm involved with another woman is, for·me, almost like taking a drink again.

One day when I'm ready to allow myself the luxury of being happy and content, maybe I'll treat these urges the way I treat alcohol and just not *go there*. But on this particular morning I wasn't quite so evolved. So I followed this mysterious, amazing creature into a hip coffee bar to get a closer look, hoping that she might be wearing Nazi artifacts or similarly horrific tattoos or possibly have no teeth so as to instantaneously get her off my *jones* list.

No such luck. It's never easy. It wasn't easy giving up booze and it isn't easy to stop fucking around. (Liquor stores and beautiful women are everywhere. And to me this woman fell into another category altogether. She was killer. She was Queen Rush.)

In fact, I realized that she was even more beautiful than I'd thought, as I tried to order my coffee and snatch a look at her at the same time, with about as much finesse as a python gobbling up his nearest snack. I was again powerless over an unknown woman who I knew I shouldn't be messing with. This addiction had me by my balls again.

We were standing right next to each other, and it was now or never. Years ago, particularly if I were high, this would have been a piece of cake. But now, sober and loving another woman, I felt both strangely mature about recognizing how wrong it was to even think I would pick up this stranger, and also impotent, because at "penis control" all systems were "Go." It's hard, trying to have principles when your cock is hard. I was a wreck. If I'd ever been cool in front of strange women before it certainly wasn't showing. I was the polar opposite of the kind of cool Marcello Mastroianni always seemed to exude. I was the new me. As embarrassed as I felt, at least I was being myself. And as strange as it seems to say, given the circumstances, I know that's a good thing.

I had made up my mind that there was no way I was going to try to meet this woman. I ordered something robotically, then listened as she ordered in a voice with more sexuality and heat than I could stand to be around. I tried to find a way out of the place to save my nervous masculinity, which was rapidly slipping away.

She was dressed beautifully and was very tall with enormous breasts. Having an overpowering need to at least say something, but also making a valiant effort to preserve my monogamy, I chose simply to tease her by pointlessly commenting to her that the pattern on her shoes was intimidating to me and probably to other men as well and asked her how she could walk around like that and expect to meet anyone. She was instantly confused by this pitiful if quasi humorous observation, yet still managed to whimsically retort, "I've had these shoes for many years and you'd be shocked how many intriguing people I've met just because of them." Fuck! What an opening. She was playing along with my weak little conversation, and I was convinced that I could've gone from nerd to gigolo in a flash, but didn't. I got back home in a few minutes and went into a deep funk. But I didn't act out. I didn't cheat on my girl. I acted responsibly.

Painfully slowly, I strangely started to feel good about myself, even though every addicted fiber in my body was fighting it every inch of the way. Taking on good habits is a bitch.

Dates from Hell

In my thirties and early forties I had a pattern of chasing, dating, and ultimately pining over women who were out to do me no good. These were "dates from hell." I was a date from hell too, though, and would remain one as long as I was an alcoholic, yet I would be the last guy to admit it and the first guy to deny it.

During my drinking days the majority of women I felt I loved, or who loved me, were an odd assortment of femmes fatales who led me to experience a vast array of dramatic events and feelings, including, among other earthly delights, stealing, cheating, being stalked, lying, enabling, ruining happy moments, competing, jealousy, infidelity, lengthy sexual abstinence, manipulating, having my friends turned against me, chronic depression and anxiety, hopelessness, feeling emotionally impotent, feeling near suicidal, never being comfortable being my true self, being nudged into the world of drugs, humiliating scenes everywhere imaginable, sabotaging my own career, and more often than not forgetting those wonderful people in my life who sincerely loved me and whom I loved, in favor of hating myself—and *that* was on a good day. But until I stopped blaming my misery on every single, rotten woman I spent time with, and started shouldering the responsibility for being incapable of expressing, on a consistent basis, real love and joy towards myself first and then to others, the joke was ultimately on me. Although my "dates from hell" riffs in concert halls might've killed my audiences, in truth my relationships were just another diseased manifestation of the ways in which I was really killing myself.

Mixed in with these horrific dames during my mad drinking and using days were a few gems who I was blessed to have enter my life. My first true love had me before I was alcoholic—I think. The one after that tried gently to address my problem; another, who was not ultimately right for me, helped me sober up. My latest love has never seen me drink a drop. My love life sounds so simple when I paint it with such broad strokes, but for the most part, up until recently, it resembled postwar Europe, riddled with sudden bursts of emotion and cum that ended in smoky ruins and my revisionist, hazy accounts about how none of it was my fault.

The truth is that at the time I couldn't trust anything or anyone except my comedic instincts and the companionship of the bottle. Consequently, since I was sort of in and out of a fog from all the carousing, I found myself very comfortable with women who validated my shitty feelings about myself. I know now that until I stopped drinking no mature, loving woman would want to devote herself to the Richard Lewis Reconstruction Project unless she was a martyr of sorts. I tended instead to attract fellow addicts and, generally speaking, extremely intelligent, selfish women. They did enough to excite me and keep me in the game, used me, and I soon became uncomfortably dependent on their "feelings" for me until finally the pointless relationships imploded. Even if I was with the Wicked Witch of All Time, my alcoholism made it easy for me to beat myself up for allowing her to beat me up (emotionally). I was absolutely incapable of knowing when I was in a shitty relationship and how to get out. Once the disease kicks in, it's impossible to get anything close to a real understanding of who one is or what one wants or who one is with. This minefield of socializing lasted the better part of fifteen years. The list of romantic failures seemed as endless as my self-loathing.

In the beginning of this crazy-go-round of ceaseless bachelorhood, I would always have just enough alcohol in my system not to really care who I was, how I acted, or what impression I made prior to or even during sexual relations. I was a madman when it came to chicks. I wanted almost every attractive woman I spotted. It didn't matter where I was or what condition I was in, if I saw a woman that visually made me *crazily* stimulated. I was addicted to beauty and instant gratification.

Cumming was a major form of stress management for me. Stress management that lasted just a few seconds. As quickly as my orgasm became a memory, then either loneliness, guilt, disgust, or an intense desire to be alone swept through me with enormous psychic force. This made being alone a foregone conclusion, way before I started making believe to whoever it was that wandered into my dysfunctional lair how happy I was to be in their company.

I can go on forever taking responsibility for my laundry list of defects in relating maturely to women. But believe me, I have made my amends to the handful of wonderful, kind women who sadly were trapped by our mutual love at a time when I was not fully aware that I was a certified alcoholic, clueless about "recovery," unable to really feel loved or progress to any higher ground of involvement, and always subconsciously or consciously looking for a way out. And I always found the door and hurt them.

I feel even worse about the women I hurt who I didn't truly love than I do about escaping from affairs that could have amounted to real love and even a family. I'm not talking about the assholes who had an agenda that only Satan could've dug, but about the women who fell in love with me because they didn't have the wherewithal to see trouble and get out before they got slam-dunked by a lover-boy who was petrified of surrendering both to his disease and to the love of a significant other.

It was far easier for me, a hopeless romantic with a drunken, chicken-shit heart for commitment, to get hot over a woman with no heart at all. I don't have to rack my brain for examples of the living hell I put myself in, a hell that made it seem only logical to yearn to bolt from being a couple, and most depressing, one that validated my unrealistic feelings of worthlessness.

It's amazing how powerfully debilitating self-loathing can be. On the surface, to most people, even pals, I was a shiny coin who had no problem getting attractive, slightly amazing women to appreciate and love me. And yet, secretly, all the while, if the coin was flipped over it would reveal an emotionally crippled mess of a man who kept himself in a pathetic prison of self-doubt and an overwhelming fear of being smothered if he allowed himself to accept the love of any one woman on a continual basis of trust and faithfulness. This of course was particularly heartrending for me when the woman was glorious, sweet, and honorable. Hence, to avoid such complications, a true "date from hell" myself, I had my antenna out for female counterpart "dates from hell" and I really picked some *doozies*.

Come to think of it, even when I masturbated during these lonely times, I usually had to conjure up the most hateful woman I could think of in order just to get a hard-on. Back in those days, the last thing that got me aroused was a sweet, nurturing, loving woman— no matter how good a lover she might have been. That kind of person was a threat—not a safe bet.

I can just see myself in bed, alone, dying of alcoholism and dying to cum and having the hardest time getting hard while I searched my cloudy memory for any woman who had recently *really* fucked me over. I dove right into the world of show business, and just like that, bingo! I had my conniving, manipulative bitch just ready to rock my cock and fuck up my world. Regrettably, these women weren't fantasies but blasts from the past that really existed. So there we were, in my head, with my other head in my closed fist, working and working and working and working until I thought I would drop dead before I got an erection and it wasn't until I blurted out, "Hurt me you cunt!" that I struck pay dirt. I came just like magic and many times so did the tears.

It was so simple. I had to go to the pitiful bottom of my emotional well to get it up, only to be fucked (in my mind) by someone who treated me like shit. That was my ticket to get me hot and erect.

Dates from Hell, #389

The easiest way for me to find a female nightmare was to make a stranger laugh, a gorgeous woman who I knew recognized me, and I would take absolutely no time in finding out much about her and within hours, sometimes minutes, admit that my heart was pounding and that we must be together.

Here's a pitiful example of my shallowness and fear at work during my inebriated days. I recall in the early eighties, after a great set at the Hollywood Improv, very single, just hanging by the jukebox, drinking and praying that I'd find a woman to lust over. On this particular night I drank more than usual and although I thought I was seeing double it was in fact two women who eventually approached me. They didn't seem too high but I must have slurred my intentions clearly enough because somehow I wound up at their hotel within a half hour. I was so drunk at that point that not only didn't I know why I was there but didn't remember what we had discussed back at the club, and I must have alienated one of the women because once we got into bed there was nothing but hostility from both of them and it was a sexless affair.

They had driven me to the hotel and my car was parked somewhere near the club and I sort of begged them to drive me back but they refused. Too loaded to put up a fight, I passed out.

Fortunately when I awoke the next morning in my clothes they were willing to unload me back at the club. I had absolutely no recollection of who they were or what we said and I guess that was what I know now to be a blackout. All I could think about when I got up, with the sun seemingly singling me out with a beacon of light directed straight toward my migraine, was to get back to my car. All sorts of paranoid thoughts—from never performing again to being murdered to wanting to puke endlessly—played around in my unfocused head. Suddenly I was back in front of the club and they sped off leaving me to what I felt blessed to be able to do—find my car and get home. Easier thought than done.

I started to walk to familiar places where I normally parked . . . no car. I couldn't believe that I couldn't find my car. It never dawned on me that I was in a drunken fog. I was so many years from thinking that I had a problem with drinking, denial was not even in my dictionary. And my car, too, was nowhere to be found. I walked what seemed like hours, slowly panicking, not knowing whether to call the police and report my car missing. Of course I wouldn't have known what to tell the cops because I was totally blank and the idea of being so dumbfounded in front of a cop seemed senseless even to me—a man with a car and a home who was parading around the streets of Hollywood in the early morning as if I were homeless. I began running down the many streets around the club, scared without really knowing why and simultaneously *praying* that my car would materialize. Finally, it did.

The memory that is so striking to me now is that as soon as I spotted my car any sense of responsibility for all the wasted time left me. I instinctively took no blame for the whole stupid escapade or for whatever it was I'd put the women through and drove home. Although I felt like shit physically, emotionally I was totally without any concern that my life was out of kilter and heading down a path of mindless destruction.

It had been yet another blind date and there was no end in sight.

Last Tango in Paris

I think I was in my very early twenties when I first saw *Last Tango in Paris*. Who am I kidding, man, I know *exactly* when it was and thirty-two years later, I probably own about fifteen or so rare movie glossies of that flick, including a hard-to-find X-rated original poster that hangs in my bedroom. To me this poster is a derisive symbol of the seemingly impossible task I always feel I have before me of trying to experience anything remotely close to a mature, dynamic, or even, God forbid, nurturing lovemaking session with whomever might be lying next to me without taking clandestine peeks around for other women's artifacts that may (tragically for me) have gotten stuck, decades ago, between my erection and a soft place; artifacts I may "accidentally" have left for a current lover to find, like some foreboding, "handwriting on the bed" as it were, of my pitiful lack of faith in women.

At a moment's notice, I can relive that feeling I had while first watching *Last Tango*, after Marlon got shot and the film faded to bleakness, of trying to keep myself from vomiting. When the lights came up I skulked out of the Upper East Side theater in N.Y. and was blinded by my own fear that a man could really turn out that way.

I was already a basket case, reeling from my father's early death, practically broke, and trying to figure out what "love" was supposed to mean. I was living (albeit cluelessly) with (rumor had it) a wonderful college sweetheart; and we were *double-dating* (wow, what a groovy phrase) with an allegedly happily married couple from my alma mater. We all made it out of the cinema to eat at some uppity, rip-off, crazily overpriced deli. We clamored blindly with the rest of the kosher groupies for a fatty, laughing stock of a corned-beef sandwich on stale rye before any orthodox cockroaches crashed our table for a nosh.

Our foursome engaged in pretentious critiques of this already overly, deservedly, well-hyped, butter-up-your-ass movie. But I knew instinctively that what had really struck me about *Last Tango in Paris* was that, whatever it was that Brando's character was trying to avoid, I would too, maybe forever, from that day on.

And so far, I have. Just as I had cringed at the young boy's alienation in *The 400 Blows* and feared for things to come in *Clockwork Orange*, Bernardo Bertolucci's film symbolized for me the out-of-intimacy feelings I somehow instantaneously knew were my destiny as soon as I saw the disdain and confusion his "murderess" felt as the *Godfather*-to-be jerked off uncontrollably after his *last tango*. I was already paralyzed emotionally, and already believed that I would never find real sustained happiness with a woman *till the cows came home.*

To all my future girlfriends' dismay, I had from then on an over-powering need to privately screen this film with each and every woman I ever fell in love with or she me, in the hope that at least, when my inevitable, sudden departure from the relationship occurred, they wouldn't be completely taken by surprise.

As *unevolved* as I remain with loving the opposite sex, I'm no dummy in general, and even I knew that there were a lot of layers to this film, not the least of which are the director's and star's political leanings. Nevertheless, my cock always leaned to the left anyway, and once I related to Mr. Brando's existential hell I didn't give a shit whether he was a right-wing fundamentalist or a fez salesman. He was fucked and I've felt fucked ever since.

A pathetic footnote to my love-hate relationship with this break-through film is that now I'm older than the fucked-up main charac-ter, grumpy, orgasmic Paul. Even worse, he seems less fucked up than I am at this point. Although in the movie Paul doesn't have a need to know anyone's name, certainly not that of a new date he picks up and hours later literally fucks up the ass, I, on the other hand, love to recognize and be recognized, since I am not ever con-fident of my identity. Still, whatever thrills I am getting are purely due to who I really am. And, very much unlike my celluloid coun-terpart, I do, gratefully, speak a little more clearly and am never thrilled fucking a woman up the ass because of my excruciating fear of having my penis break off. If that ultimate nightmare ever hap-pened, given my luck with women, I would no doubt be saddled with an unsympathetic partner who—unlike the heroines you read about helping lovers pick up their dismembered member and make tracks with it to the nearest emergency ward, all the while comfort-ing the weeping, horrified, genital-less casualty, and even making sure the "joint" rests comfortably on the ride to the hospital in a decent-looking tray, with enough ice underneath to make even the limpest mishap look cool—would be fed up with my crying and complaining and leave me stranded.

Worse yet, and this is all my fault, because of the history of heart disease in my family I have a real problem even purchasing butter without thinking that I'll drop dead a few hours after enjoying some lightly buttered toast. You know, come to think of it, I blame this movie for every single, fuckin', goddamn hang-up I have.

Cool! I'm finally off the hook! I'm blowing off my shrink! I'm ready to rock! Thank God! Bring on the babes! I'm fearless again!

Foreplay Man

It's not like I'm some Valentino or something. I mean, Christ, if you look close enough you can usually find itchy flakes in my hair. Also, ever since I was a small boy, I have demonstrated episodes of involuntary nose and eye twitching. I live practically like a recluse and have always been pretty up front about being terrified I'd be swallowed whole by just about every woman I've ever adored (even when smitten immediately on a blind date, over dinner—before the appetizer yet) to whom I ultimately say, "You're the one." I have been known to go absolutely wild when I first meet someone who excites me and then slowly pull back from any promises I might have made, using anxiety or, once in a blue moon, actually feigning an exotic disease (which then of course requires a quarantine) to bail out of being with someone. Even though I've been told that I'm a passionate lover, I could care less what a woman says about me sexually, sensing that it is usually intended to mislead anyway; still I find myself on a mission to get the kudos, and then perhaps needlessly feel paranoid, and then ultimately move on to other pastures, as it were. I'd much prefer to feel legitimately paranoid. All that being said, I still consider myself one hell of an eligible bachelor.

In actuality, this deep-seated problem is not so much me as it is the types of women who lust after me and what they expect from the relationship. Whether they are younger or magnificently getting on in years, the common thread is still always desperation. You show me two desperate people trying to build a relationship and I guarantee you that I'm one of them. I'm desperate to make anyone happy but myself. I please them, hobble off, then guiltily howl into the night calling out for new prey to confuse and help keep me in my intimate, solitary confinement. On the brighter side, I'm like an old wolf with a conscience. In truth, conquests never interested me, but I seemed to revel in the bloody consequences.

Cutting down the ring of hope with the tenacity of Joe Frazier, initially I like to corner any new object of my desire with praise, emotional support, heat, promises, and boundless attention. I am particularly in rare carnivorous form when my lover is bouncing back from a drought of fondling and hasn't felt too attractive in quite a stretch.

Then it's Mr. Hoax to the rescue! Leave it to me to turn a vulner-able, given-up-for-lost female instantaneously into a carefree nymphomaniac, with all her well-intended systems go for yet another brainless attempt to get (in this case, me) to become a mature, devoted, dynamic, unconditionally loving better half of some exclusive pairing of the species. Have I got news for her . . .

Red-rum. Red-rum.

I'm not a womanizer. I'm not a pig. I'm not a misogynist.

So sue me, I just love being with women! I love being loved by women. I want women to feel loved like I have yet to figure out how to allow myself to feel loved. I guess I'm sort of a kosher guinea pig for out-of-kilter sexual appetites.

I must enjoy making women (many of whom are either as scared as I am of getting close to someone, or after having gone through a real dry spell are feeling asexual) feel good about themselves again. I do this almost altruistically, if one doesn't scrutinize, without ever getting even a simple, "Thanks, Richard."

After the mission is accomplished, I go on automatic pilot, plan my courteous yet expedient escape from responsibility, and count on get-ting hell's wrath from this rejuvenated woman over my disappearing act. But boy oh boy oh boy, that next guy in line is really a lucky camper. *Foreplay Man* has done his work and not only will the next beau reap all the benefits but will most probably feel even better, hear-ing one put-down after another, on the last "misfit" she tried to love.

This dating style is not just an avocation with me but rather, upon reflection and rigid self-examination, a dirty, rotten, selfish conflu-ence of unshared emotions, stemming from my seduction and need-iness, that never leaves me or my accomplice in this hologram love better off than before my unconscious ruse started.

I am ashamed of myself.

I can't believe that I ever went beyond a flirt while knowing that, as typical a practice as it is to kiss and hold and feel affection from someone, a simple common part of what humans do, somehow the humans I do it with always wind up thinking I misled or even betrayed them. If you only hurt the one you love, then they got it backwards. I was the wrong man. I doubt that I ever knew for sure whether or not I truly loved them. But I can safely say that I hardly, if ever, love myself. So ladies, I beg of you, before you splatter me all over the sidewalk with vicious epithets, consider the source. Moi.

Could it be that I'm being far too ethical considering that most of us know more scumbags than decent people, or is there honestly some intrinsic problem with *doing it* with someone, when you pretty much know down deep that the other person will never wind up being your ongoing partner; even though you feel certain that he or she would want that more than anything else in the world?

The biggest problem I have, right out of the gate with this, is that I've never wound up long term with anyone yet, for better or for worse, so consequently I have fucked over everyone who has ever fallen in love with me. Ouch! I feel like calling 911 on myself.

"I'd like to report a sick fuck."

"What seems to be the problem?"

"I'm about to see another chick who digs me and I think I want to make it with her."

"Sir, you're gonna have to speak slower."

"Sorrrrrrrrrry. I'mmmmm about to seeeeeeeee another chick who digggggggggs me and I think I want to maaaaaaaake it with herrrrrrrrrrr . . ."

"Sir, you're tying up our line for real emergencies." Click.

"This *is* a real emergency, you jerk-off," I bellow into the void of a defenseless receiver.

My **Wife,** My **Daughter**

If history repeats itself and I continue to date women much younger than myself, then it looks like if I ever marry, my wife will (more often than not) be mistaken as my kid. Do I really have a choice? Probably not. Why? Easy. I'm too much of a baby and I think being with someone my age would be like settling for the *mother* of my dreams instead of the *woman* of my dreams. It's a shame that after all of those years in therapy it will still most probably fail to kick in when I might need it most.

There's more to this embarrassing scenario. Death. From the first time I began to mentally double my age it dawned on me that I could easily be dead sooner rather than later. I freaked fuckin' out. This hasn't made it any easier to commit to anyone because I constantly visualize her wearing a black veil shaking hands with legions of neurotic mourners.

The truth is that even though I still have long hair, can get a decent erection, and continue to play the same music I loved thirty years ago as a student at Ohio State, I feel that marrying someone particularly close to me in age or generation is pretty much the last nail in my coffin and flushes any hope of eternal youth down the toilet.

I guess I just feel washed up. Over-the-hill. Way too old. I missed the boat. I passed up an opportunity to have a family. I lived a lie. I constantly feel like a heterosexual who missed his *procreation calling.* Unlike most mammals I feel more like an insect than a human. Too selfish for words. Killer of my father's name. One big, adult failure. Just an old Jewish turtle with two feet, in a shell big enough for ten men.

Yeah, that's how I feel. So now, it seems scary whenever I'm told by a real young chick that there is love in the air. There's no way that affection from her, for me, can be anything more than a pitiful deception on her part. Let's face it, either I'll drop dead early into our marriage, or she'll be fucking every repairman on the face of the earth at the first sign of me wanting to nap, which out of necessity will be, say, a few hundred times a day.

The irony of all this is that when I was at a more suitable age to take a bride, I took a drink instead and became for the most part (when not working on my comedy) an *MIA* (Missing In Alcohol). In sort of a cool way I guess, the part of my brain that was too impressed with champagne somehow kept me from tying the knot prematurely and screwing up some unfortunate bride who would have had to be either an enabler or as twisted as me. By some angelic luck, as isolated as I felt, I lived, didn't kill anyone while driving under the influence, and basically stayed all twisted up solo, keeping it together just enough to try to entertain millions of strangers.

So after all of this drama, what is it that has me teetering on the brink of maturity? Age . . . Sure, sure, as long as I stay sober I'll make better decisions, but now the prospect of hanging with a real young babe for any length of time strikes me as being pretty fuckin' silly. I mean, after a while, her looks will fade, as will mine (and say I live a really long life), I'll be around 150, she'll be maybe 110 and I won't be attracted to her anymore, plus we still won't have anything in common. If you start out bored with someone it doesn't get much better.

I have a feeling I lived my social life inside out. Rather than get married to a hot, young chick when I was a perplexed, young man, I opted to stay single and grow older without a wife and kids. Now, the prospect of impregnating a hot, young chick with my limping, middle-aged sperm seems a tad silly. Perhaps it's not so much silly as that these hot, young chicks are the same age as my friends' children; and the younger the woman I date the zanier I feel, and the zanier I feel the more pathetic I look, and the more pathetic I look the harder it is to feel realistic, and the less realistic I am the closer I feel to immortality, and the more immortal I feel the less spiritual I become, and the less spiritual I become the closer I am to wanting to drink, and the closer I am to wanting a drink, the closer I get to the end.

So I guess I'm torn between growing old gracefully and not growing at all. In a way, I can understand how lots of guys my age can't stomach the idea of getting close anymore with a woman their own age, having spent the bulk of their life with someone who withered at the same rate and gave them their children, and ultimately drove them crazy. And more times than not this has aroused nothing but cynicism in them towards marriage, and to women in their peer group, consequently giving them the jones to be with as many hot young chicks as possible. I get it. It's laughable to everyone who watches it go down but it makes sense to me, and I feel sympathetic towards these guys.

I'm just the opposite now, and am so outnumbered by friends who have grown-up children and have been married many times and are full of hostility from those many broken marriages, that it seems like a no-brainer to them that hot young chicks are the answer. But I am slowly but surely getting in touch with the beauty of accepting who I am; and being with a hot young chick is something that might be cool for a moment but within a few hours, a few seconds even, I can't help but feel like a human-sized cartoon man being led around by his cartoon penis in a cartoon world. The real human in this undynamic duo is the hot young chick, who I ultimately feel responsible for after dragging her life down the inkwell as fast as I can by saying, "Hump me, you hot, gorgeous, crazy, motherfucking savior!"

The sex thing is *really* crazy. Assuming I asked a young starlet to marry me and she said yes (despite a frantic fax from the Supreme Court telling her to bail), and we had sex at some *normal rate* for married couples for the next twenty years, what exactly does that come to mathematically in erection and orgasm time? Say we screw twice a week, no weeks off for anything . . . okay, two, carry the one . . . hold on . . . times fifty-two weeks is . . . okay . . . then times twenty years . . . Got it! I would have an erection if we fucked non-stop, for a total of about four and a half days. So, what do we have? We have under a week of fornicating and screaming with joy and 19 years, 51 weeks, and 2 days of feeling totally isolated with each other.

I just can't imagine that if I'm drooling, muttering obscenities, and mouthing off to strangers in the street for showing optimism, that my much, much younger fantasy wife (bearing witness to all of this) will be dying to get me back to our place and tear off my boxer shorts that I accidentally shit in, then begin the progressively routine regimen of cleaning and powdering me, then *still* want to suck me off like I'm some matinee idol. Instead, I'm cocksure she'll be planning my murder for the life insurance. I'm also sure that whenever she can get away from me, she'll be balling and blowing every man in sight. *Next stop, Viagra Falls.*

Doesn't sound like a plan. I'd rather be in prison and be let out for five one-night stands. If I know anything, I know that I can't bear to be bored with a significant other and, superficiality aside, if I settle for a gorgeous "trophy" who insists that I am the love of her life I would be killing two birds with one ego.

I think I have to boast for a second to put things in clearer perspective. You see, I've spent most of my adult life feeling the joy of being seen with a lot of beautiful women, and feeling privately the pain of knowing it was a charade. The boast is coming. *Now*, I might have the chance to actually jump into a relationship with someone who doesn't have to watch documentaries on the sixties to see what the landscape was like when her lover went to school. I swear, most guys I know (at least the unstable ones) seem to think it's insane to date women close to their age. I think they feel that way because they never spent thirty years (and endless hours) like myself, trying to explain to various lovers *what we were actually seeing, hearing, or, oh fuck it, practically anything we were experiencing,* just so we could have a conversation.

Good luck guys! I've been there (and barely came out alive), and now I'm dying to be able to be myself with a real woman and not someone who is the woman of someone else's dreams. The beautiful nightmare is over because I'm starting to wake up. And dig this: I can't even jerk off to young chicks anymore. Imagine that? It even gets me hotter to masturbate now when I imagine that I am making love to someone who understands me, accepts me, adores me, and wants to love and take care of me.

Those lucky chicks—to be young and hot and not be bothered by me anymore. "*Me, me, me, me, me, me, meeeeeeee.*" I'm finally ready to sing for my supper. It's now or never. I'm just dying to get out of high school.

A Lone **Assassin**

We just stood by my front door holding each other, sort of awestruck by the past twenty-four hours and by how we had never felt so comfortable with anyone like this before.

"I'll call you," I managed to spit out, doing the best I could to stem the onrushing tide of fear.

"Oh no!" she quipped with a tinge of sarcasm, looking so fuckin' happy and full of optimism because maybe she'd met her man.

I let her out and gingerly closed the door, then watched her drive away before I slumped down on the nearest chair and began to shake.

I had had a great time and that didn't bode well for my mental health. She was great and I knew it. I also knew she was one of the few women I had dated in recent memory who was actually alive when JFK got shot. That was indeed a sign of maturity for me because most women (as opposed to this one; let's call her "Oh No!") who I was more inclined to romance had actually played with *Sesame Street* dolls in their youth.

Oh No! and I shared an amazing amount of similar experiences, passions, emotions, and sensibilities and, yeah, she thought I was hilarious. That's beyond important for me. It's more than that, it's a fatal psychological defect of mine, because if a woman doesn't laugh enough or at the right places, I'm convinced she could never truly love me. This comedic neediness has no bounds. Once, when I had serious doubts about some younger woman's claims of loving me, the death knell tolled when her golden retriever, Fiona, didn't seem amused at my wildly funny antics while I tossed a bone, and soon after I bolted from the relationship.

Back to Oh No! I didn't have that much experience dating women who wouldn't inevitably prompt snickers from close friends of mine as soon as we would be out of earshot. My rule of thumb has been: the younger the woman, the less baggage. So when I stumbled across a real, live, possibly mature candidate, history sadly documents that I instinctively began building my case that every honest thing she had told me that evening revealed some terrible flaw in her character that would sooner or later make my life a living hell. While tricking myself out of any chance of love, I of course rarely took into account my rocky side of the story. I have millions of eccentricities and fears—oh well, that's their problem.

When I first became aware of this unfortunate habit of building an immediate wall between me and any potential, dynamic relationship with a woman, I must have been, I don't know, maybe four or five. Just joshing you. I was more like in my late teens. And to come clean, many of my irrational fears, to this day, began just moments after my first penetration. Yup. I felt trapped the moment I lost my virginity. For some odd reason once my "thing" enters that "place" (and the act can be performed in any location—a drive-in theater, an off-limits room on a tour at the Palace de Versailles, or in a stall at a mutually agreed-upon delicatessen) some sort of heaviness creeps in and covers me and my lover like a sort of lobster net, and things are never the same again. The sex might continue but honest conversation abruptly ends.

I don't mean this to be a cocky statement. It's not that the woman necessarily wants to trap me or that the sex is so great. But rather, I feel pressure, whether *she* gives a shit about me or not, to immediately be a "boyfriend." From early on, I have somehow mangled my long-ings for love from a woman by fearing her returned desire as a tricky way to eventually manipulate me out of whatever bliss I think I might attain. I've had more blisters than bliss. It's all about me. It's hard to expect love from someone when you don't think you are worthy to give it yourself. So, historically speaking, in a long line of broken rela-tionships, it's fair to say that I've been their own worst enemy.

This, for me, is a novel and stunning admission. I guess that I never wanted to take the blame for failed relationships even though I must unconsciously have perceived them as doomed before the first kiss. Until recently, to rationalize my aloneness, I have sadly concocted some sort of personal, revisionist history for every failed love affair. It seems that not only have I shot myself in the foot but also in the heart. The woman of my dreams is so desirable in reality yet so undesirable in theory, I kill the relationship before I imagine it will kill me. And up until now, I almost never blamed myself. All right, I *never* blamed myself. And not all the women were good for me but I ultimately could never have been good for them. Not as long as I'm trigger-happy. Not as long as I remain a lone assassin.

I have been so twisted in my thinking about women I almost got thrown out of junior high school for suggesting on a midterm that John Wilkes Booth had a perfect right to murder Abraham Lincoln. I simply gave him the benefit of the doubt for being lonely and emo-tionally drained after some fictitious woman I drummed up in my head led him into committing an infamous, boneheaded move that altered the course of history.

I saw John as a struggling actor who must've had a steady com-panion, "Candy," who pressured him into making a name for him-self in six months or she would continue to fuck the wig maker. As fate would have it for lovesick Booth, just as he was about to grab the role of Hamlet in a small theater group outside of D.C., not only did the producer pull out because he caught his wife (the set designer) fucking some schmuck who was considering creating "slave trading cards" with bubble gum, but he also contracted what we know today as the crabs from his wife's dalliance (and since little was known or written about this phenomenon at the time, to this poor contaminated guy, it just looked like mini lobster tails eating his dick off) and he committed suicide, leaving John out of a gig. Making no bones about it, Candy told John that in her eyes he was a failure and could never live up to what she wanted in a man. She wanted someone who people would really take notice of. He wasn't good enough.

Not for long. Driven by lust, confusion, and self-loathing, he darted off to Muskets & Things and bought a gun. He made himself famous and lost the girl.

Just another lone assassin.

Phone Sex

Although the ear, nose, and throat guy dismissed it out of hand, I was still convinced that the sleazy advertising executive whose phone number I got at a bar in Soho—where we met and made out briefly while standing next to the jukebox—was the sole reason for my inner-ear infection, and that I had contracted it only moments after my orgasm during phone sex with her the night before. It came as no surprise, really. Because when Charlene came over the phone, she shrieked in a way I had thought, up until that moment, was reserved only for struggling young actresses in the middle of a desperately off-the-mark audition for a role in some exploitative horror flick.

If the truth be known, I believe that I deserve any hearing problems I get from this charade of intimacy. I really do. I'm just nothing but a "phone-orgasm junkie-monkey." That's how an ex-girlfriend labeled me at an emergency counseling session just hours after she caught me (in our bed, alone) fucking someone else (verbally)—or so she thought. She barged into our bedroom with the force of the LAPD on an ill-advised drug bust, flaunting the Polaroid camera she niftily grabbed on the run from out of the hall closet, and all the while screaming like some aboriginal chieftain.

At any rate, you can imagine my soon-to-be-ex-girlfriend's embarrassment when she caught me in bed whacking off to the juicy delivery by my phone mate on the other end of the line. It was none other than Janus, a showgirl from Pittsburgh, an old acquaintance of mine whom I'd met years earlier, backstage at one of my concerts. She was on my A-List of aural concubines as she, very much like myself, had suffered through countless years of disillusionment in the relationship game. This, of course, fostered a tremendous fear of intimacy, a predilection to talk dirty, hang up, and go about her business—alone. My kinda gal.

And I've got to tell you, I rarely cheat on my girlfriends unless the relationship has pretty much gone south. Hey, that's no excuse, but I'd be lying if I didn't admit that talking dirty on the phone to an old lover, from some distant hotel room, then hanging up and immediately ordering room service, left me much less racked with guilt once I got back home than if I had done the deed in the flesh.

On top of that (and even sadder) is that I firmly believe that I'm better in bed on the phone than in the sack. I mean, up until the age of about thirty-five or so, I was a pretty damn good lover. My biggest problem was blurting out promises and lies during my orgasm. Once I even practically yodeled in ecstasy that I could actually abandon show business for her, and hang out in Egypt for a year while she went over and studied King Tut or one of those old guy's remains, to complete her master's degree. But then, what with my bad knees acting up all the time and my ever-increasing anxiety over misleading lovers and with my libido getting cranky, I finally gave up, opted to just pull back, be alone and talk dirty to Ma Bell.

"Who is this?" I reply uncomfortably, over the phone, responding to some pretty provocative sexual come-ons for what feels like the millionth time today.

"Who do you think it is, you flirtatious, sex-crazed, repressed animal?"

"I give up, Marilyn Manson?"

"I'd laugh but I'm already wet, you crazy maniac. When can I see you again?"

"Oh, Christ, I haven't been feeling too well."

"You never feel well . . . I want you inside me so badly."

"I'm expensive."

"Fuck you. Are you touching yourself?"

"I'll call you right back, some whacko is at my door," I lied and hung up and then kept the phone off the hook as I tried to discern just exactly who that was. I also tried to figure out why and when I'd been intimate enough with her that she would feel comfortable—after so many months, maybe even years, of not talking—calling me like that. I didn't even recognize her voice.

That kind of call happens to me all the time. I obviously have more problems with the telephone than choosing what long distance carrier to use.

By the way, I'm not talking about those 900 numbers. Those are bullshit, a pale imitation of the real thing—you know what I mean. A person you *really know* on the phone is a big difference. Isn't it? Maybe not. I mean statistics can lie, but I have to admit that about 98 percent of all the women I've spent most of my time in bed with, on the phone, had a big problem with it. I'd hear things like, "Are you ashamed to be seen with me in public?" or "Since I've started dating you, Richard, my phone bill has gone up 75,000 percent and I've never even met you in person." Okay, fine, so maybe I have a little problem, I'm afraid to get close to a woman. There, I said it. Now that the cat's out of the bag I can readily admit that, as a member of this frightened species, I've devoted myself to becoming one of the world's best damn phone lovers and it works. I can actually stay home, do my work, have sex on the phone, and not go out until my excuses start getting shabby.

I'll freely admit that telling a rational, fairly sensible woman I'm dating that "an apparition sent from the Lord appeared on my refrigerator door and told me in no uncertain terms that I was quarantined" generally left them cold and me in "whack-off hell." I'm starting to freak out about this because it's becoming a dilemma.

Most of the women I've met in the past few years, who were justified in splitting after I failed to convince them that there's a much bigger, psychological safety net, if we focus primarily on improving our love life on the phone instead of striving for an honest-to-goodness, adult, loving relationship, left me with no option but considering using those disingenuous sex lines. I'm screwed either way. If I give up phone sex with a real woman, I'll be forced to grow up and get real. And if I decide to cave in to the sanctuary of anonymity, my cover will surely be blown after the first month, when my ultraconservative, squeaky-clean accountant (in a panic) might clandestinely meet me at a restaurant on the outskirts of town to chastise me for spending $12,786 on the phone, in June alone, calling the number 1-900-SUCK-MEE! He might, also, meaning well, think it timely for me to let Jesus into my life.

I'm still looking for a new accountant.

By the way, know any hot, single women with commitment issues?

An Open Letter of Apology to Practically All of the Women I Have Ever Gone Out With

. . . And with whom I somehow found myself in the uncompromising position of saying "I Love You" to, knowing full well that it would never work out. However pitiful and grandiose this seems to be, first off, let me just say, I *am* pitiful and grandiose. When I try to be myself around women, these character defects alternate with one another like evil twins, each selfishly jousting to be crowned with the victory of love, so the other is saddled with making up the excuse to get out of love once I've achieved my victory. I'm not too proud of this but historically, when it came to sharing real intimacy (or more importantly, trusting it from a girlfriend), I've always felt safer figuring out how I was going to take care of myself than I did giving up that responsibility to anyone else, even for a few minutes. So I guess all you dames are *off the hook* . . . I was just unavailable, and still might be.

The only thing I'm certain of now is that I had more to do with why things never worked out than any of you could ever have dreamt. *I* didn't even know. No one told me, until now. It was shocking that I sort of heard this so late in life, but I did, and once I accepted it, I felt this need to come clean as soon as I got the bloody news. I'm leveling now! I have no fear! I have already lost too much time to lose any more! Look, this isn't easy, so take it or leave it because if you're out there, *this Bud's for you.*

Yeah, yeah, I know, too little, too late. But it wasn't until last week that someone told me this about myself. Let's just say a little birdie told me. (This sounds like a lot of bullshit but I'm just trying to honor my doctor-client privilege.) And I figured that for any of you who are still alive and holding a grudge (having bought this book to see if you could spot yourself) this shrink-aided epiphany may help. It made me realize that somehow, some way, I'd left my teenage years and entered adulthood petrified about deserving to have my own free will and exasperated with my overpowering drive to feel my own authenticity. Couple that with my *Shaq*-sized paranoia that any woman would—if I really let her in and she got close enough to me—kidnap my spirit. I am so desirous of experiencing a life companion, yet so crippled by the brainless fear that any one, any size, any color will sap me dry of who I want to be. So strangely enough, I either found a frighteningly safe haven in suffering the indignities of being fucked over by angry women or was lulled into a comalike existence by people-pleasing chicks who spun me around in so many directions that all the pleasing canceled itself out. *Oh, baby,* give me that dictator to tell me I'm a piece of shit or that weakling to tolerate my excesses. Either one.

And even more pathetic is that while neither of these types of women gave me much pleasure or hope on any consistent basis, I still made them feel loved, I think; although deep down, I had no intentions of ever really coming through for any of them or being there "till death do us part." Even though I said "I love you" thousands of times, mostly during foreplay to help myself get an erection, because nothing is hotter to me than my fantasy of being one half of an honest-to-goodness, dynamic, mature, nurturing relationship, I had the tools but no manual. And what might have been Houdini's greatest magic trick, had he been as fucked up as me, was now mine. I completely managed to escape any *healthy* sense of history. You might call me a liar but I was just plain chicken-shit. The line was drawn in the sand before we ever met. It was "give me liberty or give me life-support." Consequently, I lied to everyone, in the most profound way, whenever I said, "I love you." Sorry. I didn't know what else to say. I was a moron . . .

If this is any consolation to any of you who are still smarting from my dysfunctional departure, perhaps you might like to know that I suffer from frightful, recurring nightmares of cross-dressing. I propose to myself in a mirror. The male part of me (out of costume) considers this. I ask the "pretty me" to sit down and relax. Maybe I even consider ordering out for some food, because I'll easily need a couple of years to decide whether to accept. Then the "she" part of "me" takes a handgun and with firm conviction, aims it right at my head and says in a scary whisper, "You told me that you loved me," and then fires! Happy now? Good. Enjoy it? Terrific, because the moron misses me in every dream and I go on to better things: I get counseling for this brief, experimental, "dark sexual period" and somehow move on to become a sexaholic and a "groupie" for every hot, killer-looking, heterosexual, single (I do have *some* scruples) ball player in the Women's National Basketball Association. Though you will no doubt be pleased to see me with the point guard of my dreams, considering how much taller she'll probably be than me, and how she'll perpetually have to look down at me in some sort of metaphoric state of condescension.

Well, that's all make-believe, just like my whole life with women. Play-acting. I've been nothing but a child. Nothing but a kid in a candy store, looking for one sucker after another. I can't tell you all how sorry I am. I guess I just had to reject you before you would maybe do it to me. I was thin-skinned in this area from the time the doctor cried, "Mrs. Lewis, it's a boy!" I beg your forgiveness. I mean, we laughed a lot didn't we? I'm on my knees. No ring, no lies, no promises, just the truth. I mean it. This is no joke . . . I'm the joke. The joke was on me.

God bless all of you and may you find a lover and companion who is willing to accept the fact that, as incomprehensible as it still seems to me, a loving relationship takes two people. Ciao.

Don't Tell Anyone, But I Have

This Really **Gross Eating Disorder**

I have a million addictions. If I'm not careful almost any of them can bring my life to a screeching and untimely halt. I drank when I was scared or miserable or happy. I fucked around on women for the same reasons. And for a long time, even before I became an alcoholic, and even now that I have stopped drinking, I have been battling a pretty dreadful eating disorder. I crave sugar. I'm afraid of getting fat. I always think I'm overweight except for those few days when I really know I am too thin and usually hear people tell me things like, "Are you okay?" "Are you sick?" "Don't you eat?" Those kinds of comments would be annoying to most people but to someone with an eating problem they are music to the stomach.

The same emotional shit that used to trigger me to want to forget my feelings and drink them away are also those that enable me to want to hurt my system and feel humiliated by eating (or rather, not eating) in a very unhealthy and, quite honestly, very unflattering and sickening way. I'm not anorexic and I'm not bulimic but whatever psychobabble there is to describe this food problem of mine doesn't concern me. What concerns me first is that its root emotional cause is the same low self-esteem and self-hatred that coddled me throughout my drinking days. *This disease has great patience—usu-*

ally much more patience than the alcoholic has. So, it has found a few areas in my life like women and sugar to torment me with in the hope that it will finally hammer me again with my drug of choice— booze.

Here's what I do. If I'm anxious or nervous or bored or happy or have any feeling that I don't feel comfortable handling, I will have an overwhelming drive to get in my car and go to the local grocery store and usually get these supplies:

One big box of crunchy-type granola.

One quart of milk.

If I'm really feeling whacked—about ten bananas.

And the most important ingredient of all—two pints of the most exotic types of ice cream with the most chunks of chocolate or candy or nuts or cookies in them as possible.

At one local store I go to (where I have at times done this ritual daily, and during some runs of depression for weeks on end) many of the clerks are perplexed that I rarely buy anything else. And I'm talking for years. Maybe some water or diet soda without caffeine, or if someone is coming over I'll ask if they want anything in the house; otherwise that's it. I eat at restaurants for real meals and rarely keep food in my house because I'm afraid I'll eat it all. It's the same reason I had to go back and forth to liquor stores before recovery, because I didn't think that I would ever stop drinking if I had an endless supply. So, brilliant me, my way of cutting back on drinking was only to have three or four bottles of champagne in the house. If I ever had a wine cellar back in the bad old days and had actually stocked it, I'd probably be dead.

I do have a freezer but when I get home from the store there is no time to store anything in it anyway because now the very crude, very private food disorder takes over. I have sanctuary to act out yet another addiction.

I'm alone. I crave the sweetness. I won't swallow too much of it for fear of the calories, so I take out a big bowl and first fill it halfway with the cereal. I rip open the bananas like some ravenous ape and throw in a few pieces, pour in a little milk, and then comes the precious ice cream! It might as well be a line of blow or a huge mimosa or a strange woman's naked body. The rush is exactly the same. I scoop out almost half the pint and put it in the bowl, trying to make sure that nothing spills. I mean I do have *some* manners during this barbaric event. I feel very alone and very excited at this point, even though I know I'll be depressed in a matter of minutes when the awareness kicks in once again that, one, I feel like I'm out of control; two, I'm not eating a good meal; and finally, that I am powerless over yet another addiction.

Be that as it may, I sit down if the spirit moves me but I usually stand and read the sports pages while I begin shoveling this concoction into my mouth. I swirl it around and around and chew it and feel the chunky cereal, the smooth and somewhat healthy taste of the banana on my tongue, and, best of all, the occasional sugar from the ice cream that sneaks down my throat. Oh, yeah, I know I'm getting some calories but to make sure I don't get many *I spit it back into the bowl*. Yeah, that's right, I spit it back into the bowl. I spit it back into the bowl. I fucking spit it back into the goddamn, fucking bowl!

This is just another dark and lonely manifestation of this disease of alcoholism. Nonetheless, now you know another of my deepest secrets. I feel lighter already—pardon the pun. And, you know what? Telling you is a first step toward maybe stopping this behavior. Not that I'm ready to stop. I'd rather just describe the whole sugary affair and get it out in the open.

So, anyway, I do this wolflike dessert sucking until most of the ice cream is done. If I throw away the cereal with half a box still left, or maybe even most of the ice cream from one of the pints, I tell myself I'm getting healthier; to me this is progress. But deep down I know better. I'm a sick puppy. And I'll be a sick puppy forever. Getting healthier depends on how many of these addictions I can admit to being powerless over and pray for help to let go of.

Sure, I know it's not alcohol, or cheating on my girlfriend, or doing blow or something that can really bring my life to a stop, but it still sucks. It makes me feel ashamed and alone and out of control and bad about myself. I thought that once I stopped drinking and lost the obsession for alcohol everything would change. Well, a hell of a lot *has* changed, and my life has become amazingly better, and I've never been happier or more creative. But as long as I'm an addict I will have to keep my eye out for ice cream and granola and almost anything else on this planet that can become an obsession. My disease still has its eyes only on one thing—to hurt me or kill me.

I know two things for sure—at least for today. I'm not going to drink and there's no fucking way I'm going to that grocery store for my favorite dish. Christ! After sharing this with you I'd be too self-conscious—at least for today. In fact, I might just have myself a real meal at a restaurant and tip the waiter and everything, just like a normal person. I know I'll feel a lot better about myself if I do that.

Man, some of this stuff seems so stupid, but if you're an addict you know how powerful something so stupid can be, and how something that seems, on the face of it, so easy to stop can feel like an unachievable task.

Lustville, USA

Overnight, I somehow became a mature, middle-aged guy, thinking I might be in love with an extraordinary woman, and that remaining monogamous, once and for all, through thick and thin, is the road to be on. That said, I must quickly admit that somewhere in my brain there must be a synapse missing that poisons this mysterious progress. I feel this way yet I also feel like a dead man when I project that I'll never allow myself the chance to fall in love with another *babe* again. And what about flirting, French-kissing, grinding, or, God forbid, fucking?

Just the thought of not being naked again with another chick is so inconceivable and terrifying that it brings me to my newly born, principled knees.

I don't know whether to celebrate my growth into a potentially more decent human being by allowing myself to experience some actual satisfaction, or finally break down and take that inevitable ride to the cemetery and pick out my final resting place. I've been putting off this appointment forever and eternity is catching up with me, and if I settle down for good with one good woman then life will, I'm sure, be nearly over. It's not that I'm cheap and waiting to see advertised some "Save Bread at our Drop Dead Discount Weekend," it's just that I'm afraid I might freak out, go berserk, and punch the living daylights out of an overzealous, graveside sales rep and it would truly be a *death of a salesman*. Even with these negative projections, I still plan to cordially buy two plots, one for me and one for a wife, who I probably will never know, but still somehow believe would want to lie permanently next to me, the man she always wanted but, of course, never met.

So here's the scenario, as I see it from my fucked-up perspective. I die. It's 2026. The funeral that I never got around to paying for (because the salesman pissed me off, insisting that he would find me the "funniest-looking" coffin, because he was a fan) will be taking place anyway. Payment was arranged last minute by a pal who was thrilled to be part of my last gig because he thought I would give a shit that my plot was near the plots of several famous comedians, not knowing of course that old comedians repeat stories every few hours when in groups. The notion of this going on everlastingly is soul-boggling. Nevertheless, I'll be a goner, and will either have my wife at the burial (perhaps this latest girlfriend), getting hugs from the throngs of tear-jerking lunatics that I was blessed to know, or else, if I continue to choose the lifestyle I have chosen so far, I can see the scene in quite a different light. Instead of having a wife with whom I would have spent almost twenty-five years laughing, loving, sharing experiences, and caring for each other, hold a tearful yet loving court on my behalf, lots and lots of the great-looking, much younger chicks I cavorted with in superficial high gear would all be there, all still looking hot, *and all looking for acting work*. They'll be wearing tight black dresses in my honor, showing off their fake tits and grief. Not one of them will know any of my buddies, and quickly kissing my casket after briefly looking for Hollywood types they can hit on for a gig, they will split, leaving me buried, with lots of memories of innocuous orgasms.

Is that what I want? I don't know. But I'm getting to the finish line and my puzzled penis wants an answer. No wonder my erection is in the shape of a question mark. At least I'll have an eternity to find out whether or not I have a soul.

Lust or just human nature? That is a question that has plagued me since I realized I could make most women feel that I'm moments away from devoting my life to them while quietly knowing I was a fraud, or more to the point, shaking in my boots that they would take my love as a reasonable sign they had a right to snatch my authenticity away from me. Apparently, *intimacy* to me is a destination on a "highway to hell." Somehow I grew up with the mangled notion that it was closeness, not familiarity, that breeds contempt.

Though I swear to God I am really making an effort of late to love and accept love from a significant other without always expecting it to become yet another futile attempt on my part to pretend that companionship isn't some CIA sting operation.

I mean, after all these years of being my own partner in loveless lovemaking or that glorious alternative of flaccidly sitting back, forced to listen to women chastise me for not screwing enough (actually because I was feeling too close to them emotionally and sex was the first thing to go south), I've realized there just has to be another way.

Yet curiously, with all these mature realizations going on in my head, why is it that only seconds after I meet any dark-haired beauty across a crowded room, I still can't resist? Even though I am fully aware of my pointless modus operandi, my soon-to-be-erect member, like some dysfunctional weather vane, points me on a foolishly accurate path, right into the headlights of an oncoming vagina.

There is going to come a time in my life when lusting after someone I shouldn't have (who's just really an unsuspecting obstacle to someone else, not to mention a thorn in my conscience) will be the final nail in my imagined cushy coffin of loneliness and endless options.

Lust is a *trip* when you have no place like home. This time I think I'm down for the count. I pray to God that my libido stops the fight. I can just see the headlines now.

LEWIS ENDS BACHELORHOOD IN DISGRACE
FAILS TO ANSWER BELL
TRAINER THROWS IN THE CONDOM

The worst that can happen is that I can be content.

Find the Relationship in This Picture

INSTRUCTIONS: READ THIS ESSAY WITH YOUR CURRENT LOVER. I can't tell you how many mornings I have spent with ex-girlfriends in conversations like this. To really get the full effect of this kind of pointless waste of time, please read the dialogue fast! Now, if it doesn't sound familiar, consider yourselves blessed, put down my book, and immediately celebrate by screwing your brains out.

FADE IN:
INT. ANY ROOM—LIMBO

Richard
Should we talk about it?

Ex
About what?

Richard
You know.

Ex
No.

Richard
That we haven't had sex ever since you thought I smirked at you right after you served that shitty, rotten-tasting granola, with no preservatives, at my 50th birthday brunch and it made my buddy with cancer puke and . . .

Ex
Wait a minute, Richard . . .

Richard
Don't cut me off . . .

Ex
I'm not cutting you . . .

Richard
Jesus! This is exactly the time when I wish to God my shrink was just sitting right here and seeing this shit when it actually happened, and then she wouldn't . . .

Ex
Why does it have to be your shrink?

Richard
You don't have a shrink anymore, remember?

Ex
I can call her when I need her.

Richard
Really? I thought she died last year.

Ex
What makes you think she didn't give me a referral?

Richard

You're amazing! How do you always seem to get me off the fuckin' subject?

Ex

Oh, so you can curse and be provocative?

Richard

Who fuckin' cursed?

Ex

So all of a sudden saying fuck isn't raising the ante?

Richard

Raising the ante? What are you talking about?

Ex

Don't make believe you don't remember the fight we had while watching *The Cincinnati Kid*.

Richard

What the fuck are you talking about?!

Ex

There you go again!

Richard

I've never even been to fuckin' Cincinnati!

Ex

The *movie*, asshole!

Richard

Asshole!?

Ex

That's right! If you can say fuck, then I can say asshole.

Richard

Whatever happened to our love affair?

Ex

Now look who's getting off the subject.

Richard

Huh? . . . Yeah, right . . . Look, this is the time one of our shrinks told us to take a deep breath . . .

Ex

It was yours . . .

Richard

My what?

Ex

Your shrink . . .

Richard

Whatever . . . but look, we're going crazy again and your shrink . . .

Ex

Your shrink . . .

Richard

What's the difference? The point is, no one has a gun to our heads . . . no one is murdering anyone around here . . .

Ex

Who said anything about murder? You're scaring me . . .

Richard

I'm just saying that this too shall pass and . . . well . . . I'm a little hungry and I admit I can become pretty relentless when I want to make a point and historically, you've told me many, many times and I think you are right, I do have a tendency to escalate our arguments on an empty stomach.

Ex

And what are we arguing about?

Richard

I forget. I'm starved. Let's order out. What do you feel like having, honey?

Ex

Anything you want.

FADE OUT:

THE BITTER END

Is This My **Last Lay?**

I don't know what women and sex and cumming mean to me anymore. It's been a struggle, these past six years, having sex without the aid of feeling inebriated beforehand. I haven't been with too many women since I got sober. I got out of relationships that weren't meant to go anywhere, yet now I don't know where I ever wanted them to go; or, most horrible, where I want this new one I'm in to go.

I don't give a shit that I'm in my early fifties. I couldn't care less that I can't go back in time. I just don't know how to shake the nasty sensation that if I remain with my girlfriend and grow old with her and am faithful, then *this is my last lay*, and in some corner of my adolescent head, I'm left feeling like a dead man.

People in Mozambique are dying tonight, and flood victims have eyes that can only see as far as the raging river, and yet I can't shake my vision of only one last vagina. It's pathetic. It's like I am at the mercy of some divine other, making me incapable of just being able to relax and be happy and content with one woman. Women are drugs for me. Loneliness is a drug for me. Paranoia is a drug for me. Drugs, drinks, women . . . The prospect of one last anything reminds me of my own mortality, and the terror of sharing (which to me is like giving my whole self up) with someone else.

Sure I'm sometimes self-centered and selfish, but I also have genuine fears about being dragged down by people who will suck me dry of my destiny. The sober me can't stomach the prospect of having my own traveling time dictated by other people's selfishness and insanity. I already did that—to myself. The challenge for me is to learn to distinguish someone's love from my perception of it as a control mechanism. I'd rather bring myself down. It's simpler and less expensive.

I'm not whining but I was hurt emotionally as a kid, mainly by being treated much of the time like I was just a little sideshow getting in the way of everyone else's desires and goals. I can't recall the moment when I first felt that I was something other than a shackle on everyone's lives, but I do know that tonight I still feel like a nothing when I contemplate that I'm probably with my last woman, even if she's the best. This sickens me to no end. I have a recovering buddy fighting cancer and he told me that he almost died so many times overdosing, that he wasn't afraid of dying anymore as much as being taken by the cancer before he really got to know himself. Now *that* shit really makes me feel pitiful. Here I am, a recovering addict, who isn't dragging my ass in for radiation and chemo, but punishing a healthy body by being fearful of trusting love. I'm afraid that it might take a stroke of bad luck, like a stroke, to force me into some pathetic last-ditch effort to love, and be loved.

It's criminal that I haven't been able to shake this self-hatred. I can battle back from alcoholism, but continue to batter and imprison myself from real love. It's surely not this glorious woman who is giving me the willies, but an emptiness that seems to strike me so effortlessly, paralyzing my heart whenever someone really loves me;

inevitably I feel forced to sabotage the relationship. Now that I don't run to the bottle anymore for imaginary strength, I run into well-traversed alleyways in my head where I can hide out, rationalize hiding out, and escape feeling human again. This is alcoholic thinking without the rush, the most boring, painful catered affair that money can't buy.

I'd love to be able to love her, be loved by her, and never get laid by anyone else again before I'm laid to rest, rather than pursue this childish hard-on for sexual barrenness. Otherwise my soul will most probably wander down the streets of the universe, unhappy and pouting, as I'm forced to look aimlessly, with my newly acquired death-ray vision, into the homes of happy people still alive, and actually treating themselves to a little bit of tenderness.

If this is my last lay I'm a lucky man. If it isn't, although *Mr. Integrity* here believes it should be, not only won't I probably live to understand myself, but I honestly feel that I'm somehow trivializing my buddy's bout with cancer, who doesn't come close to having the odds I do to celebrate a healthy serenity, once and for all.

If I got sober to stay stupid it's the biggest practical joke I could ever pull on myself.

"Marry Her, Asshole"

It's near the end of the millennium and I'm near the end of my fear-of-intimacy rope. I have experienced tidbits of closeness with many women but what I've experienced much more is fear. Fear of being swallowed up. Fear of being criticized. Fear of never doing enough. Fear of her leaving me, out of the blue, for reasons she can't explain. Fear of being fearful that I don't deserve to be with someone I dig. Fear of having double the fear because I'll become guilt-ridden and take over her fear of me leaving her. Fear of being funny when the moment maybe didn't call for it and being chastised for it. Fear of basically never being myself again, even though I've never really been that content with myself. Fear of always thinking that I'm with the wrong woman and always having the need to search for the unobtainable, real Ms. McCoy. And the fear of never ridding myself of the despicable habit of being unable to restrain myself from occasionally "acting out" sexually with other women while I'm involved, probably hoping to get caught, or instead copping to it, thinking I'm being astonishingly honorable with my mate, while privately hoping to be rejected so I'll be free once again of the scary bonds of a committed relationship.

I think it was FDR who said, "There is nothing to fear but fear itself." Thanks again, Mr. President, for nothing. Not only did you react tragically slowly in recognizing Hitler's atrocities but now I can just hear your booming voice, once again blundering, this time on a much smaller scale, and making people like me feel that being riddled with fear is simply a walk in the park. What bullshit! Do you have to rub it in? You're dead. Let me live in peace with my own fear. And let's face it, you didn't have the perfect marriage. A little shrinkage for you and your First Lady might have been a good thing. Unless you were too afraid. Wimp.

Presidential history aside, the lowest point in my confusion about the subject of finding "the one" occurred after dating someone I was convinced was the best woman for me, based on where I was at in my life, that I'd ever dated; and yet I suffered through one of the oddest, most disconcerting and humiliating events with her, an event that wound up making me feel like I was really just full of shit about ever truly wanting a relationship.

Two hours prior to this experience I had spent what I had thought to be some of the most honest, revealing minutes ever with my therapist. I had gone on and on and on and on, listing every incredible quality my girlfriend had and how meaningful it was. Then I went on and on and on and on about how odd it felt being comfortable, instead of lonely and always on the make. Much to the apparent delight of my shrink I seemed to be feeling very positive about it being about time that I accepted love from one woman without always being halfway out the door. I mean, I don't know if my therapist really was happy or not but she seemed to be. Perhaps she felt she was actually winning the war we'd been fighting ever since I'd first sat across from her and went on and on and on and on about so many women and so many fuckin' issues and enough unhappiness and uncertainty for at least two middle-aged Jewish men. Stupid joke. I mean, twenty middle-aged Jewish men.

So, the session ends. I always end it. It's a therapy quirk of mine. I hate being told when to stop feeling. So during my visit I usually take a few furtive glances at her many clocks, all placed perfectly around her office so she can help me and tell the time simultaneously, and I can boast that I have always started to leave her office before she has ever said, to the best of my recollection, "We have to stop now."

Anyway, moments later I was in my car, trying not to dangerously daydream too much as I am prone to do when feeling euphoric after great, eye-opening sessions. Over the years I have come frightfully close to running down pedestrians simply because I was light-headed with enlightenment and somehow driving without looking consciously through the windshield.

Then it happened. The disease struck just like it used to when I was mainly battling alcohol. Back then, when I thought that I could just deal with my drinking problem by cutting back, it never failed that as soon as I was "good" one day, I partied the next. It never failed. I felt I deserved a reward for my maturity and abstinence the day before. So in this instance, I was so thrilled with at least sounding to my shrink like an honest-to-goodness adult in a loving relationship, I again felt deserving of a nasty reward, and must have unconsciously put out my antenna while driving back in search of any hot woman, in any car, in any crosswalk, at any intersection, just to take my mind off of all that growth and perhaps get myself in trouble like always.

It didn't take long. There she was. Although it was a little past twilight I saw enough of this beauty's profile to slam on the brakes of any maturity I might have displayed just moments before in front of my doctor. Her windows were a little tinted in what looked like some sort of Jeep (I'm as bad at describing cars as I am trying to make small talk with my internist when he is sticking his finger up my ass during a physical), but I saw a woman who from the looks of it was so beautiful and hot, who made me so crazy, I immediately started driving like a desperado. All the sanity I felt from my session was drained from me like a great cum after a great fuck with someone with no baggage. I tried to fight off the overpowering urge to catch up with this mystery woman. No dice. I was hooked. Like any good addict, I didn't think about the consequences.

I drove like the crazy man I am, weaving in and out of traffic, trying to create a simultaneous stop for both our cars at the nearest traffic light. I'm occasionally good in bed but I'm even better at this. I made it. No ticket. No guilt. Total excitement. The rush was there. I stared shamelessly at this woman's car—it was rapidly getting dark and the stunning shadows made her look even more beautiful through her passenger window. I prayed that she would open it. I didn't care if she recognized me nor did I know what I would say. I knew only that there was a chance that if she really blew me away, and smiled back at me, I might ask her to pull over, and worry about the shame and guilt later.

She made it easy. Her electric window came down real fast. I was in a state of shock. She was amazing-looking. I knew my insane car chase hadn't been in vain, but for a whole different reason. The fantasy woman was my own girlfriend. I didn't recognize her vehicle, but it had to be pretty obvious to her by the look on my face that I hadn't had a clue it was her, until she'd opened her window.

She started to laugh and just before the light changed she asked, "So, just how long was it until you knew it was me?"

I immediately lied: "Oh, please honey, don't be ridiculous."

"Uh-huh," she said with a smirk, then added, "I'll speak to you later."

I was humiliated. Caught with my pants down in rush-hour traffic. The horndog without his clothes. Move over, Mr. Emperor. I'm center stage now. This was a first. I tried to pick up my own chick. Holy shit! What was that all about? I was flabbergasted. I mean, the odds blew for that to happen, but it had happened and I didn't know what to do.

When I got home I finally admitted that I hadn't known it was her, and being the cool woman she is she was flattered and mocked me a little. Although she did ask me what I would have done if it wasn't her. I told her I didn't know. I guess my honesty pushed her into admitting that for a few seconds before she opened her window, she didn't know it was me either. Cool, but she hardly risked her life in traffic chasing after a fantasy mate who could have been married, a lesbian, a leper, an escaped mental patient—anyone. But it was my own woman! I'd hit on my own woman.

I felt pathetic. And then a few days later I ran into some rock star acquaintance of mine, who in his prime must have had a zillion women and a whole world of unknown wet female fans from every country wanting him. I told him the story. He chuckled for a second, knowing me pretty well and how tortured I was being with one woman, and then he got this really thoughtful, yet sorry look on his face. He said one sentence and split.

"Marry her, asshole."

You Would Even Feel Bad About a **Hooker**

I think I like this woman. I think she likes me. I'm not sure if she is telling the truth. I'm not sure if I know what the truth is. I think I know what I want. I think I want her to want me. I don't know whether I want her to count on me. I'm not sure if she really wants me or if I just happened to come along. I don't know why I put myself in the position to be wanted by someone who needs someone. I'm pretty sure if she needs me she must be too needy to really feel comfortable alone. I have always been alone and never been comfortable. I have very little notion of what loving another person means if it means that I lose my freedom. I have always had my freedom and felt helpless to express my love without doubting it. I never doubted that other women loved me but never felt it would last as long as I wanted it to. I never wanted to be loving someone who decided not to love me. It has always been easier to keep my options open even though I have never been clear what my options are. This woman who today says she loves me makes me want to drink again because her love is filling me up with something strange and I don't trust it. If I don't drink I might need to make believe that I want affection from another woman. I feel sick and tired of feeling sick and tired of hurting other women after I accept their love and then want to disappear. I don't even know how to show up with someone who claims she loves me when I think I may love her. No one ever told me that love could occur without me getting obliterated. Maybe I need to accept the fact that I can never love anyone because I don't love myself. Maybe I was custom-made to live out my life with hookers. But I am too afraid of unknown diseases and my pal told me that I would even feel bad about taking the love from a hooker. I would need a hooker to tell me it's all right to pay for an orgasm and that it gave her life added value. I wouldn't believe her and would feel I was just enabling her to live out a loveless life even though it is pretty much similar to how I love but I don't charge anyone. I've been screwing myself for so long by keeping myself unhappy I don't even know if I want to try and make someone happy. It's impossible for me to accept the fact that I could without doubting that that person is really happy. I'm even afraid that I will want to love and be loved (just moments before I die) and will have the wedding, honeymoon, and burial all within a period of a few minutes. That would be great but I'm worried that none of my friends whom I might want to be my best man will be alive. This fear indicates more and more that I would only be getting married on my deathbed to prove to everybody but myself or my wife that I was human. I'm not sure what I have ever done in my life just for myself except stop drinking. I don't even know if I stopped drinking for myself or for the people I hurt while I drank.

Don't get me wrong, I'm not whining. *This is a good day.*

Joseph and Mary and You Gotta

Be Kidding Me!?

Talk about dysfunctional families! They broke the mold. They take the cake! They won the jackpot! They rule! Hey look, I'm no New Testament scholar (in fact I'm not much of a pundit on anything) but I do happen to recall being told that God blessed this dynamic duo, Joseph and Mary, with *his* son, which would have made them what, second cousins? No . . . mothers- and fathers-in-law? . . . No, wait a minute . . . how can that be? Let's think this through. It means that if Mary gave birth to Jesus and there really is a God who would do that sort of miraculous chicanery and Jesus really was his son, for openers, what chance do you think Mary would have to be *pro-choice?* But before we delve into these heady issues, let's get down and dirty first. Let's, for argument's sake, use any biblical polls at our disposal and we will probably find that Joseph and Mary had your typical marriage back then, with men using excuses about sheep outside their bedroom window making them irritable and getting them out of the mood for sex. Or perhaps even having an affair and coming home late saying that some workers were constructing a miracle and it held up traffic. Whatever. So, here we have Joseph and Mary going through the tedious shit of sleeping on different beds of straw, acting out their resentments of each other, and basically not having sex for the better part of a year.

To darken the picture, let's say they despised one another and it wasn't accurately reported. On top of that, it's very likely that Joseph, being a man, might have been sleazier than his wife and might even have been in some hot water with the local rabbi for possibly committing a busload of adultery. Problems had to start with someone. He was a typical Jewish guy with his fair share of jealousy, possessiveness, hang-ups, and a need to wander, be it in a desert or into a nightclub. And even if we assume Joseph was an okay guy but his sex life with Mary had gone south and the nearest shrink was three oceans (or twenty centuries) away (and so he was hoping for a libido miracle), one miracle we can't expect him to buy, knowing that his sperm had abso-fucking-lutely nothing to do with his wife's pregnancy, was that she didn't cheat on him. He may not have been a genius but he was no fuckin' dummy.

"Joseph, we've been blessed."

"How so?"

"I'm pregnant."

"No shit."

"It's a miracle."

"Oh, really. I think it's that asshole, Irving, the retarded shepherd boy you always feel sorry for."

"How dare you!"

"Well, what do you expect, Mary? We haven't fucked since 1 B.C."

"What's that supposed to mean?"

"I don't know, stop bugging me, it just came out."

"You're jealous, aren't you, honey."

"Fuckin' A, I'm jealous. How would you feel if I was pregnant and we hadn't . . . no wait a minute . . . that's stupid."

"Not really, sugar. I am pregnant but not by you or any other man."

"I'm going down to the bar and I want you out of here by dusk."

"Ohhh sweetie, won't you give me a chance to explain?"

"What's to explain? I married a slut and while we're at it, maybe I haven't been totally faithful . . ."

"What!!!!!!?"

"Oh, please, we haven't fucked like forever and now someone knocks you up and I'm supposed to feel guilty over a stupid blow job I got last month at the Purim Carnival after I had a few too many red wines?!"

"I forgive you. I love you. I want you not to be argumentative. I want you and I to be filled with gratitude."

"What's with you? You join some cult or something? You're a Jew and never forget that."

"Honey, we're more than Jews now."

"You found some extra cash? I suddenly know how to use a screwdriver?"

"No honey, I'm pregnant with the Son of God, the Lord, Jesus Christ."

"I'm going drinking and I don't know when I'll be back. You need help and I don't think I can love you anymore."

"I love you."

"Blow me, you lying sack of shit."

Well, this *version* was obviously cut out of most Bible printings but my feelings are that Joseph had almost a bigger cross to bear than his (ha-ha) Son, at least on a day-to-day basis, on earth, trying to keep his marriage together.

Hey, look, I'm no saint. You understand. I'm a street kind of guy and I'm telling you, even some whacked-out bozo on blow, smitten with some drop-dead, kick-ass, gorgeous floozie, would have to have gone deep into his nose to fall for any of this bullshit. Sacrilegious, or just plain common sense, I ask you?

Mary has a pretty cool role in this mystery, but let's consider her husband, not her purported platonic affair with God; just poor, incredulous Joseph, who rumor has it was called "Dickless" behind closed tents by his lovely, if not delusional, wife because of the marital difficulties they were having in the sexual arena. To worsen matters, Mary is rumored to have been very grouchy as she worried over the difficulty she would likely have with her temperamental hubby concerning his inevitable shared visitation rights squabble with God.

Poor bastard. I take my tallis off to the guy. I wouldn't have believed a word of that cockamamy tale. True or not. I'm thinking that it wouldn't have been so crazy or unprincipled for Joseph to call it "splitsville." But don't go by me. I'm the last one to preach about lasting relationships. I'm a pathetic hypocrite. To me, what's good for the goose isn't anywhere near acceptable for the gander. I have a double standard. It sucks. I'm not proud of it. I'm working on it. Still, it's just that I can see me being really paranoid if I were in his shoes. I mean, it's *very* conceivable that if I were Mary's husband, knowing myself as I do, the marriage would have really been on the rocks. With all due respect, who gets married knowing your wife is the Blessed Virgin? What a nightmare! On top of that, I can't imagine forgiving Mary for her seemingly adulterous ways, based solely on her *divine explanation*. What do I look like, a fuckin' idiot? No way I would have forgiven her and moved on if she couldn't shake what I would've been sure was a sloppy, mentally disturbed piece of "immaculate" bullshit about being faithful to me. We'd be arguing all of the time and yet, there she'd be, telling me that she was pregnant with God's only son. Check, please!

With all due respect to the Creator, what about me? I'm supposed to compete with that? I'm supposed to have an open mind and really try and work on the marriage after hearing that bullshit? Give me a break! Then, to make matters worse, heavy-hitting disciples and some wise men get involved and help spin this thing, perhaps way out of proportion, to all the tabloids (which back then were probably chiseled in stone and had to be schlepped around by the publisher and read by small groups, for a small fee, while the curious were tending their sheep). But before you know it the news would've been all over God's creation!

I would have been distraught and felt impotent if I was forced to believe her and stay married. I probably would have opted to pity myself, and, if horny, whack off to some sketches of hot Roman babes and pray that the real God might make things change and Mary would come back to me, admit her licentious ways, have some goodwill left for me, and together we could look for a decent couples' therapist.

Now, I kid the New Testament but I'm Jewish, and from Hebrew school on I really and truly wanted to believe in our Old Testament. Sadly I had as much trouble buying those stories as I did in the "rewrite." It was impossible because it was my feeling that, unless I could believe in the whole Bible, every exquisite tale, I would have a hard time believing any of it. For openers . . . Noah's Ark? It's cute and sweet, but animals two by two? What's that all about? Was there some giraffe dressed in a tux working as a maître d' . . . you know, like the old days at Studio 54, only letting the better-looking cats in (and dogs and donkeys and ostriches and God knows what else) and of course allowing only the famous, more religious ones entrance to the VIP room to snort wildlife delicacies, if they really wanted to party? That's a tough sell! I'm not sure how the giraffe communicated to one of the foxy-looking animal-waitress-actresses that Noah hired to seat people, but what would he say, "Two porcupines, no smoking?" And, with all due respect, can you really visualize Jonah's mother screaming out to him that lunch is ready, and while she is barely able to make him out on the seashore (apparently they lived in a resort area), her son bellows (while making it out after escaping from inside a whale's belly) "Mom, you're never gonna believe this!"

If memory serves me well (which if true, is in and of itself a cause for celebration), when a couple gets a marriage license, they have to swear on a *Bible*. Given my gut feeling about the "greatest book ever written," I'm a little shaky about how forthright that covenant could ever really be. I'm probably better off staying single.

I swear to God.

Mirror Mirror on the Wall

After not seeing her face-to-face in years, it nearly killed me when my former lover of decades ago, now very much involved with someone else, left my hotel room without so much as kissing me. We were both very horny and dying to make love. Maybe she a little more than me, although she was too cool to let on. When she left and I hadn't *gotten off*, and although I knew I had done the right thing by not enabling her, I felt torn apart with loneliness. Worse and even more frightening was that I started to feel hopeless, just like I felt soon after admitting to my alcoholism. When my very stunning and sexy former flame split, I realized that I probably was addicted to *just about everything on the planet.* Having orgasms with any number of close female friends was very high on my list of cross-addictions. It became crystal clear. For the rest of my days, I would have to fight the urge to always get what I impulsively want when I want it, or my life would deteriorate rapidly and most probably I'd die much before my time, due to a relapse.

Irony weighing in, the locale didn't help my melancholy. There I was, in my beloved New York City, on a gorgeous fall day, looking out of my Central Park South hotel window, seeing the splendor of the park below with all its mysteries waiting for me; yet feeling that I could do little more than be paralyzed, lie motionless in bed, and sob uncontrollably. I was an unhealthy psyche trapped in a healthy man's body. I was unable just to be with myself.

"Depression" is what my therapist called it on the phone from the coast, an hour or so later. My heart floundering for a purpose, I listened to what I already knew. I was feeling like shit because I wasn't acting like I used to. Withdrawal! I'd have to go through these jags periodically in order to evolve into something better for myself. Someone more responsible, decent, and selfless. Christ! I felt like a fuckin' saint. *Saint Boredom!*

Yeah, yeah, yeah, I thought as my therapist reminded me what growing pains were for. It was still an almost intolerable place to be. I wasn't drinking. I wasn't stoned. But I wasn't happy either. I wanted to fuck. So did she. It would have been consensual. But I didn't push it. My penis was shaking its head in utter amazement. I was doing the right thing. It made me feel good for a moment and then I felt cheated. I felt cheated even though I had acted appropriately. I had an epiphany that I would suffer through lots of these lows, unless I started to feel some sort of new inner strength. Others had told me as well that if I grew spiritually, these bouts would be less frequent.

Fuck it, man. I just wanted to get laid like I used to when I didn't think so much. Nah, that isn't it. I can't even lie to myself anymore, without feeling like an imbecile! *I just didn't want to grow the fuck up!*

And this was supposed to be the new *improved* me? This is all because I'd been trying to lead a more principled life ever since I stopped drinking? Somberly, I was coming to realize just how simple it had been for me in the past to act like I had nothing to do with consequences. For the record, staying in my room for ten hours staring at the ceiling turned out to be a better alternative than fucking a woman (a recovering alcoholic herself) who doesn't consider sleeping around too big of a deal. I felt "good" being such a mess.

Here was the dilemma. At the time, I was dating a woman who didn't appear to want to fuck anyone else. I thought I loved her. I knew that she loved me. I knew that if she found out that I made it with any other woman, she would be repulsed and most probably would leave me. I knew that if she made it with anyone else I would leave her. I was Mr. Double Standard. I also knew if I made it with my ex (who was just leaving my room) nothing could change between us but it would fuck up my head. I know that having an orgasm behind someone's back isn't like committing a murder, but for some reason, I knew that when I got back home and saw my old lady, I'd feel like a scumbag.

But if I don't feel like a scumbag, I still won't get any awards from my new partner, because she won't know that I don't feel like a scumbag unless I tell her why I don't feel like a scumbag. Of course, if I tell her, it makes me as stupid as someone who believes that making it harder to buy handguns doesn't save lives.

So maybe it's true. I'm trying to save my life. Again. Spiritual awakenings alone aren't enough. The crude awakening is, that it isn't enough to just stop drinking, either. I'm certain that slowly but surely, after the glow of feeling proud from being able to get through a day without any booze fades, the same old asshole intentions and actions in me came back with a vengeance!

Getting sober early on is no rush. If you do it right, it involves getting to know yourself and others for the first time. You feel like a baby taking on man-size responsibilities. Saving your life from drug or alcohol abuse doesn't mean that you have the right to reward your clean and sober self with reckless actions. In fact, from what I know, if you go down that path, it will almost inevitably lead you back to the bad old days when the shame and self-loathing kick in, the whole world becomes one big, two-drink-minimum gin joint, and suddenly scores of bartenders are on a first-name basis with you, all over again.

So I just lay there in my hotel room, as sober as could be, with unrelenting misery my just deserts. No confusion, no drama, no orgasm, no excuses, just fidgety emptiness. I wasn't getting anyone in trouble, or making anyone feel badly, not even myself, unless you count the temporary despair. I was hiding but not from my feelings. And believe me, that's a big deal. That said, it still felt like shit, being a moral guy.

A newly recovering drunk once looked at me with great confusion, as I told him how much better he looked after his first thirty days of sobriety. I tried to tell him how inspirational it was to me, almost five years sober, to hear him clearheaded and to see how courageous he was being in comparison to the angry, fearful, resentful *boy-man* he'd been, just a few weeks before, who had chosen to stop drinking but still saw no good reason to live.

The more praise I heaped on this guy the more he seemed to resent it. After all, he thought he had fun living out of control. Who doesn't? Unless perhaps you inadvertently slam into a school bus while driving unconsciously and kill twenty-seven rosy-cheeked innocent kids. He was lucky. He only lost his family, job, and savings.

Feeling the desire to give him some sort of life lesson before I left (the remnants of my self-centeredness hungry for attention), I told this guy that I could only speak for myself, but I was convinced that through my years of recovery, one thing was crucial, "I acted like a better human being."

This newly evolving soul, covered with scars and doubts, then managed a slight grin and took almost no time to look deep into my eyes while his own mustered a glimmer of a twinkle, as he told me something, even if it was only for himself to hear.

"Well, they can't blame us for that."

Amen, brother.

She's Sitting **Upstairs**

I know I need to be with her, and she with me, but I can't shake the depression. She seems happy and can't see the ever-growing fear I have that I can't live out the rest of my life without her in my corner; and yet I am amazingly annoyed at the same time that I can no longer dream about and pursue the wrong women.

She sits there with a smile just like I used to have after bringing a beautiful, polished apple to one of the few attractive grade-school teachers I had, who somewhere down deep, I felt, maybe wished I was a grown man so we could be married.

Maybe that's it. I finally want to be a man to one woman forever and I don't know how. Dare I tell her any of this? She might just stare at me. She might even feign some sudden female problem and split, sighing with relief as she drives away from my home. Slowly but surely she'll turn up her car radio, she'll sing louder and louder to drown out her second of sorrow over losing me, yet at the same time be kind of happy about gaining her freedom from my self-imposed exile in sharing my trust.

I sort of feel like I do everyone a favor when I drive them away. I never factor myself into the equation because, to be frank, I think I'm sort of happy to be "un-bugged." I get on my own case constantly and get over it, but when someone who claims to love me gets in my way, I see no way out, except perhaps to disappear.

I have always felt trapped by women. I mean, perhaps it would have been better if I had somehow spent the nine months getting ready for my birth outside the womb, like some lobster tail that a waiter made sure was served out of the shell. Sure, it would have been weird for my mother, but I might have felt less controlled as I grew up, in some sort of mysterious, psychoanalytical, bullshit way.

Recently, a woman who professed to love me told me in no uncertain terms, "I think I want to spend the rest of my life with you."

I freaked. As is usually the case when I hear this type of sentiment, I instantly go into a shell and see and hear the world as if I'm in some crazy diving bell designed by Jules Verne, and actions and speeches around me all seem slowed down to a crawl.

"This has nothing to do with you," she exclaimed, trying to calm me down.

How funny is that? Of course it has to do with me. (When I became an alcoholic and I'm not certain exactly when the disease took over, *everything* had to do with me.) Now I'm a little more serene and have much more *acceptance in my life.* I might even be a little spiritual. Yikes! Hard to believe that, as cynical as I am, I can believe in some sort of higher power. But I do. And yet, when true romance enters the scene I become a self-doubting, blithering idiot, full of fear and paranoia, while my faith in God and myself leaves me.

I became a comedian because I had a sort of faith in myself that I knew when a joke was right. I never practiced guitar because Hendrix was the God and I insanely felt I had to play up to that standard. I never studied painting because I felt I would never know when to finish a canvas. I never settled down because I never felt settled.

So what if she is sitting upstairs? She can't sit there forever. I mean, the housekeeper will move her eventually, right? Aah, shit! I'm fucked! I just don't know whether I still feel like I'm not worthy of happiness, or if a woman who claims she loves me is inevitably lying, or whether I'm just (like many women contend) a typical guy who loves women but can't grow up. On top of that, I'm also crippled with the fear that as soon as I say, "I do," my new bride will collapse with a new and exotic disease that will keep her bedridden from then on and my secret life with other women will slowly drive me mad and get me institutionalized. And while there I'll think, somewhere down deep, that it's where I have always belonged anyway.

Nah, I really don't sound like the marrying kind. More like *The Fugitive Kind.*

I'm like some middle-aged Jewish sociopath when it comes to intimacy, living out an experimental lifelong play that Tennessee Williams (if alive) would keep faxing me daily, to act out and keep myself unhappy.

Maybe that's why so many of those Chagall paintings always made me feel hopeful. The way those grooms would hold on to their beloved wives and levitate with joy. What a great notion.

Don't knock it till you've tried it.

She's sitting upstairs. Maybe she's my soul mate.

Uh-oh. "Checkmate."

I Guess **It's True**

I guess it's true. You can't have it both ways unless you're fucked up. If you're not fucked up you *can have everything you need with one person.* You can surrender yourself without feeling you're held prisoner.

It doesn't matter to me much anymore what other people want or say is the right way to feel about love. I know what I want. I want to stop wanting what I don't have. I want to feel, for once, grateful and able to love someone fully. I want to accept someone without looking to make them something they aren't. I want to finally admit to myself that I'm good enough to be loved. I'm getting tired of the chase. I'm getting tired of the manipulation. I'm feeling stupid thinking I'm not being who I really am. I'm exhausted from looking for someone who *won't* tell me what they want from me. I'm gloomy over the prospect of thinking that I always need new prospects. But I think I'm just about at the end of my rehearsal at being a man.

"Ready, Mr. Lewis?"

"How's the crowd?"

"Sold out."

"Really?"

"Are you kidding me, Mr. Lewis? It's standing room only."

"No shit . . . Hmm . . . That's nice . . . That's, uh, cool."

"Are you all right? Want me to hold the curtain? You need a drink?"

"Huh? Oh, no. Ha! That's funny. No, I'm cool, really . . . I'm just a little nervous."

"You kill me, Mr. Lewis. You're always nervous. That's your

whole shtick. You kill me. And I gotta tell you, my wife loves you. She's your number one fan. She always believes you when you're on the TV and say how unhappy you are."

"No kidding?"

"Yeah. She once told me that she felt that what you really needed was a good long hug from a good woman."

"She said that?"

"Yeah. She worries about you. Tell you the truth, it pissed me off a little. I got a little jealous but now that I had the honor to meet you it doesn't bother me as much."

"I'm glad."

"So, you ready?"

"Yeah . . . Tell me something. How long have you been married?"

"Me?"

"Yeah."

"You really want to know?"

"Yeah."

"Let's see, Joanie and I will be married . . . holy shit . . . twenty-eight fuckin' years, pardon my French, this September sixth."

"Isn't that something. Are you happy?"

"Mr. Lewis, I really think you should get out there."

"Seriously. Are you happy?"

"You really care?"

"Yeah."

"I'm the luckiest motherfucker on the planet. I mean she has her faults and stuff but if she stuck with *me*, I mean, shit, I'm one lucky motherfucker."

"Good for you. Okay, get me out there."

"You got it, Mr. Lewis . . . you'll be great. They all came for you."

"I know. Mind if I ask you a personal question?"

"Anything Mr. Lewis."

"Did you ever fuck around?"

"Not once."

"I'm ready."

"Ladies and gentlemen, Richard Lewis."

PART 3: Another Beginning

Right **This Second**

One of the toughest things about recovery from alcoholism, on a day-to-day basis, is that you have to learn that your only real reward is just getting to live your life without having to be God. I have found, so far, that if that unexciting game plan doesn't lead you to drink or prevent you from becoming a more decent human being then you're on the right path.

It's weird trying to be normal. Only someone who has spent years avoiding everything that stood in the way of real happiness can truly grasp the exhilaration of this meaningful boredom. The whole she-bang is so much easier now because I have given up caring about the outcome. I can say with assurance that nothing I ever wanted or predicted came out the way I thought it would. When I started to try and make what *I* wanted to happen *happen,* and forgot about the rest of the world, I probably resembled a funny, hunched-over meteorite just looking for a place to crash. Somehow I crashed into the loving arms of friends or I wouldn't have the luxury of *right this second.*

A few years after I stopped drinking, I had the sobering realization that I was the same guy. I also realized just how much time I'd missed spending with the people I loved. I think I made my amends to most all of them. However, I also concluded, with great sadness and trepidation, that even though I had decided to take the burdens of the world off my shoulders, I couldn't stop others from being assholes. Starting fresh and with nothing to medicate me anymore, I needed a new technique to approach the rest of my life with, or for sure I'd wind up drinking again and probably changing my name. "Ladies and Gentlemen, the comedy of Ricky Rage."

The clearer my thinking became the crazier people appeared. That wasn't what I'd bargained for when I decided to give up champagne. I figured I would stop drinking and everyone would automatically be great to me. Boy, was I wrong. On top of that, I still wasn't so great to them, either.

I was a sober mess. Instead of waking up the next morning in the same clothes I'd had on the day before, I woke up with no desire to put on any clothes, or get out of bed, see anyone, do anything, or even express myself creatively anymore. I didn't want to talk to anybody or, God forbid, listen to my own rationalizations anymore. I knew I was back from the grave but I had no place to go. Even my own shadow seemed embarrassed to hang around.

Early sobriety is hell. Every bad feeling that you ever had about yourself and all the resentments you held towards others rapidly become so obvious that without drinking them away you either have to deal with them, relapse, or pray for some UFO to transport you to another place where it might be okay to get high again without feeling like you're a lost soul. A condo on Mars didn't feel right. I stayed calm, sober, and hopeful, and slowly I started to feel a little bit like my old self.

I'm all I've got these days. And I'm happy for that. It's wild. I like being all I've got. I'm not afraid as much anymore. My fear, I'm discovering, came mainly from my own crazily motivated, self-centered obsessions. Now, no longer drinking and having a little faith has helped me restore myself to a glorious, mundane sanity. I still feel insane from time to time but hardly act that way anymore.

The insane thing really is that if I act sincere and with principles, others can still think I'm off-the-wall or even unscrupulous. That really pissed me off for a while. I didn't know what to do. I felt impotent. My life was becoming unmanageable again and I wasn't even getting high. What the fuck was that all about?

Acceptance. That's what it was all about. I still cared way too much what people thought of me, whether they loved me or despised me.

If they loved me I still didn't trust it and if they despised me, particularly if I acted rationally and even generously, I was at a loss for how to respond. I know better now. It's so simple. *It doesn't really matter*. I don't even have to respond. I don't have to do anything anymore that would create a messy situation for me. Every day is a war when you battle yourself. When you stop fighting yourself you also have to stop going into battle against others. If you stop battling others you have to ultimately accept their behavior and move on.

Peace of mind takes a lot of work.

Peace of mind is a moment-to-moment thing.

Peace of mind is always there if you let it in.

So is a piece of ass.

What price, serenity?

King Fear

"And you think *Lear* had problems? You're like King *Fear*."

That's a nickname, spontaneously given to me ages ago by a substitute shrink. I'd been referred to him by my regular shrink while she was vacationing as far away as she could get from clients—somewhere near the equator. When this idiotic, stand-in quack ad-libbed that nonsense during *my* session, I bolted, slammed down a hundred-dollar bill and screamed, "Sticks and stones will break my bones but words will never hurt me." King Fear has left the building, the doctor probably thought to himself as he happily contemplated telling his shrink pals at a dinner party later that night the tale of how he taunted me into better health.

In my gut I hoped this doctor was trying to make a joke to the self-effacing *comedian* in his room. But, considering he knew that I'd had a huge anxiety attack the day before, his comment felt inappropriate. But to give credit where credit is due, I must shamefully admit that, joking or not, he was right on the money. More amazingly he only had to listen to me moan for about three minutes before he intuitively knew he could heckle me into making a quick exit and force me to fend for myself. He had a method for my madness.

Only one day before the "Fear" session I was an immobilized wreck who couldn't get out of bed for the better part of twenty-four hours, except to take a dump. And when I did get out of bed to move my bowels, I had forgotten that I had loaded up on stomach remedies the night before so that my *stool* (pardon me) was a really strange color, and true to form, with an anxiety attack drawing near, I instantly concluded that I had contracted some terrible stool-coloring disease and would die in a matter of moments. What a *shitty* way to live. I was like a one-man, anxious talk-radio station . . . K-FEAR. "ALL FEAR, ALL THE TIME."

I lived through my imagined fecal cancer-warning catastrophe but still fell into one of my *depression stupors*. Do you know the kind? For me, it begins immediately the moment I first open my eyes in the morning and begin to list all the negative stuff waiting for me. Without much effort I can even do it alphabetically. The list of potential problems both real and imagined can render me frozen with negative coming attractions. If I already have a rash and it didn't go away overnight I immediately leap to skin cancer. If it does go away I wonder whether it will come back or whether it migrated to somewhere else on my body that I can't readily spot. I worry that my girlfriend will hear lies spread about me or truths from angry ex-girlfriends and hold it against me. I torture myself with not having made funeral arrangements for myself, forcing a loved one to scamper around and get a quickie funeral home for me. I can actually visualize my body lying there with my soul hovering around aimlessly, having left hours before with no place to go. These are just the tip of the iceberg, and occur usually well before I have my first diet Coke in the morning, and when I finish the diet Coke I immediately realize that all the chemicals I just drank will contribute to yet another early demise.

I start feeling like every fighter must have felt being pummeled in the clinches by Marvelous Marvin Hagler. In my case, on mornings such as these, the Not-so-Marvelous Lewis throws in the towel, the day, and his hope, and opts for the fetal position method of dealing.

After I quit drinking, for a long time I was shocked by the day-to-day anguish of just getting through life without booze. Not drinking was just the beginning of my dealing with my problem and wasn't close to the cure. Even when the craving was over and some spirituality materialized in me, I still had to be alone with myself; and oftentimes that has been an almost impossible task. It's especially nerve-racking when I have to keep myself company all day. I'm my own worst neighbor. I hear myself say to myself, "Keep it down, asshole," to that negative voice, but I continue to ridicule myself.

Adding insult to insanity, I found it hard to truly understand how practicing *acceptance* would help me evolve into a happier person. This whole *acceptance* thing was just a word until it slowly became a way of life for me after I sobered up. Simply, when alcoholism ruled, nothing much mattered, including what others wanted or even who they were because I wanted to drink more than anything else. When the disease was in high gear, it exercised so much control over me that my self-centeredness blossomed from perhaps a healthy narcissism to a sloppy, self-absorbed monstrousness. I learned then that one of the things I had to give up was my ego, which in turn made it easier to surrender to my drinking, and then made it easier to accept others for who they were rather than as obstacles to the satisfaction of my own needs. When it worked I loved it; when it backfired, I lost confidence in the whole *acceptance* idea. It has taken me a considerable amount of time, *almost a lifetime*, to accept others without being so self-involved as to think that their actions only really revolve around the effect they have on me. I soon not only had a bigger picture of life and the universe, but of all the people, particularly those close to me: of how they were just other people who for better or for worse had their own agenda and goals. So long as I didn't let the fact that they had perspectives different from my own bother me, nor let their journey interfere with my newfound serenity, I soon found that my self-centered thinking was quieting, and acceptance of others, which was a natural segue, just happened magically by itself.

This realization took a lot of pressure off me and even, almost mystically, improved my posture. Unfortunately, this evolved state of mind seems to come and go with the tide.

And on that particular morning before my emergency session with the interim headshrinker, like many another morning, I woke up feeling so overwhelmed with anxiety, so unable to simply let life take care of itself, I could only sweat it out. So I just lay motionless. I stayed in bed, *worrying in place*.

Within an hour, I heard answering-machine messages from several business associates who seemed to be forming a *vast, antihappiness conspiracy* to make sure that I felt my life was totally crumbling around me. My mind zipped into high gear and before I knew it my depression and anxiety started to gather steam and project themselves far into the darkened future, and I didn't think I had a chance of turning any of it around. I felt much more comfortable just staying in bed at my newly christened *Misery Motel*.

In passing, I will say, it wouldn't have been the worst thing if we Jews had had someone in biblical times die for our anxieties. I mean—and don't get me wrong—God is plenty, but a nice little Sol or Myron savior would have been cool. He could've taken *the big panic attack in the sky* for the rest of us, so we wouldn't have to start so many mornings feeling like we have this boulder on our chests with graffiti on it, spray-painted by a sociopath, listing all the people and things that we think are standing between us and peace of mind.

I know now that I was the one standing in my way. I didn't know it on *that* morning or countless others, but I do now. In the past, I felt I had to address every single fear and resentment instantly, or risk feeling like a phony. Now I take great pride in doing nothing a lot of the time. I learned that when I do nothing, often the creeps go away at their own pace to a safe distance from me.

It's a new way of living for me, to feel like life is not passing me by just because I am standing still. I never used to live as I do now because I thought that the bogeyman would catch me and declare me an impostor. So I lived in a constant state of anxious alert, ready to attack anyone who dared call me on my insecurities, or judged me, or tried to fuck with my future. Plus, I had to *always* be right. There was no room for anyone else's opinion. When the anxiety got too overwhelming I either made jokes about it, or for the better part of a dozen years drank to make it disappear.

It used to be that when anything in my life, even something good, was making me miserably anxious, dawn seemed more like the continuation of a jail sentence than the start of a promising new day. I would open up one eye and peer around, hoping that my other eye might see things with a better frame of mind. But it didn't work that way. Instead, I would start concocting my own inedible *complaint casserole* ("mm mm good") for my already taxed mind to torture itself with, gourmet-style. Within moments I had so much ill will toward so many people, places, and things, that there seemed no point in getting up in a universe that contained them.

I felt like I must have continually cut the class that taught about *tools* that could have helped me deal with my anger and frustration, by simply taking an action, trusting it, and moving on. It was almost as if having integrity wasn't enough. Something was missing. There must have been such a big hole in my confidence that I continually needed some sort of validation from anywhere, a burning bush, *anything*, to make it feel like I knew what I was doing. Instead, I either swallowed how I really felt or just let it simmer, sometimes for years at a time, only to see it resurface light-years later, generally in response to the wrong person—in response to something else altogether!

Now when I get overwhelmed with free-floating anxiety, I hardly do anything at all. I try to stay still and listen to my heartbeat. I did this very thing yesterday, when the morning started out in piss-poor fashion and made me wonder what the point was to staying sober if I was going to be so stressed and miserable. I had again lost sight of the fact that life *can* be miserable, and that more often than not, people like me *create our own misery*. As I lay in bed, listening to a new set of wackos on my answering machine, I did not elect to go back to sleep. I didn't lose my sobriety. I didn't even do anything that could be labeled as foolish or unprincipled. I swear. I could only hear my heart beating really loud, which to me was a reminder that no matter what, I had myself; and most of the manipulative, lying, guilt-tripping, full-of-shit people who were trying to take advantage of me or make me feel bad *couldn't*, if *I* didn't empower them. Could it be that simple? That I actually count? I actually don't have to meet someone else's needs and demands without feeling like a scumbag? You mean, maybe *they're* the scumbags? What a cool concept. Perhaps for most of my life, I've been *a dyslexic neurotic*. It makes sense to me now in a backwards kind of way. I put everyone else first, then resented it deeply, and then oftentimes ended up acting like a tremendously insensitive, self-centered jerk.

This time, I made a list of all the things and people pushing me to feel so hopeless and helpless I could not leave my bed, and calmly figured out what I could do about each, *if anything*. Some things I could do made sense and others were insane. So one by one I made a decision, took an action or decided not to take an action, and let it go. I let it go. I let it go. I let it go. I let it go. I let it go. I have to repeat and repeat that, because I have spent most of my life hanging on crazily to resentments and other bad feelings; then ultimately I let go of my own self-esteem. This time I called the villains one by one and told them the truth and my anxiety seemed to melt away. The truth may not always set you free but it sure as hell scares the shit out of liars and scoundrels. Try it sometime. When some unscrupulous person is obviously fucking with your head, just stand tall, tell them how you feel, and watch what happens. Sometimes nothing happens and that's fine, because it usually means only that the big "bad guys" might put up a little stink (the *skunks*) before scurrying off in search of easier prey.

That's what I did the other day. Quite a step for *this* lunatic! It was so fucking easy I could hardly believe my own self-esteem. I just went down a laundry list of assholes, told them how I honestly felt, and they started to shrink, like obedient, trained hemorrhoids. My problems shrunk too, and my hope started to grow again as they fled like cowards!

Okay, maybe I never left the house but I didn't lose my mind either. I know the outcome was right because it feels pure. I spoke from the heart and watched from the sidelines as life took its course. I just let it play out, for a change, and let it go.

I had an *out-of-calamity experience!*

I had one full day and didn't do a goddamn thing. It was near midnight when I got off the phone and finished doing "nothing." I was really exhausted. Luckily I was still in my pajamas. So I just closed my eyes and slept like a baby.

King Fear has left the building.

Unfortunately, he knows where I live.

Powerless

I knew a long time ago or so it dreamily seems, that when the mind-bending, body-crunching, notorious roller coaster at Coney Island, the dreaded *Cyclone*, plunged practically at a ninety-degree angle on its first amazing drop, *someone was looking out for me in a big way.* Most riders had their hands outstretched to the heavens, like a bunch of overzealous members of some gospel church undergoing another grueling test by God and, finding themselves in the wildest pew of their lives, screaming *bloody murder.* Not me. Whether I lucked out and got the miraculously scary front car with no loudmouthed ass-hole sitting in front of me and *infinity*, or nabbed the back car as it whipped around almost more viciously in a vain attempt to show the front car who was boss, it made little difference, I *surrendered*, happily. I sat there, quite still, trancelike, not a nervous tic in sight, just like a little Jewish choirboy, filled with gratitude and joy that for that moment, almost mystically, I felt no need to worry. I had complete *faith* in that old, gargantuan, wooden monstrosity. I just knew I wouldn't die on that insane-looking, demented joyride. It would be too obvious a way to go, man. I mean, come on, falling off a fuckin' roller coaster? Give me a break! Look, I may never know anything terribly important, but even back then I was no fool. Some-how I innately felt that God (some think the best writer around, who finished his script a *helluva* long time ago and already wrote, if not in the Bible, then at least on some legal pad floating around in the heavens, that a battalion of self-absorbed actresses would one day enter my life and turn even my most serene moments into "the parting of the Red Sea!") was way too hip to get that dramatic with my life. And besides, I didn't go on that psychotic ride to die, I just didn't know how to live without getting in the way of myself. I was as clueless as a male praying mantis must be, when, following the best goddamn blow job of his life, the old lady swallows up his ass. And for me, as I look back, the rush wasn't from the fear of it all, but from the total relief I got from letting my brain be quiet and feel *powerless*. That's the ticket to ride, man, just letting go and feeling powerless. And when I understood that in a more meaningful way, a long time after I dragged my body-weary, adolescent self off that *Cyclone*, everything fell into place, one way or another, whether I dug it or not. And that's just the way it is anyway, right? Whether I dig it or not. My crystal ball is finally in mothballs. I was the worst fuckin' soothsayer that ever lived when it came to predicting my own future. The more cocksure I was, the more moronic my predictions became. It never seemed to happen quite like I wanted it to, or when, or how. Fuck it.

Shit just seems to happen and then blows right through town, with a mind of its own, just like a *cyclone*.

Some people buckle up for safety. I just buckle up.

What do I know?

I Wish **I Could Divorce Myself** from **Myself**

I've been my own worst enemy ever since I first heard the rumor that I could actually be myself. Be myself. Wow, what a chore. I know now that I didn't have a chance of being myself while I was drinking alcoholically. The big shock was that, even after I stopped drinking like I didn't want a tomorrow, I still continued on the warpath in the war I was having with myself, trying to shoot down any self-esteem that might still be lingering. In a showbiz manner of speaking, I have been *one tough addict to follow*. Feeling comfortable in your own skin takes a long time if you really want to get it right.

The bitch to getting a handle on hopefulness on a day-to-day basis is that there are *so many* despicable events in life. They're everywhere: Events suck. People suck. Governments suck. Leaders suck. Relatives suck. Lovers suck. I suck. *Suckers* suck. And I'm in a good mood. Rim shot! Rim shots suck.

I think that maybe I have an attitude problem. But seriously! I can't seem to shake it. I'm hoping that spirituality helps me out of this zone, because all other options seem to suck. Did I mention that?

It's pretty understandable, if bizarre, that a lot of people appear either insane or headed that way. Life can be such a bitch most of the time that if you dwell on the bad shit, even suicide can look like a great getaway option. Suicide has never been an option for me. Why take my own life when I've worked so hard to figure out whose it was?

And yet, I still find it hard to try to be a decent person, principled and on some kind of spiritual path, when I am constantly bombarded by crap from unethical scoundrels who couldn't care less about what effect they might have upon anyone but themselves. There are so many people who want to have it their own way, even if it means squashing the very soul of a family member or best friend.

It's so disheartening when you realize how scared and selfish most people are. It's cool if they want what makes them happy. It seems, though, that the general perception of what's important and relevant is defined by people with money or power.

It takes a lot of balls to find your *own* true identity and self-worth. *It's taken me a long time to ask my former self for a divorce.* We're still in court but the real me seems to have the upper hand. For starters, I could give a fuck anymore what people think about me. And I don't mean to sound pompous or foolish. What I mean is, I don't give a rat's ass about what others expect of me so long as I feel I'm not being mean-spirited or too judgmental, and that I am respectful of what any other caring and reasonable people want.

For the better part of my life I have tried to please others, all the while resenting the shit out of myself for taking actions that sickened me. That *me* was ruthlessly sabotaging my own happiness. It's *that* person I'm divorcing.

I've had it with who I thought I was. I need to shed the bogus skin that others wanted me to wear, so that they felt more comfortable around me. I see life now as a great Buster Keaton sight gag. I'm running downhill, constantly avoiding hundreds of menacing boulders in the form of other people's self-centered perceptions and desires, and staying out of the way of these jerk-offs while surrounding myself with *kind* human beings.

This isn't an easy trip, even if Keaton made it look easy on film. Hooray for Hollywood! In the end, I basically believe that all we are is what impression we leave and not the blip in time we actually experience.

I think that about the best way I can conduct myself is to mind my own business, allow myself to experience joy from time to time, feel compassion for those who are suffering, and fall as far out of narcissistic love with myself as I can, so as to leave as much earthly time as possible to care about others.

My divorce proceeding is ongoing and much to my lawyer's credit, he won't take the case. I'm going to have to be stuck with some insecure, overworked, public defender.

Me.

2001—**A Space Odyssey?**

Is that what this movie is about? An odyssey? Wow! What a trip! It was so confusing. I first thought it was about how the 1962 Mets played ball. Not really, but seriously, I long ago stopped caring about what that black monolith represents. In fact, I don't even give a shit about what others think it represents. I've heard it all.

"It's gotta be Jesus."

"I'm telling you, it's only a state-of-the-art speaker system."

"It's a goof, man. It was meant to symbolize what the greatest handball court ever would look like."

I'm burned out on other people's speculation.

Even if Arthur C. Clarke himself came to me in a visualization, telling me what he meant by his book, I wouldn't give it much thought. Who knows? Within moments Stanley Kubrick could appear and tell me how *his* vision was more relevant than Arthur's. Suddenly, *my* perception would seem pointless to me. That's a slippery slope to feeling worthless.

In the last few years, I seem not to care much anymore about what anything means. I don't think anyone really knows anyway and I'm not particularly interested in listening to them guess. I've wasted enough time being interested in what *I* think things mean. And who knows how important I am? Or even what I should mean to myself? I don't want to know. I like feeling powerless over most things and laughing at those who think they're powerful.

All I know is what *I* feel, and that has always been based upon unsound proof. I just want to keep things as simple as I can, try to be a decent person, principled, keep assholes away from me, write till my brain shuts down, and try to achieve as many orgasms as possible with a tender, loving, passionate woman without having the pressing need to say "I love you" all the time. There you have it.

Life is too mysterious to be explained by self-inflated, moronic mortals. God blessed religions—but which one? Religious fanatics and people involved in cults to me are like mobsters in holy places. They seem to be hanging on for dear life to some concocted dogma to avoid taking responsibility for their own earthly behavior. Ultimately it seems, at last historically, everyone gets fucked over under the name of somebody else's god. Not my God. He's a nice person. He's helping me understand who *I am*.

Seriously, if you can actually stand on a beach and stare across the ocean to the horizon, or better yet gaze from a rooftop and spot what ages ago some inspired person once labeled a *constellation*, and then really believe that the ideology of any organization led by humans capable of inappropriate farting, belching, lying, cheating, controlling, stealing, or brainwashing has much merit, then God bless you; you'll need Him. My feeling is that if you need someone on a payroll to make sense of infinity and spirituality, that's what they call in the comedy business a joke on a joke.

I feel I know enough, have been told enough, and been hungover enough for a thousand people already, and if I could just do my *thing*, without bugging anybody or being *bugged* (by, say, an out-of-control independent counsel on my ass), I could gratefully call it a lifetime. My lifetime. I don't need any help in redefining it. So scram! Let me die as clearheaded as I came in. It's my fade-out and I'll fade out like I want to.

Au revoir. Adios. Shalom. Whatever. What's the bloody difference? *They* say, "You can't take it with you." Brother, I wouldn't want to. I've gone down that road. No thanks.

And besides, on my deathbed, I'm going to care less who the self-righteous *they* were. *It's my party and I'll die like I want to*. Really people, get a life. Leave me out of your frightened misconceptions! *They, they, they, they!* Enough already! Get lost! Read a good novel! Jerk off! Rent a video. Ever see *2001—A Space Odyssey*? Try and figure that film out.

I could give a shit. What's the point?

Like *they* say, Keir Dullea, gone tomorrow.

I Have Inoperable Lung **Cancer**

Yeah, we all heard it correctly. A group of us nutty, lovable, fighting-to-stay-clean-and-sober guys were meeting to give one another some support when, after listening to us talk about our problems and blessings for a while, our comrade-in-recovery said he felt like talking a little, too. Then he informed us that just a few hours earlier, out of left field, he was told that he had inoperable lung cancer and that the doctor said he probably wouldn't live more than another two years.

Now this was in a room full of men with all kinds of emotional problems just like everybody else but with one glorious addition—all of us are able to admit to being addicts first and foremost. Everything else that happens in our lives, like a bad soap opera named *The Good and the Shit,* we accept, so long as we don't drink or use. Well, our pal was sober. He was clean. He was looking great. He had fought long and hard and kicked the worst drugs imaginable. His life was never better.

Tell his lungs that.

A lot of happiness had been expressed in that room, before our buddy shared his fucked-up news. Now it was impossible, at least for me, not to feel like I'd been run over by a truck. Yeah, me. I mean, it's a motherfucker trying to get your life together after getting sober, but the notion that after all that effort you can still be blindsided with a terminal illness left me feeling like roadkill. Sure we all hugged him, told him we'd be there for him, and we will be, but what does this shocking, shitty event say about recovery? Why give a shit? Life blows so often and for so much of the time, why not get high?

Well, my pal is reason enough. He was like a warrior suited with perfectly tailored angel wings. He joined us first to tell everyone that he was sober, *then* that he was dying. Then. Then. Then. Then. Then. Then. Then. Then!!!!!!

That's the reason. It seems that none of us former drunks and druggies can do it alone. At least a lot of statistics seem to back that up. As for the few lucky cats who can stop cold turkey, that's cool, but I like hanging out with other former lost souls for support, because I get a better understanding of why I became an alcoholic to begin with. But when a guy can still make it to a little meeting of men to lend his support and then tell us he's dying, *that is sobriety.* That's unconditional love. That's courage. That's a million bucks of additional faith in myself and the others who were there to bank for a rainy day when we're feeling a little bummed, not because of cancer, but because the cable TV went out, or the microwave keeps burning the popcorn, or we can't feel sexually red hot at the moment with a long-standing lover, or we just feel like everything is pointless.

Why not just go back to living in fear and get a drink and start from oblivion again? *Why not get a drink?* I'll tell you why I'm *not* getting a drink. I'm not because maybe my buddy is still alive and maybe he's still getting chemo and radiation, and maybe he still has faith and maybe there will be a mind-blowing breakthrough, and maybe I want to hang with him all day or take him to the hospital for a checkup and if I drank he couldn't count on me for dickshit, and I might as well be *dead* as far as he's concerned.

If he licks this thing it'll be joyous. If he doesn't it'll be a very somber day. If he dies sober, he'll be inspiring people until and beyond the moment he goes. I pray to God a miracle happens.

And I pray to God I have what it takes to die sober, no matter what. If you're a recovering addict you sure as hell leave a lot more than possessions behind you if you go out as sober as you were when you came in.

I'm praying for my friend and I'm also praying for myself to be able to be on my deathbed when the time comes, clearheaded and sober as a saint, surrounded by as many recovering addicts as possible; still able to tell them that even though the lunch I just had tasted like shit and the dumb-ass nurse keeps bringing me pork chops when I keep asking for the broiled chicken, still, my life has never been better.

Then I want to close my eyes with a sober smile on my face *and hope they get it.*

Hey Buddy, **Can You Spare an Autograph?**

I was ready to bust. I couldn't have even beat out a bunt if my life depended upon it. I longed for peacefulness. I couldn't find it. I isolated myself more and more. I was hiding from just about everyone I feared might further contaminate me with their toxic, self-serving principles. I was turning into the first *live* audition for the Madame Tussaud's wax museum. I was losing my hold. I was sick of living by my mistakes. I was also right smack in the middle of writing this book and the task seemed overwhelming.

Then . . . Mark McGwire got ahold of one.

"And the pitch. . . . It's outta here! Number 62! Number 62! Number 62!"

Everyone was jumping around happy for everyone else and it almost didn't matter *who* had hit that ball because someone did and a little bit of faith crept back into our lives. At least it did into mine. I was temporarily put out of my self-indulgent head. I was living in my fret-free past right there in the moment and it was heavenly.

McGwire sent my mind back to the wondrous days of Little League, to the smell of the dusty infield and my carefree pals and their overzealous dads yelling hours before the game began while their good-natured moms set up the postgame refreshment stand. I remembered the strangely overconfident yet slightly retarded kid, who must have broken some psychotic record for announcing consecutive games over a loudspeaker without anyone being able to discern the players' names. I was inspired by that kid because, while he was always being teased and ridiculed about his speech impediment, he somehow remained undaunted. Mostly, there was a sense of open-ended hope floating around. It was intangible yet at the same time you felt you could bite right into it and taste it like it was the best damn apple since the Garden of Eden. But this wasn't forbidden fruit. It was happiness there for the taking. There seemed to be no downside. We all just seemed to be hangin'. It was like some old favorite camp or team picture came to life indefinitely. It was nothing heavy. We were just having fun for a few hours. *Living in the moment*. Where did that go?

Man, I have to get back to "just being." And if only for a brief taste, Number 62 put me back into that state of mind. I wish life could be a dream. It used to feel pretty sweet.

How cool it was not even to know what petty bullshit meant. What a trip to simply focus on helping to move your teammate along the base paths into scoring position and then maybe even be the one to score the eventual winning run. (Hopefully, much to the delight of pretty Doris sitting in the bleachers, wearing pink lipstick and a little pink sweater to match with its tiny pearls fastened on the collar, who was like some miniature, provocative, sexual constellation trumpeting the promise of a potential premature ejaculation in uniform, right behind the big oak tree, as soon as the game was over and all the adults had their backs turned.) Wow! Fantasy. Joy. Fun. Teamwork. Just being. What a happening! What happened?

There's so much noise these days. So much of everything that hardly matters. That's why the home run was so important. It made everyone shut up so we could listen to our own hearts and not be so concerned about bugging anybody else. Not that *everyone* calmed down, but I bet most of us did. I swear to God, I even felt reconnected to my own country again without feeling like some right-wing ultraconservative. I felt like that "little American boy," on the sandlot before I was poisoned by authority figures with hidden agendas and overblown egos. Even the *rainbow coalition* of fans I could see on the TV set with my sunken eyes didn't appear to have a racist bone in their bodies. They all twisted and shouted in the stands! Hoo-Ray!!!! Blacks, Whites, Hispanics, Extraterrestrials, Jews, Gentiles, it didn't matter; they were all hugging one another and I was sitting home alone, *high-fiving* my furniture. A burden was lifted.

Oh, er, excuse me Mark. Say, listen, do you think you might sign something for me, anything, a prescription, maybe? Or maybe just say a few words into a tape recorder to my shrink, something like, that you think I'm going to be okay one day? Will you do that for me, slugger?

Before I Visit Mom in the Rest Home

. . . Or whatever you call those places (they give them different names but, regardless, it is pretty horrible when anyone has to stay put in one, as we all do if we live long enough, and sort of wait to go on to the next dimension, if there is one). Even if it mattered, it's an impossible task to figure out who feels worse, my mother or those who watch her living the way she is living now, since she had another stroke. This last one basically left her almost blind and her memory tragically tinkered with in such a nasty fashion that she has very little short-term cognition left, and only rarely has moments of sharp recall when she hears of things from her past. Regardless of the ups and downs I have had relating to my mother throughout my life, it still humbles me when I realize that I wouldn't be here if it wasn't for her. My mother's eggs coupled with my dad's sperm have spawned quite a photo book; with their three kids, and then grand-children and great-grandchildren. And now each of us in the family, depending on our age, relationship to her, and own emotional sta-bility, are thrown into various degrees of chaos while witnessing my mother's private, slow descent into eternal peace and quiet. I sure hope that there's peace and quiet for all of us when we die. There certainly isn't much of that shit going around while we're alive.

I'm dealing with my mother's illness the best way I can. Accep-tance and compassion are the main ingredients. I don't have any pressing issues any more with her specifically, and even if I did, how

pointless since I couldn't have any kind of real closure with her anymore anyway. And that's cool. Really cool. She has enough to deal
with. Her final aches and pains make me sad, yet selfishly I can't
shut down my brain from imagining myself in her agonizing condition, years from now. I also can't stop from routinely having fire-
works displays of raw emotion bend my dreams into even more
twisted images than Salvador Dali's.

Being the baby in my family came with a flurry of early attention;
then like a quick left hook from Muhammad Ali I was left stunned by
the feeling that no one cared anymore. I think they all probably did
care but mostly in a weird sort of telepathic form, even if they were
standing right next to me. The problem with their telepathy was that
I didn't pick up a message, if there was one. Even worse, though, it
sometimes seemed they just didn't know how to care, and often hurt
me deeply and made me feel that I would be better off alone.

I know I wasn't special in growing up feeling like this. Many families I've gotten to know in my lifetime had very similar dynamics to
mine. Of course, no one had my screwball brain with which to try to
make sense of those dynamics. The scary part for me was that loving
family members who offer moments of support and affection can in
an instant become abusive, suffer temporary insanity, be incredibly
selfish and narcissistic, join cults, become alcoholics or drug addicts,
but if you're real lucky, *maybe* make the time to take you to see the
Harlem Globetrotters. Trust me, I've contributed a smorgasbord of
dysfunctions to my own family's history and thankfully, being in
recovery, I have been able (to the best of my ability) to make any
amends to those I felt I'd hurt.

My mother really couldn't let me make any amends because,
sadly, she didn't want to accept my alcoholism. Initially I was devas-
tated by her lack of compassion and understanding, and in my early
sobriety her attitude made me feel even more ashamed than I
already did. It took a while for it to become clear to me that my
mom, like my dad, often looked upon me more as a reflection of
what people would think of her and less of who I was as a boy and
then a man. Whether this had to do with self-loathing (with Mom's)

or self-absorption (my dad's), I still suffered, feeling like even my own feelings were not my own. And so, when I proudly admitted to my mother that I was an alcoholic, she felt guilty and disgraced, and was in more denial about my disease at that point than of course I was. This angered me a great deal, but soon the acceptance that I have had to practice since I became sober allowed me to move on without making it a long, drawn-out drama. Once you admit you are an alcoholic and want to get better, there really aren't any big deals anymore other than drinking and using again.

I had a dream one night that sums up my relationship with my mother. It was a typical nightmare with lots of loose ends, but it was clear that it took place at the rest home, which in reality I was getting ready to visit. In the dream my brother and sister were with me. When I walked into her nursing care room, she didn't know who I was. Her longtime boyfriend (from after my father's death) was there too, and she seemed to be making him uncomfortable by not recognizing him either, but her focus seemed to be on me. *Hey, what the fuck, it's my dream.*

Her initial reaction to me was unfortunately not far from how she really is now anyway. So even though, in the dream, I felt as if I understood her condition, I couldn't shake the longing for her to know I was there. It's almost as if I wanted credit for showing her I cared so much.

And then, almost like at the end of the film *Carrie* when Carrie bolts from the grave and even bald men in the theater have their hair stand on end, my mother scarily shouted my name. It was as if she had known all along who I was, and had just been toying with me. I was angry and felt humiliated—which was very reminiscent of how I was made to feel as a kid so many times. Yet, afraid to display my hostility as always, and in light of her state of mind, I showed gratitude for her recognition of me, as if this was a sign of her getting her health back. And then, horror of horrors! Suddenly a huge passport, *mine*, almost six feet tall appeared, and she opened it and was just about to make it official by stamping it when I woke up.

Oh, Christ! Whatever happened to *wet dreams?*

Well, you don't even need Psychology 101 to figure that beauty out. I never felt validated by my family. My folks were middle-aged when I started my adolescence and had their own shit to deal with. My older sister had long since split and started her own family when I was a little boy, and as for my older brother, I was on the receiving end, from my perspective, of a lot of abuse from him over and above just typical sibling "horseshit," which ultimately left me flat out disgusted and needing a separation. In time I came to feel that it was better to pursue my goals by keeping disconnected from him and his negative impact. Consequently, and with great sadness, I chose to wind up brotherless for most of my thirties. Eventually we forged some sort of working, peaceful relationship together, that we still try to maintain today with intermittent success. But when I was young, my brother, like my mother, would occasionally express encouragement, and then retreat, leaving me feeling as if I was more of a threat to him than a source of pleasure to be around. Very early on I learned to isolate—not to drink, not then, anyway—but to stay clear of negative energy.

My father, a workaholic like me, was clearly in charge of his own life, but offered very little guidance on mine. Somehow his absence crazily made me worship him even more. This truly gifted caterer, disguised as my father, was so rarely around, his face might as well have been on a milk carton. I tried to live up to his spectacular achievements yet never really knew why.

I guess that left me and Mom trying to figure out the world's problems and our own. *My Mother the Car*—wasn't that the name of a short-lived TV show? Well it's a fitting title for my mother and I. She *drove* me crazy. I probably drove her crazy. She came first, though. The onus is on her. And besides, I was just a kid, and it didn't seem fair to wait around for McDonald's to come up with a campaign twenty years later for me to *deserve a break*. So there I was, so young, so confused, and left to my own devices. The loneliness was overwhelming. I didn't feel accountable to anyone who really mattered. Later in life, left to my own devices, I chose alcohol to keep me company.

I actually understand, although it's a pity, that my mother wasn't capable of hearing me admit to being an alcoholic when her support might have counted the most. She felt embarrassed and almost responsible, it seemed, and probably thought my alcoholism reflected poorly on her. To her, my recovery was more something to be ashamed of than something to celebrate and root for. Like I've said, everyone in my family seemed to come from different planets and in retrospect I wound up getting more support from the knee-pads I wore for my trick knees.

Consequently, there is that dark hole in my soul or part of the brain that never got that good housekeeping seal of approval. Other than flashes of what seemed like fake appreciation, my family's approach to me took the form of a hunt for disapproval. I often wondered, in my darkest moments of self-doubt, and after years and years of psychotherapy, if being raised by wolves might have made a positive difference.

It wasn't violent, it wasn't outright abusive, but it sure sucked. And even though I make a real attempt not to dwell needlessly on the past damage inflicted upon me—except of course, joking on stage, for example, that the original Lewis home, especially during family reunions, should have had attached to the side of it a huge mirror, similar to those we have on our cars, that would read, "relatives might appear closer than they actually are"—I'm certain too that I've avoided having my own offspring in large part because I think I am all I can handle, and I haven't wanted to take the chance to let anyone of my own creation down.

So, a day at a time, I try to stay sober, try to keep my addictive personality from sabotaging the real joy of being alive, and privately celebrate the prospect of being able to show up where my mother rests uneasily, and sit by her side whether she recognizes me or not, and hold her hand. My compassion for her now is overpowering as I try to comprehend what she is going through and deeply regret what we could have had.

I know that as a young mother, she had her hands full just trying to find her own sense of self-worth. From what I picked up in the family rumor mill, her own childhood didn't resemble a happy

French impressionist painting either. And unlike me, she had to try to mature while simultaneously trying to stage-manage an entire family. She had very little help and there wasn't a shrink in sight. I wish she could have devoted more time to herself, or had someone to help her understand just how far she seemed to be retreating into her own world. She must have been hurting for so long starting at such a young age, that by the time I reached puberty she didn't have much left to give, and she couldn't easily give what little she had. Everyone in my family felt so hurt for so many different reasons both real and imagined that everyone walked around in his or her own private fallout shelter. After all, there was a Cold War going on.

As the baby in the family, I didn't initially think I had to run for cover over anything. But when I left home, I did. I ran from myself and from intimacy. *Less is more* in acting and this seemed to be the safe route to go with relationships, too. I ran straight to strangers for approval, had innocuous love affairs, and screwed irresponsibly like some crazy armed robber in the twenties making a quick score then fleeing out of town, as far away from the scene as possible. And then, eventually, I dove into that divinely medicated world of drinking, until that too let me down.

No more hiding. Come on life, give me all you've got. I should be dead. It's all gravy now. Come on, try and kick my ass, baby. I dare you.

I'm going to hold my mother's hand real tight and I just know that she'll realize that it's me and I'm struck with this slightly crazed fantasy that now that her brain isn't working that hard anymore, her heart will take over. And without all the defense mechanisms and guilt and fear and words getting in the way, it'll send a message to her hand to squeeze mine, and that'll be the sign that we did the best we could together, and that we both simply accept that. End of story.

Vacations

Just being alive is enough of a *vacation* for me. Getting away from my *work* (of nonstop creativity) is at best, from my standpoint, only a chance to contract some weird virus that will render me bedridden for enough weeks to get even more work done, and, as a bonus, is an easy way out of "people-pleasing" social events that I have tragically scheduled.

I spent so many years avoiding my feelings that the best thing for me to do if I want to get a vacation away from whatever it is that people get away from is to feign an illness and stay in bed and yank out the telephone. That's Paris and Venice for me, baby!

Of course, there are some good things to be said for seeing some of the world's amazing cities, but for me a true escape means to *get away* from my *obsessing,* not to travel with millions of others who are trying to be first in line to nab that perfect window table at a café filled with beautiful future ex's; or to land that tough, hot theater ticket; or to worry about being bombed somewhere while eating bad Italian pizza on the Spanish Steps in Rome, and reading passages from Keats, sitting, sweating, and getting nauseous, ironically, just a few hundred feet away from the very apartment where the master poet died.

Another problem I have on vacations, especially those in other countries, started well before it became chic to worry about terrorism (our ass-backwards way of starting to feel like a nation again). It's that I always have to fight off the compulsion of absurdly thinking that practically every man between the ages of eighteen and thirty who sports a turban, particularly those with lots of facial hair, is there solely to assassinate someone. Hey, don't get me wrong, I love Hindu headgear and I know this is an irrational notion—it's just that I never met a turban that couldn't hide a snake or some sort of explosive device inside of it.

Granted, *turban-phobia* is a devastating problem for me to try to overcome and managed care won't pay for the treatment even though it clearly should be a covered benefit—but wait, I haven't even gotten to my hang-up with overpacking. I pack (even just for an overnighter) with a ton of clothes. Given my usual state of mind—the crippling fear that a nuclear war will pop up just when I am starting to enjoy myself—I feel it is necessary to be able to make a fashion statement. I wish I was kidding but I really do care way too much about how I look in public and the end of the world would have little effect on my vanity.

What I think all this symbolizes is that I have always tried to get away from myself while not getting to any *place*. Consequently, wherever I wind up, I never relax. Because even if I showed up buck naked without a thing on me—money, good luck charms, whatever—I'd still have so much emotional baggage, bellhops would run for cover.

That's why I like to stay home most of the time. I mean, who wants to feel responsible for hotel and various other travel personnel losing their minds just by coming in contact with me? Rumor has it that one concierge at a pretty high-profile five-star hotel in New York City was institutionalized moments after my departure. Allegedly, physicians on the scene reported that this previously well-adjusted, top-of-the-line *employee of the month* felt uncontrollable remorse after looking into my eyes and sensing my utter desperation, even though I simply said (with what I thought was an accompanying twinkle in my eye), "Honey, thanks for everything."

It's a major burden so innocently to have an incapacitating effect on others. If I really have the need to get out of town, solitary confinement, probably somewhere in Maui, with twenty-four-hour room service, seems to be the way to go. Otherwise, there's no place like home.

As long as I'm not too conscious of me being there.

I Think I Have to Go into a **Nuthouse**

Yeah, that's what this superstar told me when she spotted me outside of my hotel in New York. It really caught me off guard, first because we were at best just acquaintances, though I've known her a long time, and second because she had no idea how depressed *I was*, and seemed to be looking to me as some sort of citadel of sanity.

As she raced over, leaving her entourage standing in front of the limo oblivious to their meal ticket's fragile mental state, she grabbed my arm, pushed me away from the others, and with tears streaming uncontrollably told me with ruthless honesty that basically everything and everyone was driving her crazy, her existence seemed meaningless, she had a sense of hopelessness, and she felt that no one really cared about her well-being, eventually blurting out, "I think I have to go into a nuthouse."

Holy shit! What was I supposed to do? Given that I am one of the world's greatest people-pleasers, I had my work cut out for me. This was a job for Superman, and God knows I wasn't wearing a cape (it was at the dry cleaners). And besides, my only real connection to her was that we're both comedians and respect each other's work and, oh yeah, one other small thing, we both know we are both addicts. The only difference, and it's a big one, is that I am in recovery and she no longer is. I knew this about her because I had seen her the past year carousing at a few parties and felt badly that she, or any other addict who knows better for that matter, was on the highway back to hell.

Knowing that she was once in recovery, and had once had the courage to admit being an addict, made a *really* big difference. The fact that I knew that she knew that I knew that at the center of everything else she might do now to help herself was the immediate need to get back *into* recovery made it microscopically easier for me to try to spit out a few pearls of wisdom.

I told her that I was still sober and that nothing that she was going through was going to get better, but could get a lot worse, if she didn't immediately forget about everything else except her sobriety. But before we could talk much longer she was swept away by "her people," back into the limo so she could make her flight. I was suddenly struck with the notion that she was flying further and further away from herself, and not to any other destination.

I felt so fucking lucky to be sober. I realized how little use I would have been to this person had I been bombed out of my mind when she approached me on the street. She'd seemed straight, just sad and lost. I was depressed, but also clearheaded and dying to help her. This is just amazing progress and growth on my part. Even though I had another hour to spend with a close friend, all I could think about as we walked around town taking in New York's infinite sensations and associations was how I could help this woman, someone I hardly knew; except that being an addict, I actually probably knew her better than most of the people claiming to understand and care for her. It's amazing how addicts instantly know what another addict is feeling. It's a bond born of hellish circumstances that lands on heavenly ground.

Back at my hotel, I called her and left a lengthy message about how she had to simplify her life now, and get back in touch with how easy it is to feel out of control and lost if she doesn't take responsibility for her once sober self. I also gave her suggestions about how she might get back on the right track, and made no bones about the fact that if she actually felt that she could get out of this funk without getting back into recovery, she was deluding herself.

Recovering addicts who *slip*, as they call it, and "go back out there" at least have the tools to put an immediate stop to the insanity, first by not medicating the situation, and then by reaching out to others who will stand by them as long as they are willing to help themselves. Whether my friend came to her senses, or cleaned up, or asked for help, I have no idea. But it's impossible to help someone who doesn't want to accept life on its own terms, particularly an addict, who when whacked is usually at the center of his or her own universe, playing God, not acknowledging they're really just looking for a quick grave to hide in. Thankfully, I haven't heard any nightmare stories on the news about my friend's untimely death.

So dig, *I just stopped writing* a moment ago and flicked on the TV in this hotel room in California where I'm staying, during yet another one of what feels like millions of nightclub engagements in a row, and there she was. There was my comedy friend on some rerun. Reruns make a lot of money for stars, but for addicts, reruns of active addiction only make a bigger mess. I hope she knows that.

I had to turn off the tube. I have trouble watching my comedy buddy without worrying. Old sitcoms give me the willies anyway, especially when I hear the canned laughter. There's nothing real about it.

Things **I Still Feel Shitty** About in Recovery

It's shocking to me that I have gotten this old and have hung on to so much of the same shit. It's astonishing to me that I have been through so much and still manage to let people get to me. I doubt I'll ever be able not to feel responsible for so many people. I am frightened of the knowledge that I am horrified by an intimate relationship because I feel that I will turn over my life to that person. I'm saddened that I don't see that a truly loving relationship can help me be happier and not more stressed. I'm amazed that my father died before his time from heart failure and yet I still have a tough time trying to manage stress any better than he did. I've come to terms with the fact that my emotional age is pretty much equal to the years I've spent sober. I guess that makes me a little over six years old. I'm unhappy that, although temperate, I'm still afraid to feel. I'm quietly humiliated that I have passed fifty years of age and still feel depressed over nonsense. I'm sickened by the inner turmoil that prevents me from ever really being satisfied with most of the things I accomplish. I'm exhausted from being on a never-ending treadmill of expressing who I think I am. I am freaked that who I am will never make me happy. It's inconceivable that I'm already at the age when death by natural causes is realistically moments away. I can't bear losing any more friends. I feel beaten down by letting myself be taken advantage of by *so* many people. I feel so hopeless when I think that everything is going to come to an end before I have more fun. I have to believe that my ability to laugh at the darkest things has kept me from going insane. I hate that I feel that whatever I do for people is never enough. I am tormented by thinking that I let people down. I feel foolish when I fail to give myself any credit for much of anything. I am practically out of steam from irrationally trying to hang on to old relationships with people who give me nothing. I'm afraid that I might burst if I hear many more people bullshit about themselves in front of me. I am close to running away from most everything and everyone that has kept me down. I'm terrified. I'm a workaholic. I'm addictive. I'm a recovering alcoholic. I feel silly that I fantasize about people who love me crying while listening to the report of my death on the nightly news. I'm stunned that I waste even a moment trying to imagine how eloquently show business friends will eulogize me. I am staggered that I long for attention even after I'm gone. I cannot stop trying to become more principled. I cannot stop beating myself up for my flaws. I despise the time I waste thinking that I'm not okay. I can never stop wondering if I *should* just wind up alone. I can't stomach the fact that I like being alone and hate living alone. I can't get over the fact that I know a woman now who accepts me. My gut taunts me that once I'm not alone again, I'll still be stuck feeling alone. I don't know if I will ever be able to trust myself. I am convinced that if I don't change, and never trust myself, no one will even know. I don't even think I have to change. I don't think anybody really cares. I hate that I'm not enough for myself. I think that I am going out of my mind in a sane fashion.

Little **Triumphs**

"Are you still sober?"

"Yeah," I replied, over the phone, almost sheepishly, to a wonderful, famous friend who I really hadn't seen or talked to much for a couple of years.

"Amazing, just amazing," she said.

"Well, it's been almost four and a half years since I had my last drink." I quietly applauded myself.

There was a slight pause. *"I don't think I know anyone who has triumphed over anything,"* she said, sort of desolately.

It was such a small statement, said faintly, and yet it rocked me. She sounded forlorn, as if she had reached some sort of bottom in her life. Knowing a little about her lifestyle I was thinking that her bottom might be located somewhere near mine, in the scarily controlling and baffling world of alcoholism. Her words showed me that she recognized that I have been overcoming this disease on a daily basis, and not only did she see the change in me, recognize it, and applaud it, but was, in her own way, I felt in my heart, encouraged enough by my recovery to begin to risk reaching out for help. Her new vulnerability was an experiment for her. Soon she would ask me for help more directly. I just knew it. And as thrilled as I was about this evidence of her progress, since I had been prodding her gently for some time to address her own alcoholic issues, I still couldn't help feeling more selfishly, if just for a few private seconds, astonished and proud to actually be in a position to help someone save their life, rather than just be their funny, wasted, drinking buddy.

I left my body for a split second, hoping my brain would stay put, and praying it would be there when I returned. *I found myself, yet again, in some kind of odd, spiritual twilight zone.* Ever since I'd bottomed and begun the journey to sanity, these moments happened on occasion and were to me real signposts of my spiritual growth. Someone I loved and respected thought I had accomplished something amazing, and maybe I had. At *that* moment, I had the stunning realization that my mere existence was both astonishing *and* insignificant. I know this may not seem *that* profound a realization to anyone else, but it didn't matter. I felt it and it felt really peaceful. I miraculously got the germ of a notion that just maybe I could, once and for all, *like myself.*

Before I started to get all grandiose and contemplate how great the rest of my life was going to be if I stayed sober and continued to triumph over my disease, I came back into my skin, flaws and all, which never felt better suited to me. And yet I also had this great feeling of remorse about my friend's sadness. I tried to imagine what could make her sound so discouraged. She's such a beautiful and giving person, and if worthiness can be defined by the love you give to others over a lifetime, this woman's got to be light-years ahead of most people I have ever met. That's why I was so floored. I saw a person who gives so much, achieves so much, and cares so much for others feel so little good about herself.

So, sort of diminishing my accomplishment (which has always come so easily for me) and helplessly trying to give her a little hope, I managed to stumble over some reply like, "Well, I don't know, I mean, like, you know, we all have little triumphs every day and life is pretty tough for most people—even for those who aren't, well, you know, uh, fortunate, you know, and I guess I just finally have enough clarity to see that."

Jesus Christ was I glad that sentence was over.

She seemed more flabbergasted by my response than anything else and after some chitchat and "I-love-and-miss-you's" back and forth, I hung up and felt in touch with a God. My own personal God. Oh my God! This can't be me writing! But it is. It really is me.

I hadn't felt this kind of certainty about God's presence since I'd bottomed out, years before. It was then, while on my back from so much more than just the alcohol, that I first had an inkling that some sort of God existed for me who had a lot more to do with things than I'd ever dreamt imaginable. Now it was astonishingly clear to me once again that there just *had to be* some sort of higher power hanging around, all the time, within me, hovering over me, in my wallet, *somewhere*, that had much more control over the way things were in my life than I did. And that was fine with me because I really sucked as a conductor.

I must've been doing something right because, for once, I was really and truly speechless. My friend's fearful voice seemed to mirror back to me my own strength, which had only evolved because I'd started on this sober, spiritual path years back. I wasn't playing God but God was working through me, making it seem easy to be there for her and others who like myself have this disease. We were all in the same boat, but I had tested the life raft and come to feel more comfortable in it than I felt sinking in a sea of booze. I felt so fortunate to be able to feel so spiritual, for once, and not convinced that only imminent doom was on the horizon for me. I felt enabled to perhaps enable her to help herself. This spirit drenched my neurotically twisted being and left me in awe.

First I was in awe in a kind of dumb, narcissistic way, like I might finally be getting a real bang out of my buck for all these years of sobriety that I have been accumulating. I felt uncommonly healthy for a change. More importantly, I felt pretty damn cool that I was able to accept my friend's small yet thunderous praise rather than quickly dismiss it in my usual compulsively self-effacing way. And then, the *real realization* washed over me. It was indeed true. The faith that I had been invisibly storing by forcing my cynical self to constantly pray, every day *(and I mean every day and every night, on my knees)*, existed! It was part of me now. From the moment I had walked out of that emergency room, years ago, my heart had begun to fill with some sort of force greater than myself, and I had started to become whole. This new strength didn't ask much more from me than that I turn my will over to it. And somehow this didn't seem to take anything away from me; in fact, this seemed to be pretty unselfish considering it enabled me eventually to look at myself clearly. I could look and see that *Richard Lewis* was unique; that I was fully alive; and that I could be proud and thankful, not just anxious, ambitious, and lost. Now this fellow tarnished soul on the other end of the telephone line was reminding me that the spiritual path was working. My faith was growing stronger, thank God, even if my addictions, always nearby, were still screaming for attention.

I stared at my all-too-vain self for a bit in my beautiful art deco mirror and saw the paunch that was announcing its arrival, but for once I didn't care. Eating disorders be damned! Not content with that sign of maturity, I then started to worry about all the things I was supposed to finish that day—and then suddenly, I didn't care about them either. I started to think that maybe I was going mad because for a few minutes all of the bullshit didn't mean a damn thing. It was too good to be true. Suddenly my past hardly mattered either and as if that wasn't enough, I was strangely reminded how the future was way out of my hands.

All I had for those few moments was the now. Not the *now* in some existential coffee shop—like wow, man, now—but like a sort of "holier than now." And I didn't mock it or distrust it or feel like some religious fanatic. I just accepted it and felt some grace.

No big deal, just a little triumph.

Actor, Writer, Comedian, **Drunk**

Yeah, that's what it said alright, inscribed forever under my name on the distinguished alumni page in the Ohio State University's 1999 basketball media guide. The communications director, thinking perhaps that he was being funny, had smeared me publicly with a word I hadn't used publicly about myself. He had deprived me of dignity and anonymity and privacy and he didn't know what the fuck it meant to be an alcoholic in recovery and how hard I'd worked to earn back my respect. I have had a love affair with my alma mater ever since I stepped foot on that glorious campus almost thirty-five years ago. Now it was the place of origin for an "unconscionable act"—as the president of the university referred to it after it had been discovered—that would soon mushroom into one of the biggest tests of my sobriety to date.

Unbeknownst to me, this story had been brewing a couple of days before I woke up to it (gratefully without any hangover) as I was edging towards my sixth year of sobriety. And then it broke wide open. For weeks, I was forced to read in newspapers about how someone had written these words next to my name, to see it on the World Wide Web, hear it on the radio, watch it on TV reports, and start getting it on the streets in the form of suspicious looks from strangers. Before this, when fans had acknowledged me on the street with a smile or a knowing glance, I'd always been able to assume it was because I was a comedian they might have enjoyed through the years. Now, instead, I had to worry whether they were wondering whether I might also be an active alcoholic.

What an odd sensation to know that you're *recovering* and yet find that millions of people might actually think that you're still drinking. What unnecessary embarrassment and humiliation. At first I prayed it was a joke but it wasn't. Then I prayed I could laugh it off but I couldn't. Then I hoped it would just go away, the way I used to think problems would just go away when I was a drunk, only to find that they didn't, and that excessive drinking made them worse. Even though I had stopped drinking years earlier, news of the "Actor, Writer, Comedian, Drunk" episode progressed into a media frenzy and I soon became filled with rage. I knew that it wasn't a life or death situation, but simply life dealing me a blow, testing me yet again to see if I could stay the course in my sober state, watch things evolve, and trust that in the end I would gain more strength by walking through the ordeal sober, by refusing to respond to the character assassination, and by trying to let acceptance start healing the pain.

Ironically, this ludicrously public slap in the face came just when I had been praying and working hard to be as candid as possible in writing this book describing the pain of being alcoholic, and the elation of working through that and leading a profoundly different existence. The whole crummy affair seemed like a practical joke of divine proportion, getting labeled a drunk when I was actually someone who had successfully fought to *overcome* being a drunk.

It's fair to say that once you've become an alcoholic, you'll always be an alcoholic. It just depends what stage you're in, whether you're in recovery or out there again, being ruled by drink or substance. I have been ruled by God since I began my recovery, and although I say I won't split hairs between the words "drunk" and "alcoholic," I will: The word "drunk" *is* more archaic, conjuring up images of skid row and stigmatizing the person in need of help. In any case, I am a recovering "everything," so to speak, but early on I might have been much less prone to get help if I'd been labeled a drunk rather than an alcoholic. The imagery I associated with the word might have made me more defensive back then and deepened the denial. It's even possible that it would have made me drink more and tell everyone to fuck off. I'd probably be dead by now. You get my point.

But I'm alive. And I'm not a drunk anymore. Okay, cool, so call me a recovering drunk if you must. But don't label me a drunk. That's slander.

Through the whole ordeal, I would intermittently be struck with how happy I was *not* to be a drunk. Then the familiar resentment would start to build, pushing away the gratitude felt at overcoming alcoholism. It was hard to stop thinking about how I'd unfairly been characterized to millions of people as the very thing I'd fought so hard to overcome, and no longer am. It's one thing to feel powerless over an addiction and to seek out help; it's another to be attacked and feel powerless again, but this time knowing my reputation is smeared, regardless of how sober or wonderful my life has been. Sure, I've struggled with depression and disappointment during recovery, but never have I felt so tested, and in an arena so vast— cruel defamation in the court of public opinion, where I make my living.

I was shocked to find that some people labeled this journalistic low as a gaffe or joke, when it couldn't possibly have had anything but horrific consequences for me. Moreover, this attitude seemed to

THE OTHER GREAT DEPRESSION   239

trivialize the daily challenge and effort needed to remain sober by suggesting I laugh it off. This was insulting not only to me, but to anyone coping with a past addiction.

God only knows what the communications director thought might happen to him. I don't even know him. He came to the school years after I was already sober. He ultimately, after most of the prestigious officials and academics from the school had already done so, sent me some sort of an apology. Then he allegedly resigned from his job at the university. It doesn't really matter what his motive was, really; the damage was done. But having it originate from my own much-loved university made it one of the most painful experiences in my lifetime.

Just as I had started to move on emotionally, many reasonable journalists suddenly came to my defense. But there were also those who didn't—for whatever reason. One in particular chose to attack. A sportswriter from the *New York Post* chose to regurgitate an "impression" he had of me at a Knicks game he'd witnessed "a couple" of years ago, painting me as a drunk. (Once again this is libel as I haven't had a drink, to this day, for almost six years.) But in this case, here's a writer not only slandering me but writing in effect that I should do all I can to help this Ohio State University communications guy get his job back! I *thought* reporters should get facts straight. The *New York Post* writer failed to report the eloquent apology made to me by the university president and the alumni, nor did he make much note of my dedication to the school and award-winning alumnus status, in particular my work helping to put an end to "binge-drinking" on campus, and to many other sober and worthwhile activities on behalf of my alma mater. No, the New York sportswriter chose to dredge up a memory he had, put it in an erroneous time frame, and for whatever reason try to humiliate me some more. How objective! How professional! How clear it once again became to me that no matter how clean my side of the street is, it often has very little bearing on the perceptions and actions of others.

I don't know either of these guys, the former Ohio State guy or the *New York Post* writer, but after their actions, I'm just grateful finally to be comfortable in my own skin. It has taken a long time to get a snug fit, and no one will rattle me enough to make me go back to a drunken tailor. I wish both of these gentlemen well, and feel personally relieved that I don't collect a paycheck by trying to disgrace someone.

With all due respect to the ladies out there, I do recall some old recovering addict once telling me, "Hey, Richard, recovery isn't for pussies." He's right. It's for strong men and women, given a chance to lick this disease, to go back and make amends and live out life with faith, and to help others the way you've been helped, the way I was helped when I was drowning in a pool of booze, pain, and confusion.

It wasn't easy to take the high road with my school, or with the New York newspaper. But the incident did somehow make it clearer to me that I had a message to carry to other alcoholics and addicts. It was simple. No matter what shit life occasionally deals you, never lose sight of the fact that it will pass. There's no way that caving in during bad times by drinking and drugging, and losing one's sobriety to avoid uncomfortable feelings, is ever worth the hell you'll slip back into. I've tried to drink away the bad shit in my life but the bad shit just smelled worse when I woke up. If it was so worth getting your life back by getting into recovery, it makes no sense to let anything or anyone, *no matter what*, be important enough to make you unconscious again to real feeling. Living can really suck sometimes, but it can also get better, if we can muster up a little grace and acceptance.

"Go Buckeyes!"

To Be or Not to Be . . . **Happy?**

It had nothing to do with being a recovering alcoholic, middle-aged, or afraid of dying. The big three didn't even enter the picture. I was just sitting on my couch in my home office, not listening to any music, and not looking out of any window in particular, just ruminating over the fact that I wasn't ruminating over anything. Then it struck me, like a thoughtful, poison dart through my heart.

Things would be easier if they weren't the way they are. Yup, that's how I've been programmed to think ever since I could remember. I don't really know how I came to believe that the way things came to pass in life was generally not for my own good. Well, maybe I do. I'm sure that with over a million frequent-neurotic miles in therapy, I've already speculated plenty about the origins of my self-loathing and self-centeredness. Certainly, as long as I live feeling like the world revolves around my own miserable perceptions of myself, I'll continue to step in shit and feel like this most of the time. It's so easy for me to immediately feel like not only am I getting shafted but that if I'm not—I will be soon.

It's inordinately simple for me to overlook joy, even when it's slapping me in the face. I not only expect joy to end, but to be some kind of setup for a comedown. I have worn a happiness-proof vest ever since I can remember. I'd joke on stage that my grandfather "left his grief to science" and that "my grandmother knitted a suicide note," but those were really my feelings: about fear, about never being able to shake the idea that I don't deserve the right to pleasure. I had to almost kill myself with booze to start from scratch by choosing life over death. I didn't realize that it would be an uphill battle to accept life on its own terms and to take the good with the bad. I drank to avoid the bad feelings but also, and this is what is so heartbreaking to me, I drank to avoid the good feelings as well.

To finally say to myself that I want to be happy when happiness is around is not that easy, given that I've spent most of my life feeling undeserving and waiting for my own personal shitstorm to suddenly appear on the horizon. My outlook in general has always sucked. But when I dropped my own perspective in favor of God's spin on the universe, I took a big step toward letting in happiness. Until I was willing to keep my usually screwball, doomsday scenario out of the way, I didn't stand a chance to enjoy my life—sober or not.

That sense of never feeling content was my scummy disease hanging around, relentlessly continuing to kick my ass until I felt so weak that it made no sense to have feelings. So far I've kicked the shit out of addiction. And although it always hovers dangerously close, it's looking mighty frustrated. It knows that I just don't want to go back to that insanity. Every experiment I ever tried with alcohol (once I even had the thought that I might have a problem) failed. I don't need my own history to remind me of that. Many of my alcoholic pals have tried to orchestrate a way to still drink and have a life too and many are dead or have very little left of what can be considered an existence. If I start totaling up the good stuff that has happened to me *only because* I have battled, a day at a time, my alcoholism, there's no contest. Sobriety wins hands down.

Now when life sucks I know that it's just life and I didn't necessarily do anything to bring it on by carousing. I also now have a great belief that things can turn around for the better. When I was a drunk, hopeless and faithless, even if life took a turn for the better, I wouldn't have had a clue.

To be or not to be happy? It wasn't until I stopped drinking that I could even begin to know the answer to that. I know now that I have tasted more happiness than I ever thought imaginable. It's a bloody miracle without a Bloody Mary. It's just being, without projecting more than what's simply going down in the moment. It's feeling grateful for just being. It's being content when things suck, because there's a good chance they'll improve as long as I stay out of my own way.

There's an amazingly dangerous line between feeling powerless and having crummy self-esteem. I'm lucky in that I have both, and make a living with the latter. I can't tell you how great it feels being up on stage, sober, mocking myself with reckless abandon for laughs, getting applause, accolades, and a paycheck on top of it.

As far as I'm concerned, it couldn't have happened to a nicer, drunk comedian.

Excuse me, *recovering* drunk comedian.

Deathbed

For reasons I never want to understand, I hope and expect (that's the sad part) to have an audience around to witness my last lucid moments on my deathbed.

If I am in an introspective mood, I may have many pressing questions to ask—and perhaps, even things to say, for the last, or maybe first, time.

Should I blow my sobriety just before I split? Will ex-girlfriends be comfortable mingling? Is there a great one-liner to have ready when I depart? Will I be scared? Will I be looking forward to finally having a really lengthy vacation? Should I cancel future appointments out of courtesy? Should I care anymore about anything? Will I have regrets? Will I feel excited about the unknown? Can I finally be myself? Will I have the need to bullshit anymore? Can I admit anything I want without feeling guilty? Will I have a compulsion to make people laugh down to my last gasp? Will I want to make some sort of grandiose statement summing up how I feel about my lifetime? Will I worry about how quickly I'll be forgotten? Will I start guessing when everyone will have their first lighthearted moment, signaling the beginning of the end of their grieving for me? Will I think about tomorrow's headlines? Will a few key moments from my past streak across my mind? And will those be memories of the very events and feelings that I chose to avoid dealing with before I became deathly ill? Will I feel badly for the time I loved women just to feel appreciated? Will I be able to "sum up," by writing feebly on a pad near my bedside table, just what it is that my life meant? Will I still be paranoid that my feelings never really meant much to anyone? Will I finally come to terms with how unimportant I am? Is it conceivable that it won't matter how I'm feeling anymore? Will I find my death both poignant and meaningless at the same time? Will I impart amazing secrets to those around me? Or will I just close my eyes and lie there like some cold, formerly hot comedian? Is there a hope that I actually can have one big motherfucker of a spiritual awakening that will be so goddamn blinding that I will at once put every tormented second behind me? Will I have enough brainpower left to ask the nurse to turn off the TV? Will I remember to tell any-one there that it's okay to dial long distance on my phone after I conk? What music will I want to hear as I fade away? Will I freak and start shrieking just before I go, when I realize that I'll never be able to do it again and maybe could've enjoyed it more? Might I pos-sibly bite the dust, then be reincarnated and although in another body, still know it's really me? Will I meet my real maker? *Is* there a maker? Will he be anti-Semitic? Will I have to feel full of remorse after I run into souls who pissed me off before I croaked and smack the shit out of them? Will I be able to enjoy holding the hand of someone I love and feel her warmth and look into her moist eyes and reassure her that there is nothing to feel badly about down the line if she is sucking some other man's cock? Will I suddenly turn into a madman, scared out of my mind, and go out ranting for real, not just for effect, as Cagney did on his way to the electric chair in *Angels with Dirty Faces?* Will I know the moment before I expire that I tried to be decent? Will I have total forgiveness in my heart for all the unscrupulous, insensitive, self-serving people who went out of their way to fuck me over?

Will my deathbed, at the very least, have a comfortable mattress?

He Was a **Great Man**

Well, not exactly, but that's probably what I'd say to the mourners if I had the luxury of eulogizing myself at my own funeral. This would be sort of a dream come true for an up guy like me. My feeling is that since everyone in my life (except God) puts some kind of spin on me as to what and why and who and where I am, I at least deserve to get my licks in when it's me in that fuckin' casket.

I really don't want to scare people who show up to pay their last respects for me, but I feel that I owe it to my soul (before it gets too set in its ways) to put in my own two cents. At the risk of sounding cocky, I expect and want a lot of people at the *last good-bye* and the more crying the better, because I suffered a lot of emotional shit and it would do my corpse good to hear a little sobbing, albeit too little too late.

I don't want a small, private funeral. Not just because I will probably be forever narcissistic but also because I so rarely left my house when I was living, I think it would be nice to see people for a change, even if I am *dead*. So come on down!!!

I have this gut feeling that if I made a "live" appearance it would be a friendly and cool visitation and everyone would have a sense of calm about it. Everyone except former "dates from hell" who are still actresses and see my demise as a great opportunity to showcase. As I've mentioned before, if I don't settle down in a good relationship but instead drop dead while still adolescently dating much younger women, I'm certain that my memorial service will mean nothing more to these vixens than a golden opportunity to display some histrionics (after catching a glimpse of some industry heavies in the synagogue) with the hopes of turning some heads (not mine anymore) and getting considered for a future role. After first feigning screams to plant a seed for future auditions for a potential horror-flick part, they would then, apparently out of the blue, go into powerful, well-rehearsed monologues from some Mamet play while paying lip service to my death by frivolously changing a few words here and there to refer to things that clearly come from my life—like too much masturbation and self-pity, my limitless quantity of neediness, or my sickening, debilitating habit of believing that I never did enough for the jerky people who knew how to make me feel guilty and worthless if I didn't go to bat for them. I always crumble, even to manipulative, unscrupulous scumbags who cry out that if I don't come through they have no options left, which to me means they will either kill themselves or worse, become impressionists. (Actually, I bet there have been a few inspired impressionists down through the ages but in reaction to the amazing lack of *really genuine* people in my life, the last type of act *I* enjoy is someone not only not being himself but pretending, and usually poorly, to be someone else who, chances are, I didn't like in the first place.)

Meanwhile back at my funeral, the last few Dylan, Hendrix, Procol Harum, Little Feat, Neil Young, Beatles, and probably Lou Reed tunes (perhaps "New Sensation" thrown in for lasting good measure) come to an end. A surviving best friend, or maybe my current lady (God forbid that I might have found a wife by then, someone who *really* got me and would be totally hip to the fact that I would get a murderous kick out of her wearing a veil, looking not unlike Jackie O. did at Jack's funeral), comes up to the mike and asks tearfully if there are any people who would like to say a few words. They do and of course someone will have the chutzpah to tell a killer joke about something that everyone knows about me and the laughs will break the ice. This sets off a mock-filled roast and everyone, out of sheer faith, thinks it is best that they all laugh (believing it will make it easier for them to leave soon; and later that night, will act as if the mourning is over, having recovered sufficiently) until yours truly shocks the shit out of them as I materialize and float upward, cloaked in a drop-dead gorgeous, timeless, black Armani suit, and set the record straight.

Although you are dead as a doornail, it turns out that you can use the shit that you request to be buried with you, and although I tried *one day at a time* to remain sober, I have a bottle of Drambuie requested just in case I decide during a bad afterlife experience to go off the wagon. I also have a tape of the Knicks beating the Lakers in 1970 just in case I locate a heavenly VCR; Acqua di Selva, my favorite cologne, just in case I go back to my whoring ways since I am very, very single again; and some risotto from a favorite Italian restaurant just in case it stays forever fresh and/or somehow keeps reproducing like some sort of hydra (that weird bug or insect or whatever the fuck it is that I just couldn't ever fathom and was repulsed by in junior high school biology class, as I chopped the motherfucker into zillions of pieces, only to have it laugh in some strange, creepy whisper as it effortlessly became a new "thing" with a new lease on life) to keep me fed. Lastly I have a few favorite albums and maybe the novel *Something Happened* by the inimitable Joseph Heller to have around to reread just in case I need my spirits lifted, which always happens when I compare myself to the miserable main character in his masterpiece, just in case I eternally remain chronically depressed in the hereafter.

As soon as I hover over and position the cheap mike (all places of worship are known to have one, as if they were some crummy coffeehouse in Greenwich Village) to make sure I am heard, I hear instead a silence unlike any I have ever experienced. It is particularly weird coming from a group of almost a thousand people, most of whom make their living listening to themselves talk about themselves (as I did).

It's bizarre. Not only does everyone just stare at me but no one (as I predicted) appears freaked and, thankfully, no heart attacks occur, but tears, and I mean tons of them, just keep rolling down everyone's cheeks. No one makes a sound or blows a nose or anything; they just stare directly at me. And I look good too, not just because of my newfound understanding and clarity, or because of the Armani threads, but because I actually have a slight tan due to a windburn suffered from my strange new way of spirit travel.

As I collect my thoughts for a brief moment and decide not to give away any of the secrets of the otherworld, I notice they are all saddened and just weep and weep, making it very hard for me to muster my composure before giving what I think is going to be an almost Christ-like speech (and don't make me tell you what I know about him now—not that it's negative but let's just say he's more human than I ever thought) intended to benefit my mourners while they still have a chance on earth to be more compassionate.

Well, long story short, "a cat heavy on the wingspread" from the *unknown* (that's sort of a little inside dope on what we hip deceased call an angel with seniority) gets my attention, unbeknownst to anyone at my funeral, and tells me that the speech I am planning to make, which had to be cleared, didn't go over with "the big guy" (yeah, he really has time for every little thing . . . who knew?— and yeah, sorry gals, he's a guy but . . . oh never mind, you'll find out) and I have to quickly plan something different to say. I'm totally unprepared but I trust it will be the right thing, because God's pretty learned about this sort of shit.

I smile, blow a kiss, take a deep breath, wait for everyone to stop crying, and say (with a big grin on my face so no one thinks I am passing judgment) "WHAT GOES AROUND COMES AROUND," and I disappear forever.

Reflections After **Seeing Mom in Her Rest Home**

When I was a drunk, I usually didn't really care exactly where I was, but sober, watching my mother die and experiencing what she probably was oblivious to, I had the odd sensation that I didn't know where I *wanted* to be. My mother's condition left her in a place that was heartbreaking. The grounds were pretty enough but the endgame was oppressive. Here she was, a pretty, eighty-six-year-old woman with three kids, tons of grandchildren and great-grandchildren, and yet it was clear she was unclear about most everything now, except her desire to get through each second with a bare minimum of anguish.

Mom would often say to me directly, about myself, "I wish he was here." I had no idea what that meant . . . exactly. Particularly on the first night while visiting her in the home, as I tickled her arms, trying to vamp in a way, to give myself some time to gather enough mental toughness to deal with a woman who clearly had little concept of what had happened to her or where she was and what the future held.

"I have to go to the bathroom," she would tell her sweet private aide, when we still had aides around the clock. But after a while it was clear that we didn't know whether she meant it or not.

She also had memories or maybe thoughts that made her feel that she was many, many years younger. Oftentimes it was hard to watch. And occasionally I would have to dart out of the room over something that I found out was commonplace with people in her condition . . . they just want to be naked. She seemed to want to assert the sexuality that she'd exhibited as a young woman, or perhaps suppressed as an adult.

Her defense mechanisms were gone.

Narcissism had lost its mirror.

She was innocent and sweet.

She stared at me, not quite sure who I was. On occasion when I would bring up old stories and somehow sneak in the fact that it was me telling them, then perhaps, and only then, did she know I was there.

But it doesn't matter. If it did I'd be beyond selfish. She mostly displayed herself, inclined to be just in the moment. And most moments were confusing, and I'm sure irritating. She was baffled most of the time. When a part of her brain tried to make sense of almost anything she became visibly agitated. Her sight was shot as well. Her memory only seemed to work if it was jarred by events of a time long past. Her eyes revealed a vacant numbness to the present and future, but she would come alive when recollection shattered the bubble, and would perk up, much like a baby being nurtured.

Before her stroke, my mother's emotional self-protectiveness made it almost always impossible for either one of us to express our real feelings to each other. Her authentic emotions were securely tucked away. She must have had them so crushed so many times by countless family members and adolescent traumas that to risk being her real self seemed more like a *punishment-in-waiting*. Consequently, growing up around her I sadly felt less like a son, and more like a peril. Unfortunately she had to trade a lot of her maternal instincts for survival instincts.

Now, it doesn't matter too much what I wanted to say to her because it really couldn't matter; it wouldn't register anymore. I felt an overwhelming sadness for this woman, who I don't believe ever had a chance to be comfortable with herself. She could never risk being authentic, and most probably felt endangered or threatened by anyone who dared to be their own person. Sure she was controlling for most of my childhood, but as I sat by her side, and she stared blankly into her futureless future, I started to sob. Intuitively and considerately, my sister left us alone. This nursing facility is so close to my sister's home that in many ways I felt it was quite necessary for another family member who doesn't live close by to be able to bear (for a change) some of the heavy burden of experiencing one's mother in such a condition. At any rate, my sister must've also requested that the aide give us privacy for an entire day, and her instincts were right on. There also seemed to be a force field that day outside the door of the little room that was keeping people away.

Loving energy was supplied by my mom's miracle roommate, Mary, who I came to call "Sweet Mary." My first day there my attention was focused on my mother, who was oblivious to my presence, but almost within moments after my sister introduced me to Mary, she wheeled over next to me.

I faintly heard my sister explain Mary's illness. Mary had been maddeningly married to a wheelchair from a very early age after being stricken with cerebral palsy, and had never had much else in life other than pity (and hopefully an ongoing, private nurturing of her own soul). Throughout this sad exposition, all I saw on Mary's face was this huge grin, which soon produced a loud, almost orgasmic moan when she and I locked eyes and fell in love. The kind of feeling I had was something that made the lust a strange couple might feel, eyeing one another after a few drinks at a bar on a Friday night, seem childish by comparison. She and I seemed instantly to attach an instant compassion and a mutual respect to one another. And my gut told me immediately that among all the people I've ever known, who will all someday meet their maker, it's a lock that Mary will be one of the few to get an eternal courtside seat next to God.

My own pity and unease around her had melted away quickly with her smile. I rubbed her back, and whispered to her that she had *God's smile*, and that I felt how spiritual she was. She must have understood because almost at once she broke into an enormous grin. She rocked back in her wheelchair gleefully and let out a soft "coo," which sounded like a mating call. At first I was embarrassed because it seemed obvious to those around us that I was having some kind of really positive impact on her, and their attention made me momentarily self-conscious. But it was clear that we had an out-of-this-world connection, and her happiness with me, her new friend (I just know she felt my compassion and tenderness towards her), made me almost want to do cartwheels. I made her smile and kick up a storm in that ever-present mechanical chair.

Mary was just one of hundreds of women in this facility playing out life's shitty hand at the end of their time on the planet, all with heart-wrenching maladies and various diseases that left them in varying degrees of pain, helpless and dependent on any decent soul who might appear. Perhaps the hardest residents for me to be around were those who were unable to express themselves: those who obviously had passions and thoughts that I'm certain were deep and profound, though hidden forever by their tortured inability to share them.

Now my mother wasn't able to express herself anymore, or at least couldn't communicate in a way that I knew for sure what she felt.

She slept most of the time I was there. This was probably a good thing because when she was awake, she called me by another name. And her dreams (provided they weren't nightmares) must've been the best time of her day. When occasionally she awoke and glanced around, she looked almost like a little bird in a makeshift nest, complete with white sheets and a bedpan, full of curiosity one moment, frightened and instinctively looking for her mother the next. She hadn't lost her mind, but it seemed like it, because she wasn't able to use it. I couldn't help but feel that my mother was a baby again, and I was a parent to her. Witnessing, in effect, the end of a personality is devastating.

Who could my mother look to anymore? Who had she ever had to look to? Her own mother had died so young—thirty-five years

younger than my mother was now. I'm not sure what kind of relationship my mother had with the rest of her family. It seemed to vac-
illate so much and also to be sort of secretive, especially her
relationship with my father. But that didn't seem to matter so much
now. The only thing that mattered was this overpowering need I had
to try to communicate to her my thought (my feeling) that she'd
done the best she could, and that I loved her.

Many times she called me "Momma." She called a lot of people
that. It was heartbreaking. She needed mothering. I wondered how
I might have responded to this before recovery, when I was still
angry for not getting the type of mothering that *I* needed. I had been
confused by the mothering I'd gotten most of the time, but now I
was starting to feel oddly guilty about having been too young to
comprehend why she may have said the things she did that angered
me and hurt my feelings. I felt guilty that I'd never taken into
account all the shit she'd had to overcome. I mean, suddenly losing
her own mother while she herself was only in her late thirties must
have been very difficult. And after not having much of a relationship
with her father, she then had to deal with a husband working
around the clock. Perhaps she was running on empty by the time I
needed her understanding.

My mother wasn't comfortable looking for the gold within herself or in people close to her, and always had an easier time praising
people who were acquaintances. She was so strung out on unhappiness, she could hardly let other people's joy in. During my career,
she seemed almost to have no choice but to appear jealous of my
successes. Now I realized that perhaps that was the only way she
could reveal her approval or pride. Perhaps I was just another threat.
Or perhaps I represented a part of her that she'd never gotten to
know or express. We were cut from the same cloth, and maybe she
couldn't fathom my good fortune so close to her. So instead of celebrating her loved ones' joys with ease, she was locked into her own
emotional prison, unable to let anyone else's luck rub off on her, or
bring her pleasure. It was almost as if she wouldn't allow herself to
feel content. She would distort—almost mangle—the goodwill and

happiness that emanated from others. And this made it feel to me not only like my feelings were being discarded, but that maternal validation was for the most part unobtainable. If you wanted something too badly, she seemed to sense it, and her own demons paraded around and blocked her attempt to embrace you in the way you felt you deserved. At least that's how I felt. And I just happened to be her son.

That was the rub, for both of us.

I left my home for college early enough in life, way before I became alcoholic. Booze didn't fuck up this relationship; a lack of communication about too many things fucked it up. But now, when she didn't know who she was or who she was talking to, it would inevitably remind me of my own occasional blackouts and how frightening they had been. There'd been times when I was completely unaware of what I might have done just hours before. And now, she was in a perpetual blackout, and it made me feel badly for her, but also feel amazingly lucky for myself, in spite of the circumstances. Because I still had the choice to never again initiate my own darkness if I didn't want to.

I started to brush her hair. She loved it. She got a weird little smile on her face that seemed to express the hundreds of thousands of hours that she was never touched gently, or stroked enough, as a woman. I don't know. Like I said, I'm very unclear about her marriage with my dad, but it's certain he was a workaholic, and she'd spent a lot of time alone. Plus, like I said, the word on the family street was that she didn't have the greatest relationship with her own father, and maybe a lot of her died along with her mother; it was hard not to feel that she was anxious to join my grandmother, whom I hardly remember, except as being kind, stocky, always smiling, and always pleasing others. I was only five when she passed on.

And my mother, who now would let me stroke her hair at the age of eighty-five, was someone I never really knew either.

As I brushed her graying hair that still looked very elegant, she managed to ask me if I was "going to sleep," but I told her no. I just wanted to keep brushing her hair. She nodded and seemed happy about that, so I just kept brushing and brushing, afraid that if I stopped she would panic. I was worried because this was the first time I was ever really alone with her in this condition, and felt helpless and almost childlike, not knowing what to do short of screaming for help.

"How does it feel, Mom?"

"Great, Momma."

Before I knew it I was crying. I just wept and wept and kept brushing over and over with this tiny brush, as she just smiled probably never even seeing me cry because she had practically no vision left.

"I'm getting tired, Momma," she weakly chimed.

"Then you can go back to sleep, honey. Is it okay if I just keep brushing your hair?"

She nodded, then slid down into a position that was more conducive to sleeping.

It was the most vulnerable I had ever seen my mother. She had no defenses, no agendas, no chores for me to do, no judgments about anything. She was able to be touched, literally, and enjoy it. She seemed, maybe for the first time I can remember, not only to be able to take in something pleasurable, but also not to be quick on the trigger to ruin it by firing off an unnecessary comment. In a bizarre way she was teaching me something. I've never been able to let people help me without feeling instantly obligated, but I have been one to passive-aggressively try to make people feel uneasy and guilty when I was *so sure* that I was right, but wasn't capable of being direct. I, too, have lived most of my life ready to fire insensitive salvos (without much thought or consideration) when I felt I was being attacked—or even when I wasn't. *The OTHER Great Depression* is not just a silly title but a state of mind I've endured that has made it almost impossible for me to enjoy life or appreciate the luxury of just being alive. As long as I felt I was going to be unfairly judged or misunderstood (which seemed like all the time) this funk would envelop me. If I hadn't become an alcoholic and bottomed, I probably never would have grown to appreciate living as I do now.

Impulsively I reached out and grabbed her hand. She grabbed mine back much the way a baby grabs onto the finger of an adult. I'd never felt as strong around her before. It is such a tragedy that I was able to feel strong and helpful and loving to her only when she was in this condition, and yet there was something strangely spiritual about it, and the room seemed to become a beautiful vacuum in time, a place where we could both just love one another without all the bullshit, the defensiveness and pettiness. I was able to remove myself from all the past crap that had prevented us from truly having a healthy, dynamic, mother-son relationship. I understood at my core just how much of a victim she had been herself, and the awful self-loathing that comes with a lack of strong emotional support. I imagined she might have had no choice but to take the path of narcissism, in order to shield herself from any further hurt. People choose their weapons precisely to protect themselves against the feelings at their center. I chose laughter for validation and alcohol for cover.

One of the most wonderful developments in my mother's middle age was how she thrived on the applause she garnered from her active role in community theater. For almost a quarter of a century after her husband died, *she seemed most alive* when on stage and away from family situations. It was astounding to me to realize that both my parents, who seemed so isolated to me growing up, sought out the very same validation—praise from strangers—that for most of my adult life was the *only* real good feeling to penetrate *my* being.

I squeezed my mother's hand gently, but firmly enough to get her attention.   ·

"Do you know who this is?"

"I think so."

"It's your baby boy."

"Richie?"

"Uh-huh. I love you, Mom."

"I love you."

"Look at me . . . Can you see me?"

"Uh-huh."

"I want you to know that it is very clear to me that you had very little help in raising a family and had so little time to understand me, but darling—I think that you did give me a lot. You came to all of my Little League games. You helped me with homework . . . you never seemed to get enough credit for all that you did."

She nodded.

I'd connected with her. She'd felt so unappreciated. No strange suit of clothes for me.

"I want you to know that I love you and care about you and thank you for everything you did to help me and . . ."

She was starting to fade out. Intuitively, as if things were back to normal, and she was abandoning me by choice rather than because she had no choice, I had a childish desire to bring up negative feelings that will always be huddling around in my consciousness about our relationship. But then just as quickly as the thought came, it left, and we broke through to a sweeter realm.

"Do you hear me, Mom? Do you know it's me? Richie? That I appreciate everything you ever did for me?"

She smiled and communicated with a tugging at my hand, then just as quickly fell asleep, like the child she now was.

I sat there just crying for about an hour. I'd gained and lost a mother all at the same time, and the experience was too complicated for anything but tears.

I'm not angry anymore. She doesn't feel guilty anymore.

All my resentments have disappeared and hopefully so have hers.

Peacefulness comes too late a lot in life.

Mom and I can't go back without a Rod Serling to help us, but we surely had a meeting of minds and finally of hearts.

Superbowl Sunday, 2000

My mother died today. Almost 29 years to the day, at around the same time, that *another* parent died. Now my mom is all soul as well, with no deteriorating body or mind to contend with. When my dad died in '71, it was my brother who called to tell me; today it was my sister who made the call. I guess I'll never have to make that kind of call to anyone. I guess that's one of the weird perks of being the baby in the family; you get hand-me-down bad news. The first thing I did after hearing of her death was mournfully embrace my girlfriend for strength. Then I told her that I'd like to be alone for a while, and once again realized that I finally had a woman in my life who allowed me to be myself. She quietly dressed and went back to her place, letting me know she was available for whatever I needed.

Within moments I felt the need to e-mail lots of recovering addict pals of mine to tell them that I'd be away for a while, and this is yet another example that *no matter what happens* in our lives addicts can't drink or use over it. I immediately felt as if my mother had given me the opportunity to spread the message that recovery is all-important. Even under the saddest of circumstances, I should try to set some sort of example for others. I sat alone for a while knowing that within a few hours I would have to get involved with canceling shows in Boston later in the week, and hoped it wouldn't cause showbiz to rear its ugly "all about money" head. Fortunately, representatives who handle some of these affairs for me took on the burden of making the phone calls, and the nightclub people were more than understanding. With the shows out of the way, I focused on how I was to deal with my feelings about being parentless for real. After I packed, I chose to sit down and write. I couldn't cry. I'd cried plenty already. I just wanted to keep my relatively new, sober clarity on things, to enable me to focus on the reality of her death, not to be blurred in any way, and really try to comprehend the loss.

My mother was sort of unselfish in a selfish way. She gave so much to others, but it seemed as though she couldn't give a thing that meant anything sacred to herself. Consequently, her giving many times didn't feel like it was pure, but rather attached to some self-absorbed notion that the act of giving was more important in what it represented to her than in what it might mean to the person who was receiving it. This was not always the case, but certainly she made it lots easier for total strangers to receive her love than those close to her. This tragic quality of people-pleasing most anyone who wasn't close to the nest was a trait that seemed to be a common thread in my DNA as well.

She seemed to have so much guilt and self-loathing that it rendered her almost incapable of rooting for loved ones. Their success seemed to illustrate just how much she wasn't able to have. For a personality like hers, an all-you-can-eat smorgasbord was a horror. She felt she didn't deserve such open-ended opportunity for self-gratification and almost always ate something at home before she got there, so she'd be full while everyone else pigged out and had a ball.

She always rooted for the underdog until the underdog started to bark with confidence. When I started to gain strength as a human being and felt more secure about who I was, my own mother sadly didn't have the wherewithal to acknowledge and appreciate my growth. When I had successes, she seemed to think they were just about showing her up, and often even wanted to somehow take credit for them. For many decades we weren't on the same team. I desperately wanted to psychically be traded for a son to be named later. She wanted me to stay in the home-team uniform but somehow bench myself. I felt like the designated loser. I felt so invalidated that it was as if even while she carried me in her womb a Vacancy sign might have been hanging there. The biggest hurt of all was her treating my admission to being an alcoholic as merely a horrid reflection of her inadequacies as a mother, and consequently having to deny the reality of it. In fact, our last blowout was her matter-of-factly denying that I was an alcoholic even when I wholeheartedly admitted it and was addressing it and in recovery. She seemed embarrassed and emotionally ran for cover, and I lost my temper. Once again, what should have been a celebratory moment about *my* success became for me another reminder of her unfortunate inability to take pride in my courage.

It's so hard to forgive someone for indefensible behavior, especially when that someone is your own mother. And I guess sometimes the act of forgiving takes a lot of balls, especially if you think you're losing them in the deed. But when I sat with her in the rest home, while she was still alive, watching her rapidly disappearing into her own memory bank, still managing to remain physically beautiful even though she no doubt felt like shit (when she could even be aware of herself), there was a period of time, like there never was before and never will be again *as far as I know*, when I knew I had finally let her off the hook.

Mother and son, both saddled with self-pity and self-centeredness for most of our lives, were no longer at odds, but finally at peace with one another.

I wish my mother well floating around in the universe, free from earthly burdens, predispositions, and pressures. Hopefully she can finally feel that she doesn't have to control everything in order to protect herself from hurt, and that she has something to give that comes from a source far greater and more accepting than she'd ever imagined.

I'm already hearing *my private* God talking through her, giving me strength to carry on. I can see now that this woman, my mom, who often fought and judged and ridiculed and on rare occasions bravely went to bat for me, always wanted deep down to love me unconditionally, but her maternal instincts were sadly repressed by her own feelings of worthlessness. She never got the kind of support that I eventually received after sobering up, and didn't have any tools to help her walk through her own fear. It breaks my heart. I so understand the kind of pain she must have felt, hearing her own bitter words that she must have known didn't come from her real self. I'm proud that I stayed sober throughout her illness and up until the time she departed, and let her see and hear the real me again. Only God knows what she is able to do now, freed from her mortal chains of guilt, depression, and self-loathing.

Finally she has a shot to be an angel, and not just for others or appearances, but, I pray, finally for herself.

I'm Waving a **White Flag** to Every Fuckin' Thing from Now on, Because Almost Every Fuckin' Thing Drives Me Crazy, and I Can't Seem to Help Myself Without Believing in a God to Relieve Me of My Pain— So, I Hereby Turn in My Agnostic Badge for Life

It dawned on me yet again this morning, for probably the billionth time, that even though I wasn't drinking today, and thankfully had no intention to, I still felt like a mess. I suddenly had this feeling that I could never love my girlfriend the way she loves me; was cocksure that without cheating on her or getting high in some way, whether through some sort of medicated buzz or by creating some drama that would make me feel that I was living more on the edge—my former comfort zone of insanity—that I was destined to be unhappy evermore.

Nice way to wake up, huh? Even though the Yankees won again and the Mets crushed the Braves last night, it meant nothing. Even though I had just hired an enthusiastic new personal manager, it meant nothing. Being alive meant very little. Not staggering around my house or some bar drunk left me feeling very short of grateful. I was on a negative roll that would lead me into a funk of hopelessness that I knew from experience would lead me to drinking again.

The only way I stopped drinking and killing myself was to one day admit, finally, that I was absolutely powerless over my craving for alcohol and had to force myself to surrender to my disease and find some sort of guiding power that I could tap into, twenty-four-seven, one far wiser and stronger than little old, self-absorbed me, to help me through life. I never again wanted to make the mistake of thinking I knew how to save myself. It was murder for a while, in the beginning, to wave that white flag for help, but I was so desperate I gave it a shot. And yet today, there wasn't a truck big enough to carry enough white flags for all the addictions I needed to surrender to.

Then it struck me like an angelic bullet right through the heart of my self-centeredness that I had to surrender to everything that was driving me mad, and at least for today, it seemed that that was *everything*; the good, the bad, and even the ugly sugar rush. And as much as I crave ice cream, probably the craving that brings me to my knees faster, even when I'm sober, is my constant torment with women. I know that I've talked a lot about my intimacy problems with the opposite sex. Christ, I could write a book about it! Wait a minute, I have. But seriously, I kid my agony. It seemed pretty clear to me that since my mother had a tough time accepting me for my true self, I irrationally proceeded to endow all the women who loved me, particularly the decent ones, with the pathetic fallout, and have for my whole life been on the defensive with them. There hasn't been a chance in hell that I would be able to love anyone real, for any *real* length of time, before I would feel that I was being slowly swallowed up and practically having my soul snatched. I don't blame Mom anymore and I certainly don't blame the women who have done battle with my well-documented paranoia about succumbing to a significant other.

I blame me. I blame me for everything. And I don't mean to sound pitiful, just responsible. It took a long time to come to that conclusion, and I know that just admitting it won't instantly make my pain go away, just like admitting my powerlessness over alcohol didn't make my need for a drink instantly go away. I need to surrender again, and yet again. This time I need to get back in the ring with my fears and addictions and obsessions and just give up and let my God take care of everything. What a concierge this cat is, man!

And I've been doing so well these past few years not people-pleasing, I won't even think about how much to tip God if I run into him on the street. I'll just plan on tipping him heavy when I'm dead, if I'm lucky enough to meet him. Who knows, he might just accept my graciousness. After all, I finally accepted his grace. I just won't have any ice cream with him. I'm sure he'll understand.

I Forgot I Was **Jewish**

I was sitting in temple this morning waiting for a friend's newly adopted baby to be blessed by her rabbi. I am a Jew myself, but after listening for almost an hour to the congregation pray and sing along with the cantor's melodic voice, I felt like nothing more than a *Jewish Stranger in a Strange Land*.

It was like I was an extra in this passé science fiction film right out of the late fifties, the ones that as a kid I would watch over and over again, memorizing every line. But this was a sacred house of worship, not a scene out of *Godzilla*, and the words were a tad more significant than Raymond Burr saying something like, "He's big all right."

The prayers, at least, used to be more significant to me. Now, though the words were the same, I'd forgotten how to listen. And yet on occasion, the service sounded joyously familiar, and when I eerily recognized a certain portion, I nostalgically and pleasantly connected with my Judaic roots. Still, I wasn't connecting as much as I thought I should have.

Through the years I just sort of retreated from getting to know more about what being a Jew really means. I think I did this because, even though I felt Judaism had a very fair belief system and didn't impose on others of other faiths, the fact that fanatics—however unrepresentative of the majority—still pop out of every house or temple of worship turned me off to organized religion. Being a member of a people with such an uncanny determination to stay alive while on the run seemed more meaningful to me than the ancient theology of it all. Also, I withdrew because I couldn't shake the notion that, as beautiful as Judaism is (equally as beautiful as other religions—not cults, mind you, but the original ones), the dictatorial nature of most religions, which turns the children of all these Gods into such pitiful, hateful, and divided creatures, made me prefer to remain an observer of the bigger picture, rather than a participant who fosters the continuing divide. I like to plant my feet on the ground on a starry night and look at that moon and beyond, and think about nature and about whoever or whatever said "bang," rather than attaching it to all of this earthly chaos.

And yet, sitting in temple this Sabbath morning and taking in my people around me, their quiet reflection alternating with rousing praise of God that was so embedded in my Jewish upbringing, left me sitting there blankly, realizing how much tradition I'd walked away from. Even though I was really there to bear witness to this wonderful event, I was nevertheless ashamed to be sitting in a Jewish place of worship feeling like such an outcast. My skullcap felt more like a beret than anything else.

Many people in the synagogue recognized me and so I tried pathetically, mainly out of embarrassment, to mouth the words of some of the most well-known sections of prayers. I was very rusty. My acting sucked. If an anti-Semite was there, incognito, spying on me for some trashy flier, he or she would have realized that I was lip-synching—poorly—merely to make an impression of devotion. My chanting fell so far behind everyone else's it was as if I were taking Quaaludes again, and that my smile to my congregant fans was more of a prop showbiz grin than the dignified nod of a normal, average Jewish man partaking in a ritual that has been going on for thousands of years. But I sensed that there was this little holy kid inside of me from another era, who I have kept hidden from myself, most probably since the day after I had my bar mitzvah. Back then, with the pressure off at such a tender age to understand God, I ran away from my religion as if it were nothing more than a vice-principal standing in the way of my learning how properly to French-kiss a willing female admirer, or orchestrate an afternoon stickball game. No one close to me ever told me that God was an option that could possibly lessen the confusion and self-doubt that were already festering within me.

Almost forty years after I "became a man" at thirteen, and got all those fancy pens as gifts just a few months before Camelot came to Washington, I was still running away from the sacred traditions I'd studied in Hebrew school. And except for some sporadic Hebraic PR appearances down through the years, and those on only the holiest of Jewish holidays, I'd somehow misplaced my heritage. To me, being a Jew had more to do with reading the words on deli menus than it did with reading the Torah.

Maybe sitting there so soon after my mother died had something to do with me feeling so alienated from my own "chosen people." I was speculating during the service more than I was praying. Perhaps it was my hard work in *recovery* and its focus on taking some sort of spiritual path—which for me was a nondenominational process— that left me feeling so curiously isolated. I mean, on the one hand it was like I was home, and on the other I felt like I was crashing the party of my own religion. I had believed in a God who helped me stop drinking, but it dawned on me now that my God was faceless, and that left me panic-stricken.

As soon as the beautiful baby boy was blessed, I felt a pressing need to make a run for it. I split early and walked the streets around the synagogue to try to figure out if it was possible for me to actually begin to relearn and participate in the "story" of God from the Jewish tradition that was both born and instilled in me. Or was this impulse just hypocritical and guilt-driven? Did I really want to be a more engaged Jew, or did I just long to belong somewhere, spiritu-

ally, that would feel a little more concrete to me than my own lonely
spiritual path?

Or maybe what interested me had to do with getting me back *as a
whole person*, before I'd started to define my identity with booze, ova-
tions, and ejaculations with strangers.

There are certain beliefs in Judaism that I'd always found, and
still find, beautiful and believable. Yet through the years, after all the
bloodshed and murder and hypocrisy committed by different faiths
in the name of God (though I think it's fair to state that Jews have
long been far more persecuted than persecuting), I have soured on
most belief systems, particularly those so defensive of their own the-
oretical righteousness, so singular in their vision and their interpre-
tations of historic tales that people who differ from that conviction
are deemed not only outsiders, but souls without a compass.

That said, I still feel like a coward. Or maybe it's just that man-
made guilt shit creeping in. Jewish guilt. Now that's bullshit. Everyone feels guilty from time to time, except perhaps sociopaths and
attorneys. But I kid the legal profession. Seriously though, I wasn't
really a deserter so much as I was faithless. I had so little faith in
myself to begin with, let alone in some sort of God, that I just
couldn't get behind faking a huge orgasmic religious trip.

Since getting sober I have tried to develop my own faith in a
divine power, as far away from organized religion as possible—*until
this morning*. I don't think I was born-again but I was captivated,
especially watching the Jewish children who were worshiping, not
unlike myself, decades ago, all dressed up and glowing with innocence and blind faith. I was struck more by jealousy than by anything divine.

I felt like it was the forty-first year in the desert and all the other
Jews had gotten out and I was still wandering around like some poor
schmuck looking for a rabbi or a decent pastrami sandwich, *anything*
to make me feel like a Jew again. Either I'm just afraid to die without having an identifiable God or I actually had a spiritual awakening. When the rabbi momentarily held the baby, the little one began
to cry. He was as scared as I was, but that was because he needed to

be in his mother's arms. This was quickly remedied and the rabbi took it in stride and beautifully completed the blessings. The baby looked quite serene, although, let's face it, he has time to figure out who his God is. He has a great start. And he can even grow up and drink like a normal person. Lucky little son-of-a-gun.

I have less time to philosophize, can't drink anymore, and yet I'm certain that I can't stay sober without a continuing belief in some sort of God. I have my little private image of who God might be. I think Spinoza said that "God is everywhere." That's a cool concept and who am I to take issue with Spinoza, but winding up in temple and longing again for something more specific has left me floundering. I think I'll go and have another look at my bar mitzvah pens and see what sort of jolt I get. Come to think of it, I didn't really forget that I was Jewish, I just forgot why.

Something tells me that the answer will just come, without my screwy head having anything at all to do with it. I've played God long enough with my own existence and, oy vey, did I make a mess of things.

The way I look at it now is, there's a fifty-fifty chance that there's a God. If there is one, it would be better for me to study up a little on where my people came from, so that when I hit those pearly gates— the ones with a mezuzah on them—I won't be forced to spend an eternity in Hebrew summer school. Then I can be really psyched about starting a new sort of existence in that great beyond while looking for some intelligent, yet sumptuous angel who isn't looking for a real commitment. Look, I have intimacy issues. Old habits die hard, right? "Progress not perfection," some stranger once whispered in my ear and magically split.

Hey! I just remembered I was Jewish!

Shalom baby, whoever your God is. And if you don't believe in God, that's cool—but I have this bridge I want to sell you.

I'm Alive and That's Plenty

I'm holed up in some resort hotel in Florida, with the Atlantic Ocean just a few hundred yards away. I'm trapped in my room by my celebrity, keeping myself from happiness all by myself. The day seems endless with radio shows and TV newscasts and interviews and all I really want to do is be in my own bed and not do any of this anymore. At least for now, the three decades of making a living by trying to impress people with my humor has begun to eat away at me and make me feel like "Sober the Clown"—watch him make believe he's having a ball. I'm not. I'm tired. I'm getting over the Ohio State debacle and my mother's death and now have to promote this "person" I have become, who really just wants to be understood and appreciated without all the other perks. I mean it. I know how pitiful it sounds not to feel blessed for having led a life pretty much of my own making (though judged every step of the way) and yet, at the core of all the hard work is this bottomless pit of despair and loneliness that I somehow seem to be rising out of the longer I stay sober and the more I let in the love of my girlfriend. It's scary to think about this, but I might have to let go of the need to make people laugh because it's too hard to treat it as a gift lately, rather than as a role I took on ages ago in order to survive.

I know this will pass eventually and I will again get excited about making others laugh out loud and forget their own bullshit. I've been through this before. Yet, this time, perhaps because I've been able to come through so much anguish and frustration lately without a drink, I have a new yearning to express myself in a way that is more quiet and less public. I fantasize now not about getting laughs, but rather moving people in other ways—perhaps through drama or writing—and not caring so much about my own persona but more about my own mental health and well-being. I feel like I'm growing out of a very old, alcoholic skin and the new "me" doesn't need as much attention.

I'm alive and that's plenty.

That may sound stupid, but I think I'm finally getting somewhere. My whole life I have been searching for something, be it some purpose, recognition, happiness—whatever. But now, even when I get frustrated creatively or feel frightened about trying to love and be loved, it seems easier to get by each painful moment. It's starting to feel like I *am* the moment, and for so long the moments owned me. I could always understand how billionaires were sometimes miserable and poor people sometimes full of life. What I never understood was exactly what *I* was supposed to feel like. Man, it really is something, this sobriety. This sudden rush of inexplicable contentment amidst so much anxiety has to emanate from finally feeling and dealing sober with all the feelings I cut off for too long.

It was a bitch at first, but now I can't imagine going back to hiding anymore. Maybe this new surge of feelings and ideas has to do with the tragic fact that many people I know and love are terminally ill, unhappy, or in some sort of denial about all sorts of crazy shit, and it saddens me beyond words. I have also taken a lot of hits the past few years both emotionally and creatively, but especially in professional endeavors that didn't pan out. But I also have done my best work, and I've finally figured out that it doesn't really mean a damn thing if I attach expectations to my own accomplishments. I have slowly discounted what others think of me, and rather have started to think how I feel about myself. It's so fuckin' odd, but I swear to God, for the first time—*I'm just alive and that's plenty.*

I guess it bears repeating.

Jigsaw Man

I've been sitting around lately feeling overwhelmed with all the aspects of my life that are causing a traffic jam to nirvana. At the same time I feel a tremendous sense of pride about being a little stuck, because I'm not out of control. I not only accept all of this momentary confusion but also can actually deal with it, one thing at a time, one day at a time.

I have so many things going on in my life simultaneously—some good, some shit, some fearful—yet none of it freaks me out anymore except maybe the possibility of dying too soon. But in actuality, I'm more fearful of drinking again than dropping dead. I swear. And let me tell you, man, that's a big fucking breakthrough for a recovering alcoholic like me. It would be a glorious revelation for any drunk on the wagon. Late the other evening, and with a weird feeling of accomplishment after so many years of self-induced insanity, I realized what a feat it was to be sober and actually sit alone with all this "stuff" in my head, and to actually be able to visualize on the coffee table in front of me a huge jigsaw puzzle in my own likeness. Though not quite interlocking smoothly, each piece appeared pristinely separate and yet necessary to the whole. They represented the multitude of feelings and the many aspects of my real individuality, warts and all. In accepting life on its own terms, each piece is at last being keenly noticed, and I am held responsible for the picture I create. And I like it. I own myself again. And maybe for the first time, I'm starting to make sense to myself only when I place myself in the universe, and out of my own world. It's so much easier to just be a part of the universe than to be your own universe.

To be frank, I have a lot of conspiracy theories about myself. Especially regarding when and where and how I got so caught up in me and became so lost. But, in the final analysis, it doesn't amount to a hill of beans because all I have is today. Once I figured that out, the rest of the puzzle kind of fell into place. The future no longer exists for me and the past is easier to deal with watching the History Channel. Unless of course I'm on it.

I sure didn't know too much about me for most of my childhood. All I cared about was pleasing others. Doing things that were what *I* thought *they* expected, or *not* doing things—like being honest from my heart—because I feared that it would cause them to drop dead (my father being the prime candidate). I guess when I got sick of walking through life on that *dreadmill,* I tried to keep most of my gut feelings tucked away, and stumbled into the very secure but blinding world of alcoholism. What you don't see is what you don't get.

When I was alcoholic I never would have seen the *jigsaw man* as I did that night, staring right back at me. Call it a hallucination. I know it's not. It's a sober, visual gift to myself, one coming from a mind starting to let acceptance and forgiveness sneak in. This vision never could have existed back in the bad old days. I would have been too high, too tired, or too scared to see it.

You can't be whole without at least recognizing your parts. After I bottomed out I cracked; then, like some tragic, porcelain poseur, I fell until I hit and shattered against some sort of concrete awareness that I was fucked and had split into a million fragments. Then I slowly started to put all my tortured, isolated pieces back together again, like some recovered, lucky, neurotic, Jewish Humpty Dumpty, until finally I recognized myself again, puzzle piece by puzzle piece. There was a message in the bottle, and that was to get out of it.

The really cool thing about digging myself in this image of a jigsaw puzzle is that a lot of these parts, although they fit me perfectly, make me feel imperfect this go-round, but it doesn't seem to bother me much. In fact, it's a groove to be imperfect. There's so much more to strive for and look forward to when you feel human and not alcoholically divine. Blind faith is a hell of a lot easier for me to handle now than blind drunkenness.

Seeing is believing. Of course, I'm still insecure as a motherfucker so I tend to be on the blind side when it comes to how much progress I've made—until the puzzle appeared. Wa-hoo! Holy Mackerel! I guess I had one of those spiritual awakenings again, brother!

Hallelujah! The puzzle looked pretty damn good. Oh yeah, I mean my posture sucked and my hair is getting gray, and I even saw a little rosacea on a few of the pieces around my nose and cheeks (even the puzzle suffers from stress), but right now, I wouldn't want to change a thing.

"I put myself together again. Ain't that a bitch!" Then I think how it's downright puzzling I didn't do this a lot sooner. "Jesus, I allowed myself to feel good for a whole two seconds," I say, out loud to myself, in an insulting tone.

"Chill the fuck out," I quickly retort, sticking up for the real me. It's a start. A great big huge one.

I had a sober vision, baby! And though you couldn't see it, even if you were sitting beside me, and might even think that I have a few screws loose, I swear to God, there are no pieces missing.

Tonight at least, I'm at *peace* with myself.

Don't Take **My Word** for It

A few years ago I vividly remember sitting with the first blank page of this book, confronted by what appeared to be the insurmountable task of telling my drunken tale and frightened of its public consequences. Oftentimes I sat motionless for hours, as if mummified, just doodling random thoughts or just aimlessly wandering around my house thinking that my story was meaningless. I vacillated between feeling heroic for spilling my guts and simultaneously pathetic in even thinking that it could mean anything to anyone.

One of the earliest drunken memories I had floating around in my head back then while jotting down my history of alienation, low self-esteem, and debauchery was the night I humiliated myself, high as a kite, in front of Bruce Springsteen. This then led me to remember a lyric of his that I heard while I was still a drunk, and a year before the ugly incident.

I was in Rome, oh glorious Rome, back in the early nineties, sitting in my amazing penthouse suite at the Hotel de la Ville, just off the Spanish Steps, on some publicity tour for a film I had shot a year before. I basically had lots of time to kill, sights to see, and champagne to drink with very little PR work demanded of me. As usual (and in particular at this time in my life, when alcohol controlled me, and was unabashedly squeezing my life out of me, making it impossible to achieve any faith other than believing in the glory of getting wasted) I did my work professionally and then let the demons take over when I felt there was nothing to lose by getting unconscious.

I had also hooked up on this trip with my New York artist-genius mentor, Carl Titolo, many of whose paintings now bless my home, and who was there with his wife on sabbatical from his teaching gig. But what should have been a joyous occasion to share this splendiferous city with my beloved pal and his angelic wife turned into a nightmare.

One night they invited me to dine at a favorite eatery of theirs run by a beautiful man with rosy cheeks who was thrilled that a "movie star"—that would be me—was going to come to his family-run establishment. I had just done some local TV and plugged the joint, so when I arrived I was greeted like a superstar. Sadly, my status as a person began to shrivel in direct proportion to the large amounts of alcohol I began consuming.

On paper it seemed that I had it all, and yet I had nothing. I was in one of the greatest cities in the world, on a hit TV show back in the States, promoting a new film, and surrounded by some of my best friends; and yet at my core I was a desperately unhappy man and an alcoholic. The dinner turned into a drunken, Fellini-esque horror show. I was the director, the star, and the sole reason the evening turned into a nightmare. I was so wasted that I wound up humiliating not just myself (although I didn't realize it at the time) but almost anyone in my path. I was a drunken, selfish twister with my decency buried so deeply below my disease that the Richard Lewis people knew and loved was long gone. I was loud, obnoxious, annoying, insensitive, pompous, and out of control.

Two days later—I needed some time to sleep the disgust off—I made my amends to the Titolos and asked them to convey my apologies in Italian to their restaurant buddy. My pals accepted my amends although it was apparent that they were worried about me. Then they told me a most remarkable tale. It was their sweet way, so it seemed, to gently illustrate to me just how fucked up I had become. Apparently, the day after my drunken theatrics, this sweet, little Italian man, a man who only knew me because I had promoted his place on TV and who had then treated me like royalty, peddled on his little bicycle many, many miles to where the Titolos were staying simply to say, in very broken English, *"I'm worried about your friend."* Then he split like a chubby, Italian version of the Lone Ranger and cycled back the long distance to his restaurant to prepare for that night's dinner. His trek was almost surreal. It was a journey by a stranger who had somehow looked deep enough into my glazed-over eyes two nights before and seen a decent person on his way out. He was, as I perceive it now, an instrument of God, who needed to tell my friends what he thought. He was on a bicycle built for two even if I didn't want to know about it. At that time, his concern was not only wasted but just made me want to drink even more. I felt cornered by kindness.

Carl and his wife related this story to me while I was still hungover and guilt-ridden and gloomy as we looked out at the glorious vista of Rome. It really is hard to feel *gloomy* when you have the sights in front of you I had, but when you have no happy feelings inside and rarely feel gratitude, you look at the world through very dark glasses. Carl seemed sad and even a little angry—rightfully so, as I had made a mockery of the evening he helped plan. And as for myself, I just felt shackled to alcohol, a broken man, and a lost soul dying to get a drink. I was desperate to be alone so I could taste that champagne without them watching me crumble further into oblivion.

By this stage of my disease, drinking actually had nothing to do with thirst or taste; it was about disappearing. Even after the restaurant debacle I was still years away from owning up to this slow death wish. When my friends disappeared I began my own search for invisibility. It's no coincidence that, feeling so invisible growing up, I opted for the same feeling as an adult. I couldn't stand myself and I'd do anything to vanish.

With that night free and no business responsibilities or people to see, the prospect of becoming shit-faced was not a problem, from my perspective, so I opened up another bottle of champagne and plugged in Bruce Springsteen's new *Lucky Town* CD. I loved it. I more than loved it. I became mesmerized by its optimism. It expressed something I so longed to feel, and so different from how I felt about myself then as a man. Soon I kept replaying the first track over and over again. "Better Days." Yup, I kept playing that tune all night, singing along with the lyrics. Somehow there seemed to be a presence in the room making me play this song over and over and over because of that lyric, "But it's a sad man my friend who's livin' in his own skin and can't stand the company." That was me. That was me. That was *fucking* me. Hearing that lyric had an impact on me like some sort of sober, prophetic arrow that pierced through my drunken haze. Unbeknownst to me, it was a strong indication that my denial was crumbling and it would be just a matter of time before I either bottomed out on booze and sought help—or died.

I kept drinking and drinking and listening and listening and as the sun set on the Vatican I sat on the toilet and looked out the bathroom window that had a perfect view of the Pantheon and wept as Bruce's song kept playing through the little speakers I had hooked up to my Walkman. I was thousands of miles away from home and even further from knowing how to get back to myself. I wouldn't get help in Italy.

Back in the USA a few months later and no closer to sobriety I had another ugly drunken incident and this time it was with Springsteen himself. I was in New York just around the time he was scheduled to appear in concert at a stadium in New Jersey after he had taken a lot of time off. *This was a big night for Bruce*. I made it a bigger night for me. I was drunk, and making it all about me was a common occurrence. I felt no pain and had very little concern, when high, about other people's feelings. I was going to go to Bruce's opening night and rent a limo and invite some pals and bring a beautiful young woman with me to show off. I was beyond thrilled to be able to see Bruce live again and also hear him sing tunes off his two new albums, especially from *Lucky Town*.

By the time we got to the gig I was wasted. When we got to our seats I somehow used my celebrity to bully myself down into the bowels of the stadium, find the band's dressing room—with the beautiful girl on my arm, in order to impress anyone I could—and, against the advice of officers and bodyguards and everyone there to serve the band, I knocked on the door and finally *the man himself* came out. He recognized me but we had never met before, and this was the first impression I made on him. I was gone, man. Wrecked. Wiped. A mess. Forget the fact that I had no right to impinge upon him and the band's sanctuary. That was the last thing that crossed my mind. I wasn't in my right mind.

The little boy in me was crying out simply to express my overwhelming affection to Springsteen for carrying the torch from Guthrie and Dylan, but the drunken man didn't have a shot. I mumbled something and he quickly went back inside and I was helped back to my seat. I hardly remember the concert.

About a year later I almost died from this disease. I was taking time off. In fact I took almost a year to start my recovery the right way. During that time I started to think of all the people I had hurt or who I was insensitive to during my dark days. I was having "Better Days" now but I needed to apologize and make amends to as many people as I could if I felt it would be helpful to both me and them.

I was listening to *Lucky Town* in a beautiful cabin in Montecito, California, at one of the most beautiful retreats in the world, the San Ysidro Ranch. I was very sober. I was writing at the typewriter and stopped suddenly as the song evoked the memory of Rome and then Bruce's concert and made me sick to my stomach. I felt as if I could've puked forever. I had an overwhelming need to get my feelings out.

I finished a very long-winded letter to Springsteen and then reached out to members of his band, many of whom were great friends of mine, and asked them if they could help me get the missive to Bruce. They got the letter to him and made sure he read it. I was so grateful when I got word back that he accepted my apology.

Eight years later almost to the day, this week, I once again wrote a letter to Bruce to ask him if I could get permission to use as an epigraph to my book the lyric that had so symbolized to me back in my drinking days my despair as a drunk, and that now, as a sober individual, was a constant reminder of how much I want to be comfortable in my own skin.

Again, I reached out to his band, friends, and his management and they miraculously helped again, as did Bruce. There are so many people willing to get on their benevolent *bicycles* and pedal to come through for you if only you give them the right-of-way.

Thank God I do now.

Springsteen was going to grant me permission to use his memorable quote to start my book. I couldn't believe how lucky I felt. I really felt I was living in a "Lucky Town" and these really were "Better Days." But this time he was helping me, a sober man, pay homage to a brilliant poet-musician, instead of just witnessing a drunk sloppily and in humiliating fashion try to express himself for all the wrong reasons.

What goes around comes around. I love that cliché. It usually has a negative connotation—and yet for me, a recovering alcoholic, it is as sweet as the best bellini I ever had at any Harry's Bar in Italy.

Yeah, man, I got sober, and all the promises that were made to me that I could live a better life without alcohol have come true. If you think I'm bullshitting you, don't take my word for it; just ask The Boss. He'll vouch for me.

The Only Important Essay

If any of you are alcoholics or substance abusers I pray to God you can really hear me now. If you read anything I hope it's this. *I was lost.* I had money, fame, gorgeous women, famous friends, the greatest not-too-famous friends, a house in the Hollywood Hills, and still I reached a point one night when I could care less about anything. If I'd dropped dead right then and there, it wouldn't have phased me. Well, of course it couldn't have phased me because I'd be dead, but for sure if I'd had a long, drawn-out moment before I died, I would have been rather blasé about the whole ordeal of what was coming next.

Somehow, I didn't die. I managed to summon up just enough courage to throw the dice and see what the next day would bring. I got help, rather than continue to do cocaine that night until my heart stopped.

I have never felt so hopeless since I hit that bottom of mine. And this is only true because I had to realize, in no uncertain terms, that I was sick with this disease called alcoholism, and that if I didn't do something to help find a way to stop drinking, I would die, and leave a lot of sad and loving people in my wake.

I don't know what clicked in my head to stop me in time. But once I'd stopped drinking, I never drank again, though I spent two nights with cocaine. The cocaine on the two nights I slipped might as well have been bottles of champagne. I still had no notion of how insane this disease was and that if I didn't feed it alcohol it would happily use coke to satisfy itself instead. The first time I relapsed was out of despair. My life was making me unhappy and I felt hopeless creatively and socially. Despondency ruled between my ears. Yet, although I was new in recovery, I had learned enough to know how quickly I would lose everything if I went back to that world of drugs and alcohol, so after doing one line I quickly flushed the shit down the toilet and began my recovery again. Twenty-four hours later, I had one day of sobriety.

The second time I slipped, a few months later, I was wrapped in hopelessness. My life had seemed to get worse emotionally, even though I wasn't drinking. I was at my bottom. I felt desperate. I felt ineffectual at almost everything I wanted out of life. I was in an airtight cocoon of self-hatred. It wasn't even really that I had a craving to drink or use. It was that events in my life seemed so out of my control that I felt impotent, and without really having any faith in a God, I was totally empty. I was a human without any sense of being. For what felt like the millionth time, my emptiness ruled me, and I didn't have anywhere to turn except to alcohol or drugs to forget.

I have never forgotten since. I so recklessly put that shit up my nose, alone in my own home. I wanted nothing more than to disappear. Even though I was surrounded by wonderful memories and pictures of people who loved me, it didn't seem to matter. I was so full of fear and self-loathing and hopelessness that I had nothing to bank on— until something clicked and I turned myself into the hospital.

Since then it has been easier, because I finally realized how cool it is and how important for me to have faith in something greater and wiser and less fucked up than myself. I needed a power that was omnipotent, that would relieve me of the need to be the center of the universe and just let me be a player while I'm alive, instead of the world's chief administrator of scheduling. I had to quit trying to manage everything anymore. I mean, look where it got me. Nowhere. I was licked and I gladly admitted it. If I tried to get off the mat one more time it would have been a quick TKO. I simply surrendered. I crowned alcohol the undisputed champion over me and decided to retire. When it came to my disease, willpower was nonexistent. I couldn't drink normally, period. And if I wanted to live, it was clear that I couldn't stop all by my lonesome.

A great burden was lifted when I finally gave in, sobered up, and got a little faith in my life as a bonus. It was easy once I realized that I had tried everything I could and that nothing *I* had done worked. It was fun to feel like a quitter—especially when you are quitting something that only wants you dead. But it's not easy and this disease can find a crack in almost any faith if you let it. I let it happen to me twice—so far.

So many people are taken out of life by addiction. So many live a long life but are just going through the paces in a drunken or drugged-out fog, unable to appreciate their life, rarely having a clear moment to care about others. I don't know too many alcoholics who remain alcoholic and have much of an existence beyond self-centered destruction. Not surprisingly, the more evident my disease became to others who then suggested I might have a problem, the more I denied it and the more I seemed to drink. I would show them! The denial is so blatantly laughable it's scary.

Yeah, it really is a progressive mother of a disease! It's so wily, relentless, and uncomplaining. It just waits around until you feel the need to hide or kill yourself. It has so much time on its hands. Alcoholism is eternally grateful for each and every victim. It takes a lot of courage to fight the bastard. And the tricky part of it is that it hangs around even when you're sober and have seemingly *lost* the obsession to drink. The disease knows that better than I do. It isn't going anywhere and is always available to go out and fuck me. It's the easiest lay in the world.

So yeah, to me, this is the only important essay in the book, because I'm a miracle and I want anyone who knows someone ravaged by this disease (or if you think you have it yourself) to know that I should be dead and I'm not. That's the most important thing and the only real wisdom I have to pass on. And I don't want to see or hear about your premature death or wasted time. I really don't.

One day I'm going to die. I'm about as sure of that as I am that I'll never learn how to record a show in advance on my VCR. Maybe I'll die suddenly or foolishly be talked into spending time in a chalet on a scenic mountainside (even though I'm allergic to the great outdoors) and an avalanche gets me. Maybe some bank robbers fleeing the scene of the crime will accidentally shoot me. Something will happen to end it all but until that occurs, as flawed, ungrateful, and self-centered as I can be from time to time, and as full of fears and obsessions as I still am, the one thing I'm most proud of is that I am no longer ruled by alcohol.

Before my recovery and even well into my recovery, I made everything that was good—and everything that was shit—worse. Don't be ashamed. Don't feel like it's impossible. Don't think too much. I stopped drinking a second at a time. When I got through the first minute the second one was easier. Only now do I have a chance to live out my life with any shot at feeling contentment.

I wish that for you. Help is out there if you reach for it.

You can put the book down now, forever if you want. I mean, since I put so much emphasis on this essay, and given its title you might figure why read anything else, anyway, unless of course this is the last page.

"God bless you."

"Thanks, Richard."

I just sneezed and blessed myself.

I know, I know, I'm a little narcissistic. I've never denied that.

That's what you have to do when you live alone.

Sure, it's embarrassing to talk out loud to yourself. But I do it all the time. Small potatoes.

I'm a happy man, as long as I don't drink.

"God bless you."

I thought I heard someone sneeze at the truth.

Acknowledgments

Since I've been a world-class people-pleaser from day one, the pleasure of acknowledging those who supported me in various ways during the writing of this memoir is a daunting task and could easily become longer than the book itself.

When you come back from the dead as I did, it's not easy to recall with any great clarity the key players who I should thank. To keep it simple, let me start out first by acknowledging God, a God who loved me enough to keep me alive before I lost the unmanageable obsession to drink myself to death, even before I came to believe He existed. And then, as if that wasn't plenty, He has graciously afforded me ever since the luxury of time, not only to be alive, but to be able to pen my book to boot.

Before any of this spiritual stuff materialized, there were people without whose guts, encouragement, and brains I probably never would have made it to the first page—let alone still be on this earth.

There was a group of loving friends who took a stand against my slow suicide with alcohol and helped me find the right path. Granted, I'm still occasionally neurotic, anxious, and depressed, but those are feelings, not drunken stupors, and by and large my existence has been totally turned around for the better. I consider it nothing short of a miracle. The people responsible for helping me know who they are, and they know what they mean to me. However, even though many people play a multitude of roles in helping an alcoholic turn the corner, there are two extra-special heroes in my life, angels on earth, if you will, who spearheaded the drive, orchestrating an intervention on my drunken hopelessness and gathering the troops for assistance. That kind of unconditional love, which ironically became conditional in order for it to work, was the greatest act of friendship I have ever experienced. These angelic earthlings are Gail Miller and Jon Dembrow. They led the way that helped others help me to save my life. I love you, Gail and Jon.

Once the sobriety train picked up steam, Dallas T. drummed sense into my head to do the right thing. Then it was Bob T. and Dr. Stuart L. who helped me make sense of the new, *original* me. But I'm certain I never would have been receptive to any of these well-intentioned pals, or to surrendering to my disease when I did, had it not been for the relentless love and support I initially received (and still do) from Dr. Austin H., whose compassion and genius taught me that I could actually lead a sober life, be happy, and not feel forever empty without a drink.

I'd be very remiss not to thank the "recovery specialists" I met during my very brief stint at Hazelden. Even though they failed to convince the then-shameful alcoholic "me" to stay at their rehab facility, their forceful and prophetic words stuck with me like glue, and their wisdom ultimately made my submission to recovery much easier. Then there were the unfailingly meticulous Dr. Louis F., who kept my physical being intact while I began starting the journey back to myself, and the astonishing Dr. Lynn J., who made sure that I didn't "crack" psychologically while I was putting all the emotional puzzle parts together.

This book never would have had a life without my passionate, exceptional literary agent, David Vigliano, who believed in my vision from the moment we met. I'm eternally grateful that he got it placed at one of the classiest, most cutting-edge publishing houses in the world. I'm indebted to PublicAffairs, to Peter Osnos for putting his faith in me, and to his incomparable staff (especially Gene Taft, Robert Kimzey, and David Patterson) for helping me "come out" of the wine cellar, so to speak, and pushing me to be as rigorously honest as I could be.

And finally, the person who I initially feared the most before we ever met—my editor—who I irrationally projected would alter my expression, my "voice," and ultimately take away my authenticity, in actuality turned out to be a godsend. My glorious editor, Lisa Kaufman, one of the most brilliantly funny and serene women I have ever met, very quickly showed me that she could literally get inside my head, get a grasp of my story, and effortlessly help me make it into a cohesive narrative. She seemed magically to become an extension of my own passion and mental picture for my book. More than I ever dreamt possible, she nurtured me every step of the long writing journey and helped me express my tale with a clarity that would have eluded me.

Before Ms. Kaufman ever read a word, many friends did, and supported my early efforts. I might have quit had they not encouraged me to keep writing. Yet, no one did more for me than two very extraordinary friends. First, my private "Contributing Editor," Joanna Weiss, the wife of my best friend, Kenny Weiss, must have spent thousands and thousands of hours convincing me that I actually had a meaningful manuscript before I even submitted it to my publisher with her tireless editing and suggestions. She practically devoted her own life to helping me feel confident enough to turn in my work. I love you, JW. And then there is esteemed UCLA Film Professor Dr. Stephen Mamber, a longtime friend who to me is the first Jewish saint. He was on call seemingly twenty-four hours a day, from the moment I buried my typewriter after he set up and tutored me on my first computer, through writing my one-millionth word on my one-millionth revision. I love you, Professor.

Much affection to my longtime attorney, Peter Grossman, who has masterfully been there for me throughout my career, as has my business manager, John Mucci, Jr., both in a way that makes them feel more like family than like business representatives. They have heroically put up with my dysfunctions with the help of Sabrina Johnson and Diane Melkonian—two women who mean the world to me.

More affection yet to Michelle Marx, my publicist, spokeswoman and confidante for so long now that it's clear that I never could have gotten my creativity out to the rest of the world, all these years, without going crazy, if it hadn't been for her bottomless pit of love, brilliance, and support.

On the spiritual side, this tome is written in large measure to honor "The Monday Night Boys" who initially became and still remain my touchstone to faith.

And finally to my darling Gina Lolamatzobrie—who claims she loves me (it's always hard for me to believe *that* from a real woman)—a glorious "significant other" who never saw me drink but who saw me through every draft of this book. Inexplicably, the more revealing I got with my writing, the more she seemed to love me. Now *that's* another miracle!

P.S. Thanks also to Melissa Raymond, Meredith Smith, and Dan Ozzi for their help on this beautiful new PublicAffairs paperback edition.

Afterword

Twenty-Four Hours to Go

It's midnight, August 3rd, 2007. In twenty-four hours I will be entering my fourteenth year of sobriety. That's a cool thing because had I not sobered up, I probably would be dead. Then this book, as hip and unusual as it might've been, would instead have had me inexplicably rapping to you from some chilly grave. Granted, it would've been a great concept for the publisher, but it would also have been a shitty outcome for me. Indisputably, had I not sobered up, I would have most probably croaked from alcoholism, could easily have become homeless, would undeniably be spiritually bankrupt, and would most likely be constantly mumbling to myself, making it unambiguously impossible to make an audio cassette for this book.

That didn't happen—neither the mumbling, nor the audio cassette—though I still can ramble with the best of them. Instead I am peacefully, if anxiously, in bed in my Hollywood home—a cool house built almost ninety years ago, undoubtedly a home that had a lot of partying going on in it well before I was born. I sense that this place was a training ground for drunks. I could be wrong, but it's not often that a house is haunted, not by ghosts, but by the smell of mixed drinks. And plenty of drugs to make me forget anything I'm trying to forget. That said, having dodged those deadly bullets, I now lay here with no other objective than to stay on my back, sober, happy that I'm not in a casket, reflecting on what happened to me during the past thirteen years, how I escaped dying, and almost worse, what's *still wrong* with my brain that makes it so challenging, even now, to find serenity.

In fact, I have zero intentions of getting out of bed until midnight tomorrow when the clock strikes twelve on August 4th and I ring in the completion of my thirteenth year of sober living. With my wife on a trip for her charity (urbanfarming.org) until the following morning, and assuming that I live to experience this fourteenth birthday of sobriety, whereupon I will quietly have some cider and celebrate my temperate birthday alone, I'm still haunted by my past and worried about the future. Don't get me wrong—I'm one lucky fuck, and I am jazzed for this sanctuary and private time to ponder the journey I've been on. I'm eager to try and figure out what thirteen years of sobriety really meant to me, how it impacted my life, and how it might impact yours if you need it like I did.

Yet truthfully, from the bottom of my grape-stained soul, I also have this desperate need to tell other recovering people like myself—or those who are sadly still trapped by this disease of alcoholism and drug addiction but are willing to at least listen to me— that so far, during what are easily the best years of my life, I have sorrowfully come to an awareness that among the many recovering drunks I have met, with all their strength, courage, support, and helpfulness to others, many still manage to hang on to their unprincipled, even scummy, ways of living. Others happen to be some of the greatest, most loving, trustworthy people I have ever known and are best friends of mine. It's this intriguing dichotomy that has led me to believe that it takes more than just sobriety to change a person. Character building doesn't happen by luck. It happens through hard work. You have to crave changing your behavior for the better as much as you used to crave a drug or a drink. You can either evolve, or die without having learned much of anything. That is the choice you have when you get sober.

Of all the changes in attitude I've experienced since putting down the drink, easily the most perplexing and intellectually mindblowing is being able to acknowledge and accept my own ascent in spirituality. This divine experience, so alien to the old drinking me, did coincide with me getting sober. For whatever reason, my new belief in a power other than myself somehow worked for me, and so far has helped me be able to continue not to drink and has facilitated acceptance and forgiveness and my desperate attempts to get resentments out of my head. God knows why I am one of the few alcoholics who, so far, have stayed this fortunate.

Tragically, I have discovered that all the faith that one can boast about or claim to be the proud owner of means shit if other aspects of maturity and growth aren't developed side by side. Believe me, I can be quite an asshole, and if I don't stay as vigilant in deconstructing my character flaws as I am in acknowledging all my progress, all the sobriety in the world would be like having a flaccid erection.

So, in almost a day's time I will start my fourteenth year of having the chance to keep my side of the street clean and of having doors open for me that I otherwise might've drunkenly smashed into. Still, I need to figure out why in being sober, as important a decision as I've ever made, and one that has kept me alive and in the best physical, emotional, and spiritual shape of my life, there are still mountains on the road to better character that I have avoided, and that I must take head on, just as I did alcohol and drugs. Otherwise I will live out my life knowing in my heart of hearts that I once again took the easy way out, just like I did for years and years during my drinking life, thinking I could moderate my carousing and that would be enough. Regardless of how many years I chalk up as a sober man, if I don't own up to my character defects and try to change them, I won't be the man I could've been. Sure, I may die sober and set an example on the surface, but regardless of what people think of me, I will not have fulfilled my potential. I'm better off now than ever, but to think I deserve a sober trophy without constantly trying to be a better person is a joke without a punch line.

It's mind-boggling how I don't feel like my old out-of-control self anymore. The creative breakthroughs I have had in sobriety, especially as a comedian, have been so wonderful it's hard not to think back to the days when I was penniless, just feeling like some whacked dreamer, a loser of sorts, imagining I could actually become a comedian. Just being able to pay the bills with a life on stage seemed like a hallucination back then to that young, budding alcoholic. But the great stand-ups who came before me, the ones who seemed to help define the shapeless and pointless existence of mankind, grabbed me by the soul and helped me find my way. Now, regardless of what others may think, I know that, in sobriety,

I have hit the bar of performance and fearlessness on stage, in front of live audiences, that I couldn't even have conceived of in the early 1970s. Back then, if I'd even once had the thought that I could come close to achieving the life in comedy that is associated with me now, I might've checked myself into the nearest mental institution.

And although my work is at the core of my being, the notion that I can assist in saving other peoples' lives and get them out of the same darkness I experienced—when the prospect of going a day without a drink was as preposterous as, say, getting on Johnny Carson—is a gift of sobriety so miraculous that it is nearly impossible to describe. To be able to have a small impact on someone else who is stumbling in his own darkness, to influence him even a little to make the decision to surrender with a little faith and humility—no drink or drug on the planet comes close. Helping others is pure ecstasy. Being there isn't too shabby either. In fact, just being married and committed to one woman after well over a half a century is not just a miracle but probably won't get me a key to Hefner's Mansion. Trust me, I had my own "mansion," but the kind of love affairs and sexual encounters I chose while drunk and high don't come close by comparison with my marriage—even with the occasional rocky days we all have in the best of soulful or intimate relationships. I'm sometimes a shitty husband and not the best brother, uncle, or pal, but man, oh man, I know for a fact that in these past thirteen years of sobriety, I have behaved in a manner that showed me I had no clue what I was missing out on before I surrendered to this disease. My wife couldn't be more supportive, but she knows as well as I that if I take my progress for granted, sooner or later she'd be lucky to be single again, and I could easily be on my way to hell on earth.

I know now that putting the drink and the drug down is only the beginning. It's scary to think how much better a person I can become if I only use the tools that I am afforded now, clear-headed, to genuinely change in areas that I never thought I could. The cold hard truth is that if I take for granted the progress I have made, I'm a goner.

I have been a narcissistic, egomaniacal, womanizing, drunken lunatic, suffered through eating disorders, and always had a miserable time accepting myself when I was truly a good guy. I'm sober, but if I don't try and improve in a myriad of psychological areas, I'll be Richard Lewis in name only and merely resemble an empty wine bottle with bad posture from the same low self-esteem vintage.

Only I can choose to become a better and more principled man, just as I alone bottomed out and chose to stop drinking. If I fail at this—the attempt to become a better human being—it's apparent that my recovery is half-assed and the potential for real transformation is disastrously squandered.

Richard Lewis
Laurel Canyon, California
2007

ABOUT THE AUTHOR

RICHARD LEWIS is often compared to a jazz musician for the way his wild riffs fly out into space but always find a way to float back into rhythm as they splatter recurring themes against a spiraling, lyrical backdrop. He's spoken of by top journalists in the same breath as Lenny Bruce, Woody Allen, Jimi Hendrix, and even Franz Kafka. All in all, his career in stand-up has brought him to the top of the ranks, and Lewis has claimed a territory completely, and uniquely, his own.

Through his many television appearances, be it series, late night chat, or hour-long-Ace nominated cable specials, he's worked his way into our hearts and our vernacular. He is the personification of our cultural 'Excedrin moment,' and made his life an open book read from a therapists couch. Making great use of his personal style, he's played himself true-to-life as one of Larry David's closest friends in the Seinfeld co-creator's hit HBO series "Curb Your Enthusiasm" since 2001, to much acclaim. At an event honoring a 'fellow icon' one reviewer wrote, "Melting the house and forcing grown men to weep openly, Richard Lewis bombarded the crowd from one obtuse comedy angle after another . . . For nearly twenty minutes he induced non-stop howling by every living, breathing thing in the house." Among the accomplishments he is most proud of are: selling out Carnegie Hall, being recognized by Comedy Central as one of the 'Top 50 Stand-Up Comedians Of All Time,' being charted on GQ Magazine's list of the '20th Century's Most Influential Humorists,' and last but not least, finally having The Yale Book of Quotations credit him as the originator of the now-common phrase, "the ____ from hell."

As this new edition of his book *The Other Great Depression* goes to press, Lewis is appearing nationwide in his 'Misery Loves Company Tour' on which, he says, "I make people happy that they're not me and then I go home."

PublicAffairs is a publishing house founded in 1997. It is a tribute to the standards, values, and flair of three persons who have served as mentors to countless reporters, writers, editors, and book people of all kinds, including me.

I. F. STONE, proprietor of *I. F. Stone's Weekly*, combined a commitment to the First Amendment with entrepreneurial zeal and reporting skill and became one of the great independent journalists in American history. At the age of eighty, Izzy published *The Trial of Socrates*, which was a national bestseller. He wrote the book after he taught himself ancient Greek.

BENJAMIN C. BRADLEE was for nearly thirty years the charismatic editorial leader of *The Washington Post*. It was Ben who gave the *Post* the range and courage to pursue such historic issues as Watergate. He supported his reporters with a tenacity that made them fearless and it is no accident that so many became authors of influential, best-selling books.

ROBERT L. BERNSTEIN, the chief executive of Random House for more than a quarter century, guided one of the nation's premier publishing houses. Bob was personally responsible for many books of political dissent and argument that challenged tyranny around the globe. He is also the founder and longtime chair of Human Rights Watch, one of the most respected human rights organizations in the world.

• • •

For fifty years, the banner of Public Affairs Press was carried by its owner Morris B. Schnapper, who published Gandhi, Nasser, Toynbee, Truman, and about 1,500 other authors. In 1983, Schnapper was described by *The Washington Post* as "a redoubtable gadfly." His legacy will endure in the books to come.

Peter Osnos, *Founder and Editor-at-Large*